THE AUTHOR Dr Peter Neville t.   ,
the University of East Anglia, and Kingston University where he was Senior
Research Fellow. He is also a Fellow of the Royal Historical Society. Peter
Neville is also the author of well known studies of Sir Nevile Henderson,
Mussolini and Ho Chi Minh. The latter has been placed in the Top 14
Historical Biographies of all time by bookauthority.com recommended by
CNN and *Forbes* magazine.

SERIES EDITOR Professor Denis Judd is a graduate of Oxford, a Fellow
of the Royal Historical Society and Professor of History at the London
Metropolitan University. He has published over 20 books including the
biographies of Joseph Chamberlain, Prince Philip, George VI and Alison
Uttley, historical and military subjects, stories for children and novels. He has
reviewed and written extensively in the national press and in journals, and is
an advisor to the BBC *History* magazine.

Other Titles in the Series

THE TRAVELLER'S HISTORY SERIES

A Traveller's History of Ireland

A Traveller's History of Ireland

SEVENTH EDITION

PETER NEVILLE

Series Editor   DENIS JUDD
Line Drawings   SCOTT HALL

Interlink Books
An imprint of Interlink Publishing Group, Inc.
Northampton, Massachusetts

This edition first published in 2023 by
INTERLINK BOOKS
An imprint of Interlink Publishing Group, Inc
46 Crosby Street, Northampton, Massachusetts 01060
www.interlinkbooks.com

The front cover shows Memories *oil on canvas by Markey Robinson (1918-99)
Private Collection/The Oriel Gallery, Dublin/The Bridgeman Art Library.*

Library of Congress Cataloging-in-Publication Data
Neville, Peter,
    A traveller's history of Ireland / by Peter Neville.
        p.   cm. – (Traveller's history)
    Includes bibliographical references and index.
    ISBN 978-1-62371-798-8
    1. Ireland—History.   2. Historic sites—Ireland—History
I. Title.   II. Series.
DA910.N48   1992
941.50–dc20

Printed and bound in the United States of America

To order or request our complete catalog,
please call us at 1–800–238–LINK, or write to:
INTERLINK PUBLISHING
46 Crosby Street, Northampton, Massachusetts 01060
e-mail: info@interlinkbooks.com
www.interlinkbooks.com

Contents

Preface

The earliest indigenous word for Ireland, as Peter Neville points out in this detailed and enthralling book, was Ériu, which can be interpreted as 'the most beautiful woman in the world'. Like other beautiful women, Ireland has been greatly desired, fought over, admired, despised, imitated, passionately wooed and violently assailed. The feminine metaphor is enhanced, not merely by Ireland's mysterious and beguiling identity, but by its standing as one of the world's most fruitful mother countries, with its sons and daughters scattered throughout the globe from Boston to Melbourne, from Liverpool to Toronto.

Ireland occupies a unique geographical position among the nations of Europe. No other European country projects so far west into the Atlantic Ocean, swept by the rainstorms that ensure that the Emerald Isle stays green. Ireland was even a step too far for the legions of Imperial Rome. While the other peoples of the British Isles were subjected to Roman rule, the Irish avoided the experience. The island's distinctive Celtic culture was not, however, destined to remain in a comfortable, isolated time-warp. Where the Romans had failed to gain a foothold, Vikings, Normans and, above all, the English, were successful.

The story of Ireland has, as a central theme, a tension between two apparently contradictory roles. On the one hand, Ireland, for much of its modern history has been the victim of foreign invasion and domination. It was even the subject of a blatant piece of colonial social engineering when Protestant settlers were planted in the north to act as a counterpoise to the Catholic, potentially rebellious, majority. The continuing Irish dimension to British politics, the problem of Ulster, bears witness to the effectiveness of that earlier initiative. It has also precipitated some of the bloodiest episodes in Irish history, including Cromwell's still bitterly recalled pacification during the 1640s, and the depredations of the Black and Tans within living memory. Thus Anglo-Saxon and Gael, Protestant and Catholic, have been embroiled in centuries of conflict and disharmony.

On the other hand, Ireland has been an active and often enthusiastic partner in the spread of British and English-speaking influence throughout the world. Especially after the Union of 1800, the Irish, Catholic and Protestant, were integrated into the fabric of British political, economic, cultural and imperial life as never before. Irish MPs sat, indeed still do sit, in the House of Commons. Irish generals led Irish regiments in wars of conquest throughout the Empire, in the process suppressing the liberties of peoples with whom Ireland's nationalists were later to identify. The industrial revolution, the great famine years, and the massive urbanisation of mainland Britain, also encouraged hundreds of thousands of Irish to cross the Irish Sea in search of employment and a better life.

But even when the Irish were apparently acquiescing to English supremacy over the British Isles and throughout the Empire, opposition to Anglo-Saxon domination never ceased completely. Resistance movements, of which the IRA is only the contemporary example, fought on, and the Irish overseas, whether in the United States or Australia, often took whatever opportunity came to hand to harry and embarrass English interests. For their part, English attitudes have swung between coercion and kindness, tolerance and contempt, admiration and ridicule.

The richness and complexity of the Irish past is ably presented in this highly readable and comprehensive book. Ireland is the source of a multitude of legends, and of a history that is often stranger than fiction. It is also a land of poets, playwrights and novelists, as well as of eloquent politicians, illustrious soldiers and persistent and inspiring rebels. The Irish Republic is now an integral part of the European Community and in 1990 elected its first woman President. Ireland has always been an immensely hospitable country, despite the vagaries of its history, and remains a source of delight to those who visit it.

Denis Judd

CHAPTER ONE

From Tara to Saint Patrick

Basic Geography

Ireland is the westernmost part of the geographical grouping known as the British Isles. But it has characteristics which make it quite distinct from England, Wales and Scotland. From the northernmost tip of Ulster to the wild shores of County Kerry in the south-west it measures some 350 miles, and from north-west to south-east a further 200 miles. The island of Ireland is bounded by one great sea, the Irish, and one of the world's two major oceans, the Atlantic, and throughout its history the sea has been a dominant influence. Nowhere in Ireland is more than 100 miles from the sea.

Ireland has a temperate climate without excesses of heat or cold, although sub-tropical vegetation can be found in the south-west. Only three of its mountains exceed 3,000 feet, but there are a series of low mountain ranges in the coastal areas. Inside the mountain rings, Ireland is made up of low, marshy plain with plentiful supplies of peat, one of the country's only natural resources (unlike England, Wales and Scotland, it has virtually no coal or iron ore). These peatlands are the finest in Europe.

The evolution of these ancient peatlands has been a slow process which started when the last Ice Age left Central Ireland covered by shallow lakes. With the passage of time, lakeside vegetations died and decomposed sufficiently to change these old lakes into fens (like England's Norfolk Broads), and ultimately into bogs. At one time Ireland had as much as 311,000 hectares of bogland (where the squares of peat are cut and have been used for fuel for centuries), but by 1985

Relief map of Ireland

Land over 300 metres

there were only 54,000 acres left and the boglands are currently disappearing at a frightening rate. Their economic value has long been evident in a coal-less country, and after independence in 1921 peat was used as fuel in the great electricity power stations based around Ireland's largest river, the Shannon. But only more recently has the historic and ecological value of the boglands been appreciated in Ireland itself. For not only are the peatlands of the central plain a great reserve of rare plants and birdlife, but they are also a repository for human remains and artefacts going back to 9000 BC. Even today, the peat fire is as characteristically Irish as the national emblem, the shamrock.

Modern Ireland is divided into four provinces: Ulster, Leinster, Connacht (Connaught) and Munster. In the medieval period there were references to a fifth province called Meath or Midland, but these ceased long before modern times; nevertheless, the surviving provinces' names, like much else in Ireland, have their own ancient roots. In ancient times, according to legend, the northern half of the island was known as Leth Cuinn ('Conn's side' after a mythical hero called Conn), the southern half as Leth Moga (or 'Mug's side' after another mythical hero called Mug Nuadat). From Conn and Mug we get Leth Cuinn for the northern provinces of Ulster and Connacht, and Leth Moga for the southern ones of Leinster and Munster.

The Political Divide

After the Anglo-Irish War of 1918 to 1921 Ireland was partitioned, and six northern counties (Armagh, Antrim, Down, Tyrone, Fermanagh and Londonderry) remained part of the United Kingdom of Great Britain and Northern Ireland. Northern Ireland is often loosely referred to as Ulster, but this is technically incorrect because three of Ulster's nine counties (Cavan, Donegal and Monaghan) became part of independent Ireland. Northern Ireland, or 'The Six Counties', has a Protestant majority with about two-thirds of the total population of 1.6 million being of that religion, while the remaining one-third are Catholic.

The other twenty-six counties of Ireland formed part of what was first known as the Irish Free State, and from 1937 as Éire. In 1949 Éire opted for republican status and left the British Commonwealth. Its current population, with the highest proportion of under-25s in Europe, is just over 3.5 million; of these about 7 per cent are Protestant and the rest Catholic.

The earliest native word for Ireland was Ériu, which according to one interpretation means 'the most beautiful woman in the world'. Those who have seen the lakes of Killarney or the Mountains of Mourne on a clear day will find that description an apt one.

Prehistoric Ireland

The dawn of Irish history is as hidden from us as the countryside on a misty morning in that enchanted but often tragic island. However, geographical proximity to Britain was a crucial factor when those first inhabitants crossed the narrow channel between Scotland and Ulster around 9000 BC. The very first traces of Irish life are to be found in Ulster, in the valley of that River Boyne which was destined long afterwards to play a crucial role in Irish history. These are the passage-graves of Dowth, Knowth and Newgrange which were built around 3000 BC by New Stone Age successors to these first migrants, who have disappeared from history without leaving any artefacts. They bear the intricate carvings of a society without iron tools which wished to commemorate the tribal kings of that day in the best way they knew how. Further examples of early prehistoric Irish art can be found on the massive stones which surround the burial chambers.

Waves of new invaders followed over the centuries, leaving behind them ever more sophisticated artefacts as Irish civilisation moved through the Bronze Age and the Celtic Iron Age. These include jewellery, collars, necklaces and earrings, and when the Iron Age too was passed through, the warlike Celts left decorated weapons to demonstrate their prowess to posterity.

When precisely the Celts arrived in Ireland is a mystery, but a date in the second half of the first millennium BC (i.e. after 500 BC) seems probable. Some clues about early Irish civilisation come from ancient chroniclers, and in the late fourth century BC Pytheas described the British Isles as the 'Pretanic Isles', almost certainly a title derived from the Celtic term Priteni, which in turn gives us the Welsh Prydain. Later Festus Rufus Avienus referred to Ireland as 'insula sacra' (holy island), and a contemporary name was Ériu (very close to the modern Éire in Irish Gaelic). Ériu was probably derived from the Greek word for the island, Ierne (Hibernia in Latin), so it is not certain that it is Celtic in origin. Roman chroniclers tended, in any case, to ascribe to the Irish the characteristics of those continental Celtic societies, the Gauls and Iberians.

What is certain is that the original Celtic invaders were only a minority among the original non-Celtic inhabitants, who produced the impressive chambers at Knowth and elsewhere. Modern scholars in Ireland, like Donnchadh Ó Corráin, have attested to the sophistication of the Neolithic and Bronze Age societies, and the Irish language certainly owes a good deal to those pre-Celtic civilisations – many Celtic Irish words were borrowed from the earlier inhabitants. Latterly,

Navan Fort earthworks, Armagh. The northern rival of the Hill of Tara which historians believe may be the site of Emain Macha, the capital of legendary Ireland, and the centre of power for the kings of Ulster

too, the cultural unity of the Celtic world was shown by the fact that in Ireland both Goidelic (the Irish and Scottish form of Celtic) and Brythonic (the form spoken in Wales, Cornwall and Brittany) were spoken.

Another significant pre-Celtic site is the one at Tara in central Ireland, where a series of ring-forts or raths marks the cult of the old pagan 'high king', a symbolic title which appeared in the Neolithic Age. The title of high king continued to have great significance in Celtic and medieval Ireland, and the linguistic influence of the pre-Celtic period shows up again in the stem 'rath' in place names like Rathmines and Rathmullen. The high king had no lawmaking powers, however, and in the Celtic period spent much of his time fighting off other petty local kings who aspired to the title.

Ireland and Rome

A distinctive aspect of the Irish experience was the absence of Roman rule. It was a near thing: in AD 81 the Roman general Agricola gave serious consideration to the invasion of Ireland, but had his plan vetoed by the Emperor Domitian (81–96) who refused to supply the needed reinforcements. No Roman prefect therefore set foot in Ireland, but there is considerable evidence of trading links. For example, coins have been found on the east coast of Ireland dating from the reigns of Trajan (98–117) and Hadrian (117–138), and the discovery of most of them in Ulster suggests that they originated from Britain rather than Gaul.

How significant was it that Ireland remained outside the Roman empire? It did not prevent Celtic Ireland from achieving a cultural rather than a political unity. None the less it is a Roman source, or a Graeco-Roman source to be strictly accurate, which gives the most accurate picture of Ireland's political structure around AD 100, when Trajan was ruling the Roman empire.

Ptolemy's Map

This source was the map provided by the Greek Alexandrian geographer Ptolemy, who seems to have got his information from British sailors who were operating from Irish ports since the place names on the Ptolemaic map are in Brythonic.

The map gives a remarkable insight into Irish civilisation at the time. Some place and river names can be clearly identified today: thus Buvinda is the Boyne and Senos is the Shannon. But most interesting is the evidence that the Ptolemaic map gives about the rapidly changing Irish political situation. Thus in the north there is a remarkable degree of continuity with the Early Christian period, because the map records the domination of the Dál Riata and Dál Fiatach, both dynasties which claimed descent from the pagan god Dáire. Likewise the people called Voluntii by Ptolemy are the Ulaid, who were still the most powerful dynasty in Ulster hundreds of years later and had their cult centre (rather than capital city) at Emain near modern Armagh. Ptolemy called Emain Isamnion.

Ptolemy gives far more detail about the north-east than about the west and north-west, and it is evident that the dynasties in these areas had not been good survivors like those in Ulster. The Koriondi, for example, seem to have left no trace in South Leinster by AD 100, but were apparently related to the Coraind who survived around Sligo on the west coast. In the western province of Munster, Ptolemy shows the dominant tribe to be the Iverni or Érainn, who ruled the area until the rise of the Eóganacht dynasty in the Early Christian period. Continuity with the Early Christian period shows up again around Limerick where Ptolemy's Auteini are the Uaithne who controlled the Shannon waterway and the lands west of that river.

In political terms, therefore, Ireland although fragmented showed signs of continuity, and with this political continuity went cultural unity and even a primitive legal code. This was called the Brehon Law, which could not, of course, be centrally enforced because the country lacked any central authority (by comparison, Britain had the advantage of centuries of Roman law). Otherwise Ireland showed many of the characteristics of older Celtic society on the continent. There was a tradition of bardic praise poetry, spoken aloud, and druids or holy men (the Romans destroyed their British equivalents on the island of Anglesey) provided the link between the individual and the pagan deities. Customs like fighting with two-horse chariots and giving the best warrior at a feast the 'hero's portion', or best joint of meat, also survived. This is borne out by references in early Irish literature, but historians now stress that the minority status of the early Celtic invaders meant that earlier cultural influences remained significant even after the Celts began to dominate the island. This was especially true where the Irish language was concerned.

Links between Celtic Ireland and Roman Britain actually appear to have increased as Roman power began to wane in the face of waves of barbarian attackers. More Roman artefacts have been found dating from the fourth and fifth centuries AD, and there is evidence that there was a Roman trading post at Stoneyford on the Nore. But this renewed contact was a direct consequence of the inability of the elaborate system of coastal forts built by the Romans in Britain to keep out the Irish or the Picts (from Scotland).

As the fourth century drew on, the strength of these attacks grew in force, and they were joined by the Saxons from the continent. In 367 a joint Irish/Pictish/Saxon attack on the British coastline devastated Roman Britain – further evidence, if that were needed, that Rome was losing its grip. Further depradations hastened Rome's decision to withdraw the legions in 410.

The Irish Colonies

This left western Britain open to Irish invasion, and there is abundant evidence of Irish settlements there in the fourth and fifth centuries. A particularly large one was in South-West Wales in the area now bounded by Pembrokeshire, Carmarthenshire and Cardiganshire (which now forms Dyfed) where settlers from Leinster became established; there was also a smaller colony in North Wales (Anglesey, Carnarvonshire and Denbighshire, now Gwynnedd and Clwyd). These Irish settlers have left place names as evidence of their occupation. The ruling dynasty of the time in Leinster, the Laigin, have given their name to the Lleyn peninsula; Port Dinalleen on Nevin Bay means literally 'the harbour of the fort of the Leinstermen'.

Another colony was founded to the south in Cornwall by the Ui Liathin, who probably came from east Cork. Cormac, the tenth-century Irish scholar bishop and king of Cashel in County Tipperary, wrote proudly of how:

> The power of the Irish over the Britons was great, and they had divided Britain between them into estates; ... and the Irish lived as much east of the sea as they did in Ireland, and their dwellings and royal fortresses were made there ... and they were in that control for a long time even after the coming of St Patrick to Ireland.

Scotland was another success story. Although Agricola had won an important victory over the Highland chieftains in AD 83, the Emperor Domitian had forbidden him to try and conquer northern Scotland, but the Romans did leave defensive outposts as far north as Perth and

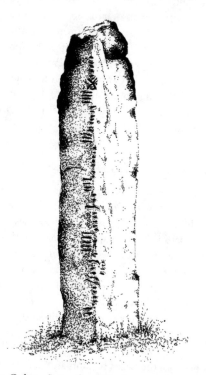

An Ogham Stone from Coolmagort, County Kerry

Stirling. Not even enfeebled Roman resistance, therefore, prevented the Dalriada, whom Ptolemy had placed in north-eastern Ireland, from colonising Scotland. This process appears, according to Irish legend, to have begun in the third and fourth centuries, but the dates are uncertain. What is known is that by 563, when the great Irish missionary Columba came to Scotland from the island of Iona, the kingdom of the Dalriada had expanded to incorporate the Pictish areas in the east. By the ninth century this dynasty had united all Scotland under Kenneth MacAlpin.

One consequence of this colonising was that the profits from the new settlements across the water were used to fund dynastic wars in Ireland itself. Another was a logical romanisation of Irish culture as the piratical Irish came into contact with the last vestiges of the crumbling Roman civilisation. Early Laigin oral history shows signs of borrowings from Latin, as in the hybrids legioń (from legion) and trebunus (tribune). More striking still are the 'Oghams' (pronounced like 'poems') which proliferate in southern Ireland today, and are also found in areas of former settlement in Cornwall, South Wales, North Wales and the Isle of Man. These big stones show the first written forms of the Irish languages, based on a system of lines and notches which clearly borrow from the Latin alphabet.

The Coming of Christianity

The other great result of the Irish settlement of Britain was that the settlers came into contact with Christianity for the first time. It is not known exactly when the first Christian missionaries set to work in Ireland itself, but a date in the late fourth or early fifth century seems most likely. So began a process which was allegedly to change Ireland from an island of freebooters and sea-pirates into an 'island of saints and scholars'. The latter description, although well known, does need to be treated with caution. Irish kings and princelings did not cease to fight one another purely because they became Christians!

SAINT PATRICK

Central to the concept of the island of saints and scholars is the career of St Patrick (c. 389–461), Ireland's patron saint. Everyone in Ireland knows the story of how he freed the island of snakes, but this legend only serves to underline how much of his life is shrouded in mystery. We cannot even be certain of exactly when he lived. From what is known a limited picture can be built up. The first point was that Patrick was British (he probably came from Wales) and that he came from a respectable family. His father was a former magistrate called Calpurnius, and Patrick was captured by Irish raiders at the age of sixteen and taken back to Ireland as a slave. He then spent six years as a shepherd, probably in north Connacht, before escaping and getting back to Britain with a pagan ship.

Patrick claimed that on his return he had a vision and heard Irish voices saying, 'We beseech you to come and walk amongst us once more.' He appears to have returned to Ireland in 432 claiming to be a bishop, and spent the rest of his life there. Fellow Christians in Britain seem to have doubted his fitness for the mission.

Patrick had great influence over several Irish chieftains and, although not well educated himself, encouraged learning in his adopted country. His memory remained especially strong around Armagh, but he also seems to have had ties with Croagh Patrick (as the name suggests) and Tara. The particular links with Armagh allowed it to claim primacy in the Irish Church, which it has retained to this day, and the city was instrumental in spreading the cult of St Patrick, so that by the seventh century it had reached down to Munster. Patrick's particular contribution to Irish Christianity was to encourage asceticism and the monastic movement, which may have been a result of his contacts with the monastic foundations in Gaul with their tough spiritual discipline. He also stressed the importance of missionary activity, and by the sixth century this was certainly one of the most striking features of the Irish Church. Lastly, he laid his stamp on the structure of the Irish Church by encouraging the development of local Christianity around monastic foundations rather than bishops and their dioceses. That old Irish habits died hard is underlined by the fact that the abbots were not above attacking rival Christian foundations.

Patrick's legacy has been a lasting one. His influence is demonstrated by his feast day, 17 March, still being a public holiday in Ireland. The Irish people identify very closely with him in a way quite unlike

England's St George, who never in fact visited the country whose patron saint he became. The strength of this legacy has also had a negative side because it has caused the contribution of others to be forgotten. Patrick's arrival in Ireland coincides, in fact, with the earliest chronicled reference to the Irish Church, by Prosper of Aquitaine, who records in his Chronicle the appointment in the previous year, 431, by Pope Celestine (422–32) of one Palladius as bishop to the Irish 'who believe in Christ'.

PELAGIANISM

The Pelagian heresy was at that time causing division in the Christian world. There is some evidence that Pelagius was of Irish origin; it is known that he was a monk who visited Rome in 400 and was rather disgusted by what he regarded as 'the low state of conduct'. He then went on to evolve his own doctrine which, among other things, denied the concept of original sin (saying that men could be free of sin and that Adam's sin did not damn the whole human race) and that unbaptised infants could have eternal life. Pelagianism was also deemed to be socially subversive because it stated that no rich man could be saved unless he gave up all his worldly goods. Those whom Prosper refers to as believers in Christ, therefore, were the anti-Pelagian orthodox Christians. Clearly, then, Christianity had some considerable footing in Ireland *before* Patrick returned, and in another work around 434, Prosper mentions another unidentified bishop being sent to Ireland to convert the barbarians. Nevertheless it was to be a slow process which got to be very much associated with Patrick's name, though seventh-century works do mention the contribution of Sachellus, Cetiacus and others. Even in his own time in Ireland, Patrick admitted in his *Confession*, he was held in low regard by the *dominicati rhetorici* or masters of rhetoric, the better educated, more worldly clerics.

THE BRITISH CONTRIBUTION

Modern historians fully recognise the great contribution made by British missionaries to the development of Irish Christianity. It was they, rather than Patrick and his disciples, who were to be responsible for the golden age of the Irish Church in the sixth century, by founding

A beautifully carved cross at Clonmacnoise monastery

monasteries and passing on learning. The list is impressive: Ninian taught Finian of Moville and St David, the patron saint of Wales, taught Máedóc of Ferns, while Tigernach of Clones, Enda of Aran, and Scuith'din of Slievemargy were all of British origin. The influence of these saints and scholars on Irish life can be discerned from the large numbers of children who still bear their names today. Nevertheless it must be stressed that the christianisation of Ireland was a slow and complex process. The historian Donnchadh Ó Corráin suggests that even in the mid-sixth century, some 200 years after Patrick's death, Cerbaill, high king of Tara, may have been a pagan.

CHAPTER TWO

Early Christian Ireland,
500–795

In the sixth and seventh centuries, Irish Christianity entered a new and more expansive phase, and began to influence others, just as it had been the beneficiary of the British Christian missions.

Saint Columba, 521–597

One of the greatest figures in this period was Columba (Colmcille in Gaelic), who was born in County Donegal in the province of Ulster in the early part of the sixth century. Chroniclers wrote that he was born in the 'land of the Scots', and in the early medieval period Ireland was often called by the Latin name Scotia. Given the intermixture of Ulster Irish and Scots, this was not surprising. He was educated at the school of Finian of Moville and then with Finian of Clonard, and after ordination is known to have helped the establishment of many churches and monasteries. He left Ireland in the year 563 with the desire to 'go on pilgrimage for Christ'.

Precisely why Columba left Ireland is something of a mystery. There appears to have been some sort of dispute about the possession of a manuscript which he had copied, and this dispute led to a war between Columba's clan and the high king Diarmait. As he had been instrumental in starting the war, Columba may have undertaken a foreign mission as a sort of self-imposed penance. At all events he set sail for the island of Iona, off the west coast of Scotland, with just twelve companions.

From this unpromising beginning, Columba was to become the major instrument in the conversion of his fellow Irish who had settled in Scotland (the Dalriada) and the Picts. Initially he did this by combating the influence of the pagan Druid priesthood, then by penetrating the royal court circles. His greatest success was to convert Brude, king of the Picts, but Columba's monks reached the Orkney islands as well as founding monastic houses at Melrose and Dunkeld.

Before he died in 597, Columba had begun the process of christianising Scotland and northern England, which was to be carried on by other great saints such as Aidan, Hilda and Cuthbert. This achievement was carried through when Ireland's links with Rome were severed during the period after the collapse of the great empire, and Irish Christianity developed special features of its own.

The Separation from Rome

The Roman tonsure was abandoned by Irish monks, who instead adopted the Druid practice of shaving the crown of the head from ear to ear. They also kept to an ancient reckoning of the date of Easter which the Roman Church had given up. All this, of course, did not mean that the Irish Church had rejected Rome's primacy, but reflected the fact that in a time of European chaos Ireland was at its westernmost fringe. It did mean that Irish monks living in societies which were semi-pagan and warlike, lacking urban sophistication, had to cut their cloth according to their surroundings. Christianity had to battle hard to survive in an era of magic, spells and ancient symbols, and a degree of pragmatism was needed. This was later to bring Celtic Christianity into conflict with the missions from Rome (originally led by St Augustine) which christianised southern England.

IONA

The monastery which Columba founded on Iona was to become one of the greatest centres of Celtic Christianity, and it is still a place of pilgrimage today. From there successive abbots after Columba controlled not only monastic foundations in Scotland, but also major foundations in Ireland like Derry, Durrow and Kells (founded mid 6th century). The most distinguished was Adomnán, who died in 704, a scholar of some repute who wrote the life of his community's founder.

In 697, the centenary of Columba's death, Adomnán held a great conference on Iona of bishops and fellow abbots which evolved the so-called 'Law of Innocents'. This said that women and children were not to take part in battles, and that the former were to be protected from violence. That such a law needed to be put forward two hundred years after Patrick's death demonstrates the savage nature of Celtic society at the time. After his death, Adomnán was also canonised.

ARMAGH

Otherwise, the seventh century was notable for the recognition of Armagh as the ecclesiastical centre of the Irish Church. Unlike most of the other clerical power centres, Armagh had a bishop who directly controlled most of the churches in northern Ireland, and gradually won the acceptance of the rest of the Irish Church as its head. This meant that the bishop of Armagh took precedence over other clerics, but there was no real hierarchical structure in the Church as there is today. His very claim to precedence rested on the links between Armagh itself and St Patrick, much as the primacy of Canterbury in England derived from its links with St Augustine.

Monastic Life and Culture

A feature of early Irish monasticism was its resilience. This was most strikingly demonstrated by the community on the bleak island of Skellig Michael (Mount St Michael), some eight miles off the west coast of Ireland, which left behind the best preserved pre-Viking monastic sites in the whole of Ireland. On a south-facing precipice are six beehive-shaped dry-stone cells for the small community of monks, specially built to keep out the rain and howling gales that blew in from the Atlantic. It is known that the building techniques used on Skellig Michael were adopted in the seventh century for other constructions, like the curious boat-shaped oratory at Gallarus on the Dingle peninsula in Country Kerry.

It is not surprising, as Donald Matthews has pointed out, that Irish monks were noted for their ascetic qualities when their foundations had been established in some of the bleakest spots in western Christendom.

And with this ascetism went a growing reputation for scholarship, as they broadened their links with the Frankish court and the Anglo-Saxon kingdoms of England. An example of this scholarship was afforded as early as 655 when a manuscript known as *De mirabilis sacrae scripturae* (Of the wonders of Holy Scripture) appeared with references to Early Christian fathers like Augustine, Gregory the Great and Tertullian.

LAW

This background of learning meant that, in a semi-pagan society, the Irish clerics were well equipped to draw up laws for both church and state. And they showed their scholarship by producing an entirely original work, called *Collectio canonum hibernensis* (Collected Irish canon law), which dates to the first half of the eighth century. The growing nature of church influence is shown by the fact that the *Collectio* deals not just with church matters like clerical orders, but also with the ownership of property and inheritance. The difficulty facing these ecclesiastical lawmakers was that in Ireland, lacking a base of Roman law, much reliance was placed on old pagan laws and customs. These monks were the civil servants of their day, and indeed much more than that because they were the only truly literate members of their society. So with the characteristic penchant of a bureaucracy for compromise the monks, as the Catholic Church has often done in similar situations, recognised the validity of pre-Christian custom laws while at the same time stressing the primacy of church law. 'The law of the church', said a contemporary legalist, 'is a sea compared with streams, the law of the church is most wonderful law ... It is known that fénechas [inherited native law] is vain in comparison with the words of God.' This was completely consistent with the doctrine of the Church throughout the medieval period which emphasised the superiority of the spiritual over the secular.

Society in Early Christian Ireland

Early Christian Ireland had a population of between half a million and a million. It fluctuated according to the prevalence of plagues and famines, which were in those days catastrophic and spasmodic (in the eyes of contemporaries) acts of God.

The slow christianisation of Ireland went on through the seventh and eighth centuries. The great monasteries of the day, rather than the kings and princelings who fought for domination throughout the pre-Viking period, were the main economic units in this society. A great monastery like Durrow could have many thousands of tenants, dependent churches with their estates, and vast wealth. By now, too, it was more common for a bishop to rule over these great monastic kingdoms or túaths, and the duties of such a bishop were clearly laid down by the eighth-century text known as the *Riaghail Phátraic* (The Law of Patrick).

> There shall be a chief bishop of each túath to ordain their clergy, to consecrate their churches, to be confessor to rulers and superiors, and to sanctify and bless their children after baptism.

The chief bishop was also responsible for disciplining his clergy and ensuring that church property and ceremonial were duly looked after and observed. In return, the laity were obliged to pay their dues to the clergy and provide for their maintenance. They did not always do so, and this meant that there were not always enough priests to go round.

If we discount the clergy, there were three other distinct social groupings in seventh-century Ireland: commoners, nobility and kings. As it was not a unitary state there were dozens of kings, but most Irishmen were commoners and this class had distinctive sub-divisions. A better-off commoner might be a bóaire (cowman) who might have considerable assets by the standards of the day. A contemporary source noted that a cowman had:

> Seven houses: a corn kiln, a barn (his share in a mill so that it grinds for him), a dwelling-house of 27 feet . . . a pigsty, a calf-fold and a sheep fold. He has twenty cows, two bulls, six oxen, twenty pigs, twenty sheep.

The chronicler went on to note that he had parkland around his houses, and that his wife had four outfits. We may conclude, therefore, that in seventh-century terms he was upwardly mobile! He certainly occupied a much more elevated place in Irish society than the bothach (cottiers) and fuidir (landless men) who came below him in the social pecking order. At the bottom of the pyramid were the senchléithe (hereditary serfs) who were little more than slaves, being bound to the lord and his land.

This fairly rigid social structure was designed to determine the degree of compensation due to a man and his family if he were the victim of an abuse. Status was everything, and if the cowman were a victim he would get more money or goods than a landless man. The higher the status, therefore, the greater the compensation. As one historian has pointed out, this meant that kicking a bishop was likely to be much more expensive than kicking a cowman!

CLIENTSHIP

The social system in Early Christian Ireland depended essentially on the relationship between lord and commoner. This system of célsine, of clientship (from the Gaelic céle or companion), was economic in origin because the lord granted the commoner a fief. This could involve either land or cattle, but its receipt bound the commoner to make an annual payment to his lord.

There were two types of clientship. Sóerrath, free or noble clientship, meant the commoner or freeman (hereditary serfs were excluded) made formal homage on his own behalf to the lord. He was then obliged to serve the lord in any way deemed appropriate, including military service. In this sense, sóerrath had features in common with the Norman feudal system as it operated in England after 1066.

The lesser degree of clientship was called gdiallnae, or base clientship. Again the lord granted the commoner a fief, which usually involved the right to milk cows but could give him oxen, land or other farm animals. A typical fief for a cowman would be twenty-four cows, and he would have to make an annual payment to acknowledge the privilege that had been bestowed upon him. In one sense the clientship was designed to protect the commoner, because the annual tribute was fixed at a level which he could pay, according to his status. Nevertheless, it was clearly the lord who got the better of the bargain. The cowman's obligation, for example, included the right to have one night's feasting a year, when his lord could bring three of his boon companions with him. It also, according to a contemporary account, forced the cowmen to pay over,

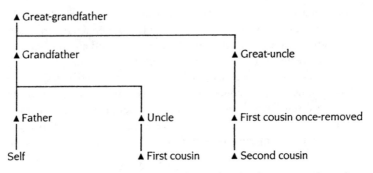

The Family Unit: the derbfhine and gelfhine. The triangles represent the males. The offspring of women of the family belong to her husband's kindred. The derbfhine was, in law, the family unit. In everyday life the smaller family unit, the gelfhine, was predominant, consisting of the male descendants of a common grandfather.

amongst other things, 'a vessel full of ripe cream, 20 loaves of bread, a slab of butter eight inches wide and four inches thick, two fistfuls of Welsh onions and two of leeks'. The luckless cowman was further obliged, as in the later feudal system, to work for the lord at harvest time and do heavy labouring work. The modern reader may be tempted to ask when he had time to earn his own living.

FAMILY LIFE

In seventh-century Ireland the family was the legal unit of the day, but the legal family was not the natural family of father, mother and children. Under Irish law this was the derbfhine, or 'certain family', which consisted of all the male descendants of a common great-grandfather. For practical day-to-day purposes, the closer, more natural unit was the gelfhine, again of the male line, but this time taking its descent from a common grandfather. Any female children belonged to the woman's husband's family.

MARRIAGE

Despite clerical influence, marriage was not the stable and holy insti-tution which the Irish Church would have desired. Divorce and remarriage were common, and so was polygamy in the upper classes. Polygamy was a result both of the desire for heirs and for additional manpower in a feuding and warlike society.

Social Mobility

One effect of polygamy was that there were many offspring related to royal houses, too many to be provided for. Those who fell outside the provision of the court would ultimately slide down the social scale, becoming lesser nobility and commoners. This process was observed by the contemporary chronicler Mac Firbhisigh, who wrote: 'It is a usual thing in the case of great princes, when their children and their families multiply, that their clients and followers are squeezed out, wither away and are wasted.'

This sort of negative social mobility was also evident elsewhere in Irish society, because members of the nobility also fell on hard times and were pushed down the social ladder. By contrast, it was much more unusual for a commoner to become a noble, although it was not unknown. The orthodox strata of society were in any case supplemented from time to time by slaves, who could be prisoners of war, unwanted children or captives from abroad.

MYTHS, LEGENDS AND MUSIC

A poem by G. K. Chesterton ran as follows:

> The great Gaels of Ireland,
> the Lord hath made them mad,
> for all their wars are merry
> and all their songs are sad.

An exaggeration, of course, but the Irish have always shown a great capacity for storytelling and singing. So although written Irish or Gaelic did not appear until about the fifth century, there was already a rich oral tradition. One of the earliest stories was the *Táin Bó Cuailnge* (The Story of the Bull of Culna) which told the tale of a row between Cúchulainn, a sort of Celtic Robin Hood, and Queen Medb (Maeve) about the theft of a prize bull. But it was one of many in a society which, even after the coming of Christianity, remembered the old tales and believed in leprechauns and banshees, a specially frightening sort of witch (they appear in many films, like the rather misty-eyed Hollywood movie *Darby O'Gill and the Little People*). By the eighth century Cúchulainn was being replaced as the great folk hero by Finn Mac Cumaill (Finn McCool) and his Fianna (soldiers).

The tradition of Irish music and song is equally ancient. In the Bronze Age, the old pre-Celtic inhabitants used the oldest Irish musical instrument, the bódhhrán, which was a drum made from goatskin which could be played by hand or with a small stick. The rib-bones of a sheep, goat or cow were also used in traditional music. Harps, so often the symbol of Irish nationalism, came in later in the twelfth century.

Kings and Conflict

Above all, Early Ireland was a country of kings. How many no one really knows but in the seventh century there may have been as many as a hundred. This needs to be compared with Anglo-Saxon England at the same time where by the eighth century there were just six kingdoms, although Cornwall lay outside the jurisdiction of the Anglo-Saxons.

This multiplicity of kings had its special hierarchy. On top, nominally of course, was the High King of Tara but his title was purely symbolic. So in reality no one king could dominate, although there were some who were more powerful than others. Old Irish law recognised three gradations of kings: at the lowest level were the rí túathe or kings of a petty kingdom; then came his overlord, the ruiri or 'great king', who demanded allegiance from a number of petty kings; and over the great kings was the rí ruirech or 'king of overkings', who was likely by this time to be a ruler of one of Ireland's provinces. Kings were endowed with mystical qualities in Old Ireland. The ancient annals are full of accounts of their deeds, and when an ancient king was crowned the ceremony was compared with a marriage, in this case between the king and his land, not his people.

In Christian times there tended to be a close alliance between the provincial kings and the Church. The kings would have divine approval for their rule, and the Church was allowed to levy taxation in the province for the upkeep of its clergy. Biblical texts could be used to justify accepting royal authority, such as the admonition by Christ in the New Testament to 'render unto Caesar the things that are Caesar's; and to God the things that are God's'.

Sometimes Irish kings seemed to want a double dose of approval from the Almighty. The Uí Briúin (O'Brien) kings of Connacht, for example, wanted the blessing of the Armagh church, and having got it allowed church taxes to be imposed in Connacht between 783 and 786 under the terms of the 'Law of Patrick'. But at the same time they wanted the approval of the church at Clonmacnoise and allowed the Law of Ciarán (Clonmacnoise's church tax) to be levied in Connacht as well. It was part of such agreements that kings must rule fairly, not abuse their subjects, and not levy taxes on the clergy.

THE MYTH OF THE HIGH KINGSHIP

It was a characteristic of Irish great kings or overkings that they aspired to the title of High King of Tara. Sometimes this involved inventing a respectable dynastic pedigree which did not stand up to close investigation, but by about the seventh century a distinct feeling of a separate Irish identity had emerged, so that the *An lebor gabála* (Book of the Taking of Ireland) could claim that the Irish had a common ancestry. It also traced the Irish language back to the Biblical disaster of the Tower

The inauguration site of the Uí Néills: Tullaghoge Fort in County Tyrone

of Babel, when God had punished the presumption of mankind in building a tower that would reach the heavens by making men speak in different tongues. The commentary claimed that the Irish language Gaelic was 'melodious and sweet in the mouth'. Vernacular or Irish law also spoke of 'the island of Ireland' even though the island was split up into dozens of little kingdoms.

The strong mythical element in the early Irish sources concerns the achievement of the status of high king. The Old Irish law defined a high king as a king 'who goes through the kingdoms of Ireland from sea to sea ... the five provinces of Ireland, he goes through all their submissions, as has been sung of Conchobar'. Many claimed the title of high king but no one royal house unified the whole island, although the Uí Néills came close to it in the ninth century. This reality did not prevent many other kings from claiming the high kingship, and investing it with a fictitious aura of authority over the whole of Ireland. In reality, the high kingship of Tara remained what it had always been, a symbolic title akin to that of Holy Roman Emperor in Germany, a title which had lost any real meaning long before Napoleon abolished it in 1805. Nevertheless the endemic state of disunity had shown signs of disappearing by the eighth century, if only because a sort of provincial structure had started to appear.

Ulster

In the northernmost Irish province of Ulster, the dominant dynasty were to be the Uí Néills or O'Neills. Their rise to power, however, was a slow one because of opposition from other families inside Ulster and divisions within the Uí Néill clan itself.

CONGÀL THE HALF BLIND

The difficulties facing the Uí Néills can be personified in the career of Congàl Caéch (the Squinting or Half Blind), who was king of Dál nAraidi whose people were descended from the Cruithin (the Old Irish word for the Picts). It is known that the Dál nAraidi kingdom covered the central area of County Antrim and that Congàl ruled them in the early seventh century.

Congàl the Half Blind seems to have been an ambitious ruler, for in 627 he became overking of the whole of the Ulaid clan, of whom the Dál nAraidi were a branch. He then engaged in battle the growing power of the Uí Néills, who at this stage only controlled the east coast of the province, killing their king and a number of Bernician princes who had accepted the protection of the Uí Néills after being driven out of Northumbria by King Edwin (links between Ireland and northern England were still close after the missionary efforts of St Columba).

This victory by Congàl in 628 proved to be short-lived. In 629 he was in turn defeated by the new Uí Néill king Dommall mac Aedo (628–42) in the great battle of Moira in County Down and killed. This appears to have been a major turning point because never again were the Uí Néills to be seriously challenged as they extended their sway over Ulster. Interestingly, the Annals of Ulster accorded the title of 'king of Ireland' to Dommall when he died in 642, which was both wildly inaccurate and an indication of the desirability of that title.

There is another interesting aspect to Congàl Cáech's short drive for power, and that concerns the sanctity of the status of king. According to the *Bechbretha*, an early Irish law tract, Congàl himself was half blinded by bee stings and as a result early Irish law was amended so that bee owners were made responsible for injury inflicted by their swarms. But the *Bechbretha* went on to assert that the law change followed 'the crime of bees against Congàl Cáech whom bees had blinded: and he was king of Tara until it put him out of his sovereignty'. Apart from the curious notion, to a modern reader, that bees could be criminal (it needs to be remembered that 'criminal' animals were being hanged in England as late as the eighteenth century), this statement conveys the mystic feeling of authority which surrounded the throne. An authority which could be apparently lost when the king was disabled in some way.

Puzzlingly, Congàl's blinding does not seem to have prevented him from functioning as king of the Dál nAraidi, although it invalidated his quite unjustified claim to be high king of Tara. Essentially trivial though this episode may appear, it does, in the view of historians, underline the peculiar aura of mysticism surrounding the high kingship, with its many taboos (gessa) and prerogatives (buada). To claim the high kingship, therefore, was to claim these rights for oneself, and the credibility of Irish dynasties could be enhanced by claiming descent from some remote high king. Conversely, when the Uí Néills had established themselves in Ulster, they were careful to obliterate all references to Congàl the Half Blind and his claims.

THE O'NEILLS

The origins of the Uí Néills themselves are obscure. By the end of the seventh century, after disposing of rivals like Congàl, they dominated the north-west and the Irish midlands, but they had claimed the high kingship of Tara from the time of St Patrick. These claims have no basis in fact. Their immediate rise seems to have been more impeded by family feuding than by the maraudings of rivals like Congàl. And this internecine struggle was only settled in the south in 743 when the Clann Cholmáin, who had dominated the midland counties of Meath and Westmeath, emerged as victors. The predictable claim to the high kingship was renewed by the Clann Cholmáin in the mid-ninth century.

Another family feud in north Ulster divided the Uí Néills there. Initially the Cenél Conaill held sway and both Columba and Adomnán belonged to this branch of the Uí Néills. Unsurprisingly, these two clerics gave their royal relatives a very good press. The reputations of rulers, until the end of medieval Europe, were very much at the mercy of churchmen as they invariably were the only chroniclers of events.

All this changed in 734 when the last Cenél Conaill king abdicated. Thereafter the dominant dynasty was the Cenél nEógain, who extended their rule over the whole of Ulster (disposing of Clann Cholmáin) and secured the support of the bishops of Armagh.

Leinster

Originally, the provincial boundary of Leinster seems to have stretched up to the River Boyne, and its heartland was the valley of the Liffey. But the northern area was lost to the Uí Néills, so that by 800 they were appointing governors to rule over northern Leinster. The rest of the province was ruled by the Uí Dúnlainge family who, as usual, took the precaution of allying themselves to a great bishop, in this case of Kildare.

Munster

The western province of Munster was ruled by branches of the Eóganacht clan between the seventh and tenth centuries. They traced their rule back to the fifth century, backing this claim with the wholesome legend that angels had shown their ancestors where to found the royal city of Cashel in County Tipperary! Their later king Oengus was also supposed to have been blessed and baptised by St Patrick. In fact, it is known that the older dynasty of the Érainn was ruling in Munster during this time, but again we see the attempt to provide the dominant dynasty of the day with a good pedigree. Common to the Eóganacht too was the claim to the high kingship which they bestowed upon their most famous king, Cathal mac Finguine (721–42), who had taken on the Uí Néills in battle. Clerical blessing for Eóganacht rule was secured from the famous monastery at Emly, and they liked to think of their dynasty as the most Christian in Ireland. This sanctity did not, unfortunately, prevent their power from waning in the late ninth century.

CHAPTER THREE

The Coming of the Vikings, 795–950

Although Ireland did not experience Roman rule, she did become a victim of a wave of Viking incursions between the eighth and tenth centuries, and shared this experience with much of Western Europe. The fjords and lakes of Norway provided an excellent training ground for the hardy sailors who raided Britain and Ireland, and the earliest raiders followed the route from the western fjords to the Orkneys and Shetlands, the Western Isles of Scotland, and on to the Isle of Man and Ireland. A second route from South Jutland followed the Frisian coastline down to the mouth of the Rhine, and so down to the English and French coastlines. This was largely used by the Danes.

The first Viking landing took place in 795, and in the ninth century an Irish chronicler lamented the 'immense floods and countless sea-vomiting of ships and fleets so that there was not a harbour or landport in the whole of Munster without floods of Danes and pirates'. The 'Danes' referred to in Irish sources were, in fact, from Norway for the most part and disunited Ireland provided a tempting prey for these marauding Nordic warriors. In their famous 'Long Ships', the Vikings swept the seas down to the Mediterranean and westwards to Iceland (870) and even the New World itself. And wherever they went in Ireland, the Vikings pillaged and burnt and desecrated the shrines of Irish Christianity. A vivid reminder of the terror they inspired can be found today in the surviving 'round towers' at places like Clonmac-noise (Co. Offaly). These combined both the functions of belfry and refuge for the monasteries, which were a favourite target for Viking raiders because of their wealth. The entrances to the round towers were high off the ground, and when the alarm bell in the belfry was rung the monks and their tenants could flee inside and pull up the ladder behind them.

The First Attacks

For the first forty years (795–835) the Viking raids were spasmodic and of a hit-and-run nature. In 795 they attacked Columba's community on Iona and Rathlin, Inishmurray and Inishbofin, following these raids with one against St Patrick's Island, near Skerries in County Dublin, in 798. A clear pattern was established hereabouts. Monasteries were burnt and cattle tribute imposed on surrounding areas so that the Vikings were provided with livestock on their return.

Iona suffered again in 802, and a further raid in 806 caused Columba's monks to make a significant change of direction. They decided, for obvious reasons of safety, to move to a new 'city of Columba' at Kells in County Meath which was twenty miles inland (and gave its name to the famous *Book of Kells*). The spasmodic raiding continued into the 820s, but by 823 the Vikings had circumnavigated the whole island of Ireland and in 824 they attacked the remote community on Skellig Michael.

The Ardagh Chalice is the finest piece of Irish metalwork of
the eighth century

Ireland in Danger

After 836 the pattern of Viking attacks started to change. In that year they made their first big inland raid into the area ruled by the southern Uí Néills, carrying many people off into slavery. The native annals recorded this attack as 'a most cruel devastation of all the lands of Connacht by the heathen'.

The next year was to be even worse. Viking fleets of sixty sail appeared on both the Boyne and the Liffey and pillaged the surrounding areas, defeating the southern Uí Néills in the process. Three years later a Viking fleet arrived on Lough Neagh, Ireland's largest lake, where they disembarked and raided the nearby monasteries.

The logical sequel to this pattern of more significant incursions was some form of settlement and this really began in the winter of 841–2, when a Viking fleet wintered for the first time in Dublin (the Vikings were to settle there permanently and adopt the Irish name Dubh Linn or Dark Pool). Evidence for this original Viking settlement survives in the cemetery in the Dublin district of Kilmainham, where ninth-century Viking graves have been discovered.

By now the Vikings had greatly increased the ferocity of their attacks throughout Ireland, and there was a serious danger that they might conquer the entire island. Their mobility was a great asset as their fleets could sail up all the navigable waterways like the Boyne, the Liffey, the Shannon and the Erne. The warring Irish kingdoms were now presented with a dangerous common threat, although it did not unite them against the Vikings. This could actually have been an advantage, and modern historians like Michael Richter believe that it was Ireland's political *disunity* which may have helped to save it from Viking conquest. A unitary state may have one power centre, while a fragmented country like Ireland then was has many.

The Irish Response

The Gaelic Irish (by the eighth century the native Irish were known as Gaels) were not the sort of people to lie down under the Viking threat, however. As early as 811 the Gaelic chronicles recorded the slaughter of a band of Viking invaders by the Ulaid in Ulster, and in the next year the Vikings suffered another bloody nose in County Mayo. In Munster, too, the Eóganacht king Locha Lein routed another band of Viking raiders. The problem was that Gaelic valour could not be utilised on a national basis.

Churchmen also showed their mettle in the Viking wars. In 845, for example, the abbot of Terryglass and Clonenagh and the deputy abbot of Kildare were killed in battle against the invaders (the tradition of warrior churchmen in the Catholic Church lasted down to Pope Julius II, 1503–12, who regularly rode out to fight rival Italian princes). But the menace of the Nordic invaders was still demonstrated in the same year when Forannán, abbot of Armagh, was captured by them while travelling in Munster.

As the mid-century approached the Viking danger began to wane. So, while further Viking fleets appeared in Irish waters in 849 and 851, they began in the 850s to turn their attentions to the equally unfortunate English. It would not be long before an Anglo-Saxon chronicler was praying:

> From the fury of the Norsemen
> Dear Lord, preserve us.

Another factor which distracted the Vikings from the possible conquest of Ireland was internecine conflict. In the late 840s a large Danish fleet arrived in Irish waters and this event started a civil war with the Norwegians. A big naval battle on Strangford Lough appears to have involved hundreds of vessels, and an extra Norwegian fleet had to be dispatched to secure their outposts in Ireland and the Outer Islands of Scotland.

In the latter half of the ninth century, Viking raiding was spasmodic and the Ostmen (literally Eastmen), as they liked to call themselves, were just part of the generally turbulent in-fighting of the Irish kingdoms. In 879, for example, Vikings based around Carlingford Lough attacked Armagh, and the city was attacked again in 898 by another force based on Lough Foyle. Another vast Viking fleet appeared on Lough Neagh in 900.

The Viking Revival

This period of quiescence lasted into the second decade of the tenth century until, in 914, another great Viking fleet arrived in the southern part of Waterford. More Vikings arrived in Wexford in 915 and began to plunder the provinces of Leinster and Munster. This in turn inspired a counter-attack by the Uí Néill overking, Niall Glúndub, who marched southwards into Munster. This intervention seems to have had little impact on Viking marauding and in 919 Glúndub was killed in battle with them, together with many of his followers. Another sign of the revival of Viking power was the seizure of Dublin in 925, following a defeat in 902 which had forced the Vikings out of their first settlement.

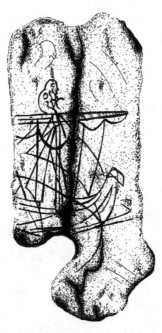

This Viking drawing of a look-out man on a ship's rigging was found in a wooden house excavated in Dublin

For a couple of decades afterwards Viking power was in the ascendant, but there was also a struggle for domination between the Viking kingdom of Dublin and its rivals in Limerick and Waterford. After about 950, Viking raids on Ireland largely ceased.

The Viking Legacy

The actual impact of the Viking wars in Ireland has been a matter of some controversy among modern historians. The more traditional view was that the Viking invasion shattered old Irish society, and had a particularly bad effect on the Church.

THE CHURCH

This view is challenged by Irish historians like Ó Corráin who suggest that, although monastic life was undoubtedly damaged by Viking incursions, the mainstream of Irish monasticism was unaffected. It is true, for example, that despite the proximity of monasteries like Swords, Glasneven, Crumlin and Kilmainham to the Viking settlement of Dublin they survived intact. This more modern interpretation rejects Professor Binchy's thesis about the destruction of old Irish society because it had long since disappeared before the Vikings came to Ireland at all.

That the Viking attacks *did* inspire terror, especially among churchmen, is not in doubt. It is not difficult to imagine the fear aroused by these hirsute and ferocious warriors, or to see in the mind's eye the terrified monks scuttling into their round towers. A flavour of what it was like to live through these times comes across in this poem by a ninth-century monk:

> The wind is fierce tonight
> It tosses the sea's white hair.
> I fear no wild Vikings
> Sailing the quiet main.

In general, historians have been impressed by the stoicism of Irish monks, who complained much less about Viking excesses than their continental counterparts. Edward James has also pointed out that one result of the Viking wars was to send some Irish scholars to safer havens in the court of the Carolingian kings of France. But there was no wholesale destruction of monasteries as there was in England.

THE ECONOMY

The real impact of the Vikings was more positive. They were responsible in particular for developing the Early Irish economy and providing it with flourishing seaports like Dublin, Wexford and Waterford. Dublin became one of the richest cities in Western Europe between the ninth and twelfth centuries, and recent extensive excavations have shown the impressive outlines of the old 'Dark Pool'. Another feature of Viking Ireland was its gold and silver artefacts. Such artefacts have not been found in excavations from the same period in Scotland; plainly, therefore, the Vikings gave Ireland an urban aspect which she had not had before 795. They also provided her with those ships and boats which were needed for commercial contacts with the rest of Europe.

In other respects the impact of the Vikings was not as great in Ireland as it was in England or France. Their attacks may have speeded the downfall of the declining Eóganacht in Munster, but this can only be a tentative analysis. Even then, Munster was in better hands under the more assertive Dál Cais (later O'Brien) kings. So the political impact of the Viking wars was small. The best comparison here is with England, where by the reign of King Alfred (871–99) only Wessex stood up against the power of the Danelaw (that part of England controlled by the Vikings). And Alfred was involved in a life-and-death struggle with the Viking leader Guthrum for most of his reign. Nor were Viking kings like Cnut (Canute) to rule over all Ireland as they did in England.

THE LANGUAGE

The linguistic legacy of the so-called Ostmen is also small, at most leaving Irish Gaelic with fifty Old Norse words. But revealingly many of them are linked to trade and commerce. Thus the Irish words *bád* (boat), *stiúir* (rudder) and *dorgha* (fishing line) have Norse roots, as do *margad* (market) and *schilling* (shilling). Small though it may be, therefore, the Norse input into Gaelic carries with it the essential flavour of those freebooting and marauding sailors who gave Ireland its first cities.

CHAPTER FOUR

From Brian Boru to Strongbow, 951–1169

The name Brian Boru is as evocative to Irish history as those of King Alfred and Robert the Bruce are to English or Scottish history. It has tended to dominate the story of Ireland in the two centuries between the end of the Viking incursions and the Anglo-Norman intervention, possibly to the exclusion of other events.

The Rise of Boru

The spectacular rise of Brian Boru (in Gaelic his name is Brian Bóruma) owed much to the traditional internecine conflict between the Irish kingdoms, which had never ceased even during the most persistent Viking attacks. In this instance, Brian's local power base derived from the decline of the Eóganacht dynasty in Munster in the tenth century and its replacement by his family, the Dál Cais of North Munster. This process was helped both by the attacks on the Eóganacht by the dominant Uí Néill family in the north, and the control of the strategic Shannon river estuary by the Dál Cais. By the time Brian Boru's father Cinnetig died in 951 he was able to call himself 'king of North Munster', but a quarter of a century was to pass before Brian mounted his claim to be high king of Tara (he also had to wait his turn in Munster because his brother Mahon was king there before him). Meantime dynastic wars raged throughout the period between 940 and 970.

At the centre of this feuding were the powerful Uí Néill clan. First it was between the northern and southern branches of the clan itself, then with other dynasties for the legendary title of high king. Initially victory seemed to lie with the northern Uí Néills and their king Domnall (956–80), who imposed his rule on the southern cadet branch and put a garrison into Meath (the first chapter of this book referred to the fact that in early Irish history, Meath was often regarded as a fifth province). However, the victory of north over south proved to be transient and the last Uí Néill king to claim the high kingship of Tara, Mael Sechnaill II, came from the southern branch of the family. He was to be an arch-rival of Brian Boru's in the latter's drive to power in the closing years of the tenth century.

Brian Boru's accession to the throne of the Dál Cais came in circumstances which were typical of the turbulent times in which he lived. His brother had been assassinated and Brian's first act was to take revenge on his murderers, who included in their number the Ostmen or Vikings of Limerick (Brian himself came from modern County Clare). The methods he employed to achieve this revenge show that, whatever his other attainments, he was no angel. For he drove Ímar, the Viking king of Limerick, and his sons, all of whom were Christians, to take refuge in the monastery on Scattery Island. Despite the acknowledged right of any fugitive to seek refuge in church premises, Brian killed them all and compounded the crime by desecrating the church where they were hiding as well. The myths about Boru tend to leave out this episode.

Boru and the Domination of Ireland

Showing, therefore, that he would use any degree of ruthlessness to punish his enemies, Brian Boru swept on to conquer Limerick and the whole of Munster in the next three years. This naturally brought him into conflict with the Uí Néills, who regarded themselves as the first family in Ireland. The actual occasion of their quarrel was Boru's attempt in 980 to conquer Ossary, in combination with the Vikings of Waterford in the south-east who provided the necessary naval power (the Viking settlers had by now become as adept at Irish power politics as the natives). This new alliance enabled Boru to hold down the small kingdoms and monastic towns of Munster before challenging the Uí Néills in Leinster and Connacht.

At this point the Uí Néill high king Mael Sechnaill II attempted to block Boru's ambitions. But he failed and in 997 the two protagonists met at Clonfert and agreed to divide the island between them. This agreement left Boru in control of the province of Leinster, his native Munster, and the old Viking settlement of Dublin.

Boru's rule seems to have been onerous because in 999 the Dubliners and Leinstermen revolted against him. It was hereabouts that Brian Boru showed his military prowess by marching north against the Leinstermen, defeating them at Glenn Máma and taking their king prisoner. He followed up this success with a winter campaign against Dublin which he stormed, plundered, then burnt down its fortress, and ultimately forced its Viking king Sitric Silkenbread to surrender. He then, according to the historian Ó Corráin, set out 'with caution and determination to dominate the whole country'. By now the Dublin Vikings, perhaps recognising a winner when they saw one, had switched their allegiance to Boru.

Boru's domination was achieved in stages. It is known that by 1006 he was able to make an unchallenged tour in the north, showing that he had broken the power of Uí Néills there, and by 1011 he was effectively (as apart from theoretically) high king of all Ireland. Yet as the historian Michael Richter has pointed out, Boru's rise to dominance was 'greeted with suspicion everywhere'. Given the fractious nature of Ireland's dynastic politics, this was hardly surprising; relations with Leinster especially worsened after about 1012, and its king, Máel Mórda, defeated at Glenn Máma a decade earlier, wanted his revenge.

In 1013, therefore, Máel Mórda put together a coalition with the Vikings of the Isle of Man and Jarl Sigurd, lord of Orkney, in an attempt to defeat Boru. This alliance sufficiently frightened the Uí Néill king, Mael Sechnaill, into abandoning his (admittedly enforced) alliance with the man the Uí Néills regarded as an upstart. Brian Boru's reaction was in character. He sent his son Murchadh to attack Leinster, and Murchadh ravaged the countryside as far as Glendalough, encamping his army at Kilmainham in sight of Dublin itself. Here he was joined by Boru in September 1013, and together their forces blockaded the city until Christmas, but without success.

THE BATTLE OF CLONTARF

Having raised the siege of Dublin at the end of the year, in the new year Boru was faced with the combined armies of Leinster and the Vikings of Orkney and Man. The decisive engagement between the rival armies was fought at Clontarf, a suburb of Dublin on the north side of the River Liffey, on Good Friday 1014. It was, according to the annals, unusually bloody and, although Boru's forces were victorious, he himself was killed in the battle. Others to perish were Máel Mórda of Leinster, Jarl Sigurd of Orkney and Boru's son Murchadh.

The battle of Clontarf has been the centrepiece for many Irish and Norse sagas, but it needs to be made clear at this point what it was *not*. Despite the myths still propagated in popular histories and tour guides, Clontarf did not mark the decisive victory of the Irish over the Vikings which ended their effort to conquer the whole island – that particular battle had long been won. Nor was it the struggle which finally broke the power of the Vikings in Ireland. Rather did its significance lie in its place in the history of Ireland's dynastic struggles, for Clontarf put an end to Boru's attempt to establish dominion over all Ireland. The death of his warrior son Murchadh meant that his only surviving son was Donnchadh, described by Richter as 'an inglorious successor', who died while on pilgrimage to Rome in 1064. Although Boru gave his name to the famous family O'Brien, there was to be no long-lasting dynasty of O'Brien high kings.

BORU AND THE CHURCH

Despite the desecration on Scattery Island, Brian Boru, like all aspirant high kings of Tara, was well aware of the need for clerical support for his title. He made his brother Marcán mac Cennétic (died 1010) abbot of Killaloe, Terryglas and Inis Cealtra, and in 1005 spent a whole week in Armagh before recognising it as the apostolic see of Ireland (that is, obtaining its authority as the centre-place of Irish Christianity from St Patrick). Church approval was further secured by the lavish gift of twenty ounces of gold which Brian Boru left on the high altar of the cathedral! The *Book of Armagh* was to describe him after his death as 'imperator Scotorum', or emperor of the Irish (Latin texts often referred to the Irish as Scotus, as we have seen).

BORU'S ACHIEVEMENT

When all the exaggeration of the sagas is set aside, what was the real achievement of Brian Boru, king of the Dál Cais and the nearest thing to a real high king early Ireland ever had? Firstly, his career effectively put an end to the Uí Néill claim to the high kingship of Ireland for ever. Secondly, Boru's reign established a new pattern of fluctuating provincial domination, described in the native annals with the rather quaint euphemism of being ruled by a king of Ireland 'with opposition' (rí co fresabara).

This fluctuating pattern of dominance, which was to continue until the Anglo-Norman intervention in 1169, also heightened the importance of certain powerful Irish families from the eleventh century onwards. Thus, while the O'Neills called themselves after Niall Glúndu mac Aeda back in the tenth century, the O'Tooles took their name from Tuathal ua Muiredaig (died 917) and the O'Connors derived theirs from Conchobhar mac Taidg (967–73), one of their early kings. Certainly by the eleventh century family names were becoming common in Ireland.

Leinster's Recovery

The death of Brian Boru on the battlefield of Clontarf meant that the process of centralisation which he had furthered ceased. Instead there was a revival of the provincial dynasties, especially in Leinster. In that province there was a notable recovery under Diarmait mac Máel mBó (1032–72), to the extent that he, too, claimed the high kingship; the annals describe him as 'king of Ireland with opposition'. In actual fact the rise of Diarmait (Dermot) involved a throwback to much earlier times because his family, the Uí Cheinnselaig, had last ruled in Leinster as far back as 738. Indeed, according to native Irish law, the Uí Cheinnselaig should have lost the title to the Leinster throne for ever. The fact that Diarmait had reclaimed it indicates that there still was a degree of pragmatism where Ireland's provincial kings were concerned.

THE O'BRIENS

Although Brian Boru's ambition to rule all Ireland perished with him at Clontarf, he had sired a distinguished family. By 1063 Murchadh's son Tairrdelbach Uí Briúin (O'Brien) had achieved a dominant position once more in Munster. From 1072 to 1086 he, in turn, was regarded as 'king with opposition'; he certainly appears to have controlled Leinster,

This High Cross at Dysert O'Dea may be a result of the generosity of the O'Brien kings of Munster. The figures are in high-relief with the back and sides carved with animal and floral decoration

Meath and Connacht. And his son Muirchertach (1086–1119) also made himself king of the old Viking fiefdom of Dublin, while claiming the high kingship between 1093 and 1114.

At this point the O'Briens sank bank into relative obscurity in their native province of Munster, their influence being confined to the area around Thomond (Tuadmumu), while in the southern half of the province around Desmond (Desmuma) the MacCarthys became predominant. The regional fluctuations which were such a characteristic of the period before Boru therefore reappeared after his death.

Ireland in 1100

The surviving evidence about what Ireland was like at the beginning of the twelfth century is fragmentary, being a mixture of documentary and archaeological evidence. Of the former the most important, indeed almost the only evidence provided from a foreign source, comes from Gerald of Wales (Giraldus Cambrensis, *c.* 1146–1223), who appears to have spent an entire year in Ireland.

Gerald wrote two major works about Ireland, *Topographia Hibernica* (Geography of Ireland) and *Expugnatio Hibernica* (Conquest of Ireland). The former was especially important in providing us with the only real description of Irish topography for some centuries, but it also contained a history of Ireland from the earliest times to the twelfth century and an idiosyncratic account of the wonders of the country. The latter is far the more interesting. Gerald seems to have believed almost everything he was told by the native Irish, and since he also believed that Ireland was on the outermost fringes of civilisation, almost anything was possible there. Thus descriptions abound of strange beings which were half human and half animal, fish with gold teeth, and corpses which did not decompose. The very stuff indeed of a modern horror film classic! The inference, of course, is that Gerald, himself convinced of the superiority of British civilisation, may have fallen victim to a bit of native exaggeration.

The value of Gerald's second work is as a straightforward history of the early decades of the Anglo-Norman conquest, the only existing one apart from another anonymous chronicle of the period, called *The Song of Dermot and the Earl.*

Wood Quay

A more reliable image of eleventh- and twelfth-century Ireland has been presented by the recent discovery of archaeological remains in Wood Quay, Dublin. These have allowed us to build up a reasonably accurate picture of how the old Viking settlement had developed.

The contrast pointed by the various levels of excavation is particularly significant. So, while the tenth-century level excavation has uncovered gold, silver and glass relics of Scandinavian origin, those from the twelfth have revealed pewter and bronze items of northern French or Norman origin. This archaeological evidence shows that by the twelfth century Dublin was trading with southern England and France, whereas in the earlier period it had been involved in the North Sea trade with Scandinavia. Crucially, this also suggests the existence of trading links with the Anglo-Norman world which *predate* the intervention of 1169. Interestingly, however, the remains of contemporary ships found at Wood Quay do not show any evidence of Norman influence. The ruling house in Dublin was still of Viking origin, although it had intermarried with native Irish families, and the actual extent of Scandinavian influence by the twelfth century is uncertain. The parameters of the Wood Quay excavation have, though, shown that the boundaries of Dublin had been extended to the north bank of the River Liffey, and that by the middle of the eleventh century the city was surrounded by a stone wall. The north bank extension was known as Oxmantown (literally the town of the Ostmen).

A good deal has also been learnt at Wood Quay about the wattle and daub-roofed houses in which Dubliners lived during the period, although these structures never lasted for more than a generation before being knocked down and replaced. They were also cramped, being not more than twelve feet by eighteen, with a single central fireplace, sleeping places around the walls, and a living space in the middle. Nevertheless historians have deduced from the Wood Quay excavations that the Ireland of that day was a good deal more complex and sophisticated than the writings of Gerald of Wales suggest. But it was still an overwhelmingly pastoral economy with a man's wealth still being measured by the number of cattle he owned. Thus while annals report that an ox was worth three ounces of silver, the silver was only used as a unit of counting, it was the ox that was important. For this reason the murrain or distemper of 1133–4, which decimated herds throughout Ireland, was an economic catastrophe of the first order.

The Reform of the Irish Church

If traditional Ireland retained its economic imperatives, so did its Church retain its reputation for learning. Ironically, it was the home-inspired reforms of the twelfth century, rather than (as has frequently been suggested) the excesses of the Vikings, that were to erode this reputation.

According to older histories it was the strengthened links with Rome which allegedly destroyed native learning and tradition, but this view has now been discredited by modern research. The links were, in fact, long-standing, going back to the beginning of the eleventh century. In 1028, for example, we find King Sitric of Dublin (note the Viking name) on pilgrimage in Rome, and in that same century a Gaelic work entitled *Betha Grighóra* (A Life of Gregory the Great) appeared as well. It showed a degree of poetic licence in claiming that Pope Gregory VII (1073–85) was Irish and had been buried on Inishmore, one of the picturesque Aran Islands off the west coast of the country. There is alas absolutely no evidence to back up this claim!

A further suggestion was that it was the Anglo-Norman invasion which forced the Irish Church to change its ways, but this too is untrue. Instead it was the native Irish kings who began the process of church reforms, although it is true that King Tairrdelbach O'Brien corresponded with Pope Gregory VII and Archbishop Lanfranc of Canterbury, both of whom advised him to reform the unacceptable (from Rome's viewpoint) Irish marriage laws. That there was Anglo-Norman *influence* in Ireland is undeniable because between 1074 and 1121 four successive bishops of Dublin were consecrated in Canterbury. It is also true, however, that the first so-called territorial dioceses, which covered a fixed area of territory, appeared in the Viking settlements in the eleventh century, namely Dublin, Waterford and Limerick.

Cormac's Chapel was named after the king of Munster, Cormac MacCarthy.
The style of the architecture is influenced by English Romanesque

The reform initiative, when it did come, started in Munster in 1101 when Tairrdelbach's son Muirchertach gave Cashel (Co. Tipperary) to the Church as the seat for a new archbishopric, and personally presided over a reform synod. Unfortunately no written records survive of what was said at the synod, but we can assume that the marriage laws and a general restructuring of the Irish Church were on the agenda. More importantly there is no evidence that Canterbury either knew of, or was consulted about, the synod. Irish kings also acted as architectural patrons, a notable example of such patronage being the chapel built in the Romanesque style at Cashel by Cormac MacCarthy, king of

Munster (1127–34), who was also a friend of St Malachy, about whom more will be said shortly.

THE SYNOD OF RAITH BRESSAIL

A much more grandiose affair followed a decade later, presided over by Gilbert, bishop of Limerick, who had also been consecrated in England. This synod of Raith Bressail assembled some fifty bishops, 300 priests and 3,000 other clerics together, and its most important decision was to create two permanent Irish archbishoprics at Armagh and Cashel. Significantly, Gilbert of Limerick presided in his role as papal legate, or papal representative, demonstrating Rome's growing influence over the Irish Church; and the Scandinavian 'territorial' bishoprics (Dublin and the others) were not invited to attend.

THE MONASTERIES

Significant changes were also afoot in the Irish monasteries. A major figure here was St Malachy of Armagh (*c.* 1094–1148), who was a friend of St Bernard of Clairvaux, a major monastic reformer in France. Indeed, Bernard wrote a Life of Malachy after the Irish saint's death.

Malachy seems to have been a reluctant leader who begged the Pope to be released from episcopal office without success. He was a Cistercian monk and is known to have founded Ireland's first Cistercian house at Mellifont in County Louth. By 1172 fifteen daughter foundations had appeared. He is also credited with introducing the Rule of St Augustine into Ireland; by 1170 more than sixty Irish foundations followed it.

THE SYNOD OF MELLIFONT

Appropriately perhaps, the next major piece of reform took place at Mellifont, Malachy's first foundation, in 1152 after the saint's death. This too was presided over by a papal legate, specially sent from Rome, who brought with him from the Cistercian Pope Eugene III (1145–53) the pallia (or symbols of office) for the three new archbishoprics of Armagh, Cashel and Tuam (Tuam had been added after the synod of Raith Bressail). This time the Scandinavian bishops were invited to the meeting, and the Irish Church was restructured into the form it has kept ever since.

The Results of the Twelfth-Century Reform

The consequences of the reform have remained controversial. Some historians have regarded them as essentially positive. The new territorial dioceses, it has been pointed out, stimulated the building of stone cathedral churches, like Cormac MacCarthy's at Cashel, which were both larger and longer-lasting than their predecessors. Their stone ruins litter the Irish countryside today. The reform has also been credited with stimulating church-building to the end of the century, and it has been stressed that most of this church-building was done by the Irish. Further reform of the older monasteries also followed the synod of Mellifont and yet another one at Brí Maíc in 1158. This decided that these ancient houses which lived by the old rule of Columba should unite together under the authority of the abbot of Derry.

Others have taken a more pessimistic view of the twelfth-century reforms. Clerical celibacy was enforced, against the old Irish tradition, as was the abolition of hereditary succession to control of monasteries and other foundations. Bishops, it has been pointed out, took over much monastic land in their new territorial dioceses, and thus some great monasteries declined to the level of mere parish churches. With them went the great schools of learning they had fostered so that, in one historian's words, the reformers 'destroyed the social, economic and cultural base of Irish learning'.

One result of this was that monastic scholars were forced out to join the so-called praise poets and make up a new class of bardic poets in the Later Middle Ages. Another consequence was that former clerical lawyers became secularised and created what remains of the native or vernacular law, which survives to this day in records. In fact, these ex-clerical lawyers founded secular legal dynasties, the 'legal eagles' of their day.

On one aspect only does there seem to be complete agreement. There never was any justification for the decision by Pope Adrian IV (1154–9) to grant Henry II (1154–89), king of England and half of France, permission to go to Ireland 'to reform its Church'. (Irish nationalists would think it no coincidence that he was the only English Pope!) This permission was enshrined in the 1155 papal bull

'Laudibiliter', meaning 'It is praiseworthy' (papal bulls are named after the opening word or words), but it was quite beside the point because the Irish Church had begun to reform itself. As matters turned out, Henry did not go to Ireland at all until 1171 and then in quite different circumstances.

Our story has come, therefore, to the fateful turn of events surrounding the Anglo-Norman invasion of 1169, some fourteen years after 'Laudibiliter'. 'At the creek of Baginbun,' runs the Irish poem, 'Ireland was lost and won.'

CHAPTER FIVE

The Norman Invasion,
1169–1300

The Norman Invasion of Ireland, which began in May 1169, was both helped and hindered by the country's disunity. Helped because it made use of Irish dissensions, and hindered because, unlike in England, there was no Irish central government for the Normans to take over.

The Norman opportunity was created by the feud between Dermot MacMurrough (*c*. 1134–71), king of Leinster, and Rory O'Connor, king of Connacht, and his ally the one-eyed king of Bréifne, Tighearnán O'Rourke (Ó Ruaric). In 1166 Rory O'Connor became high king of Tara, replacing Murtough MacLoughlin who had been high king 'with opposition' since 1156. As far back as 1152 there had been a dispute between O'Connor and Mac-Murrough over the agriculturally rich province of Meath; Mac-Murrough had also supported MacLoughlin's claim to be high king, whereas O'Connor had opposed it. More pertinently O'Rourke hated MacMurrough, who (also in 1152) had abducted his wife. There seems to be some dispute about whether this lady Devorgilla connived at her abduction or not!

The accession, therefore, of O'Connor (1166–86) put Mac-Murrough in a dangerous position, particularly as the people of Dublin joined his enemies. The Dubliners had taken exception to being ruled from Leinster and killed MacMurrough's father and, according to legend, buried his corpse with that of a dead dog under the floor of their assembly hall. Beset, therefore, by enemies, MacMurrough sought help abroad in England. So it was that internecine conflict in Ireland was to provide a window of opportunity for the Normans similar to the one in England in 1066.

The Anglo-Norman Attitude to Ireland

Apart from the ecclesiastical links between England and Ireland mentioned in the last chapter, there were other reasons for English interest in Ireland. Thriving trade links existed between Chester and Bristol and Dublin, although the chronicler William of Malmesbury patronisingly wrote, 'Of what value could Ireland be, if deprived of the merchandise of England?' It is known too that there had been talk of invading Ireland during the time of both William the Conqueror (1066–87) and Henry I (1100–35).

This became more serious after the accession of the first Plantagenet king, Henry II (1154–89), when Pope Adrian IV presented him with a gold ring set with an emerald as a symbol of his right, and that of his successors, to rule Ireland. Adrian claimed the right to do this under the terms of the so-called Donation of Constantine (*c.* 750) which allegedly made the Pope lord of all the islands of the sea. It is a profound irony that it was the Papacy, to which the Irish people were so conspicuously loyal over the centuries, that instigated the invasion which was to mark the effective end of their independence. But in 1154–5 Henry was too busy with other matters, so the intervention in Ireland was put aside for nearly two decades until MacMurrough provided the necessary catalyst.

He did so by visiting France in person and going to see Henry who had extensive land holdings there. Doubtless the English king would have remembered Dermot MacMurrough's voice, which was allegedly hoarse from shouting so much in the din of battle, but he was unwilling to intervene personally in the dispute with O'Connor. Nevertheless, he did accept MacMurrough's homage, and did not prevent him from recruiting amongst his knights. Using Bristol as a base, MacMurrough was especially successful at recruiting Welsh Marcher lords (those who guarded the Marches or border area between England and Wales), his chief success being the adherence of Richard FitzGilbert de Clare, earl of Pembroke, better known to history as 'Strongbow' (*c.* 1130–76). Other recruited families which were to be celebrated in Irish history were the Norman FitzHenries, Barrys and Fitzgeralds, and the Flemish Roches and Synnotts. Many of these soldiers of fortune were impoverished younger sons of noble families.

MacMurrough then returned to Ireland in the autumn of 1167, but was overcome by the combined forces of O'Connor and O'Rourke and had to appeal to his Norman allies for help. A small expedition led by Robert de Barry landed near Wexford in 1169, but the major landing came in the following year.

The Coming of Strongbow

On 1 May 1170 de Clare, or Strongbow, landed with his knights at Baginbun on the south-western tip of County Wexford and built a huge rampart to block off the promontory on which they had landed to make it inaccessible to the native Irish thereabouts. It then acted as a bridgehead for further Norman reinforcements. It can still be seen to this day eight centuries on, overgrown with gorse and brambles.

Who were these invaders? It is a valid question; the contemporary Irish poet, Thomas Kinsella, recently reported that, having been educated in the Irish nationalist tradition of the 1930s, he had not known

Strongbow's Seal showing an Anglo-Norman knight on horseback

that the invaders actually spoke French and not English. Historians, too, have had problems about whether to call Strongbow and his companions Anglo-Welsh, English, Anglo-Norman, or even Cambro-Norman (Cambrensis being Wales). As they came from the French-speaking ruling class in England, albeit one that had been anglicised to a degree, Anglo-Norman seems the safest term to use and it will be adhered to here. (The term 'English' in this context is too loose, as the dynasty which ruled England after Henry II is known as the Angevin (from Anjou) and he himself ruled about half of modern France.)

For the same reason the wretched MacMurrough, often made out to be the villain of Irish history, deserves some sympathy. In a world where national boundaries meant little (Ireland's happened to be provided by nature), it was far from unusual to call in foreign help. Henry II's son John (1199–1216) was opposed by barons who begged the assistance of Louis, heir to the French throne.

STRONGBOW'S CONQUEST

Between 1169 and 1171 the Anglo-Norman invaders won a string of fairly easy victories in south-eastern Ireland. The original expedition had captured Wexford, so provoking a desperate expedient by O'Connor who offered to restore MacMurrough as king of Leinster if he would send the Normans back home! Instead, more invaders followed, and in September 1170 Strongbow captured Dublin after first taking Waterford. Then when Dermot MacMurrough died in 1171, Strongbow became king of Leinster having already, as agreed, married MacMurrough's daughter Aoife (Eva).

The Anglo-Norman triumphs in Ireland were largely triumphs of technology. The native Irish never lacked anything in fighting spirit. The Normans had heavily-mailed knights who fought on horseback and were supported by well-trained Welsh crossbowmen, whereas the native Irish still used slings and stones for weaponry, and when they did ride horses, rode them bareback. Once established, the Anglo-Normans also built strongholds, usually on hilltops (sometimes man-made) with fortified houses surrounded by wooden pallisades. In this instance, Ireland's isolation from the rest of Western Europe had meant that she had lagged behind in the vital sphere of military innovation.

Even so the Anglo-Norman knights did not have matters all their own way, and their hold in Ireland in those first two years was sometimes rather precarious.

The Intervention of Henry II

King Henry did not himself arrive in Ireland until 1171, alarmed that his vassal Strongbow might be becoming overmighty. Another factor seems to have been the murder of Thomas à Becket, archbishop of Canterbury, in December 1170, for which Henry himself was generally blamed; Ireland provided him with a convenient bolthole. His claim to be fighting for Christianity, however, has to be regarded as disingenuous.

Strongbow made homage to Henry and as a reward received Leinster as a fief. In 1172 Henry took Dublin under his protection and granted a charter 'to my people from Bristol – my city of Dublin to inhabit'. He also received the submission of the kings of south-east Ireland and the entire Irish clergy at Cashel. Meath was granted in its entirety to Hugh de Lacy. Only Connacht and Ulster remained outside Henry's control and in 1175 the Treaty of Windsor secured the submission of Rory O'Connor of Connacht as well, although he was allowed to keep those parts of the province unconquered by the Anglo-Norman adventurers.

The apparent conquest of Ireland was completed in 1177 when Henry made John, the youngest of his four sons, 'Lord of Ireland'. An additional point of significance was that in 1174 Henry had offered formal penance for inspiring the murder of Becket, a fact which had previously inhibited him from publishing Adrian IV's bull sanctioning the conquest of Ireland. The new pope, Alexander III, sent Henry a letter authorising him to protect the Irish Church, but not to conquer the whole island. However, claiming as he did the Lordship of Ireland for his son John, Henry II went on parcelling out Irish land to other Anglo-Norman lords. The same Council at Oxford, for example, which claimed the Lordship for John granted Cork to Robert Fitz-stephen and Miles de Cogan, while Limerick was given to Philip de Braose. But Henry's attempt to get the Pope to legitimise his claim to all Ireland failed in 1183. Nevertheless, until John succeeded his elder brother Richard as king of England in 1199, there was still a prospect that two independent Plantagenet kingdoms might emerge.

That it remained no more than a prospect was partly a result of John's own boorish behaviour on his visit to Ireland in 1185. Historians disagree about whether he personally pulled the beards of Irish chieftains who had come to meet him at Waterford, or whether it was members of his entourage! What is certain is that John received no declarations of loyalty from Irish provincial chieftains afterwards.

As a result of John's visit a second generation of Anglo-Norman invaders were in place in Ireland, something which caused some resentment among the men who had come over with Strongbow. De Lacy was assassinated by a native Irishman in 1186 but other members of the original 1169–70 group were displaced by John's cronies. Even Gerald of Wales, who was never noted for having a high opinion of the Irish, was disgusted by the behaviour of these new men (as a de Barry, Gerald had relatives in Ireland). They, he wrote, were 'men who ... spent all their time in the greedy pursuit of wealth' and who were 'neither loyal to their subjects nor formidable to their enemies'.

The Earldom of Ulster

There were exceptions. One of them was John de Courcy who was one of the few Anglo-Norman nobles who showed any interest in old Irish traditions; he even commissioned a Life of St Patrick.

De Courcy arrived in Ulster in 1177, having gone there with a few hundred knights and foot soldiers on his own initiative after what seems to have been an invitation from one of the Ulster rulers. In Ulster, as elsewhere in Ireland, the superior weaponry of the Anglo-Norman force was crucial although de Courcy had some narrow scrapes in his early years in the province. In 1178, for example, he was defeated somewhere in County Antrim and only got back to his stronghold at Carrickfergus on foot because all his horses had been killed in the struggle. Survival also depended to a degree on making allies among the Irish of eastern Ulster. But by 1185 de Courcy was confident enough to have a halfpenny coin struck with St Patrick's likeness on one side of the coin and his own on the other. He was probably encouraged in this by Prince John's decision in that same year to acknowledge him as tenant-in-chief and self-styled earl of Ulster. Despite this, when John succeeded to the English throne de Courcy refused to do homage to him, and openly allied himself with native Irish kings like the O'Connors of Connacht. For this he was stripped of his earldom, which was formally bestowed on Hugh de Lacy's son Hugh in 1205.

The so-called 'Earldom of Ulster' developed interesting features which made it both Anglo-Norman yet distinctive from English practice. One was the specialised use of the motte or raised earthen mound on which in Ulster the lord's hall was superimposed. Over a hundred of these earthen mottes can still be found in Ulster today, although they also survive elsewhere in Ireland (as, for example, in Clonard). In England, by contrast, the motte normally supported a tower which was only used as a refuge, while the lord and his family lived in the bailey. This was an enclosure which was big enough to contain the lord's own farmyard, a feature not found in Ulster excavations. In Ulster the purpose of the bailey, rarely found in fact except in castles on the frontiers of Anglo-Norman areas, was purely military; the lord had no farmyard so the purpose of these earthwork castles was almost entirely protective rather than for living. This particular model of castle had died out in England before the end of the twelfth century, but it lingered on in Ulster where areas of the province were still under the control of hostile native Irish.

In other respects, the earldom followed the Norman pattern elsewhere. Its main urban centres, like Carrickfergus, Downpatrick and Coleraine, were laid out in the same style as any other market town in Europe, but they too were very small. Carrickfergus, which served as the capital of the earldom, probably never had more than one thousand people. Merchants and craftsmen from England were encouraged to settle in de Courcy's lands.

The international marriage alliances which were characteristic of the age were a feature of de Courcy's successors, the de Burghs. One of de Burgh's daughters married the heir to the earl of Gloucester, and of their two daughters one married Robert the Bruce (future king of Scotland) and another a member of the House of Stewart.

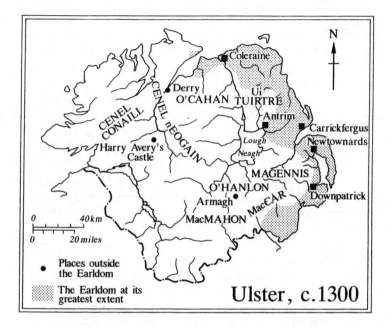

Ulster, c.1300

Places outside the Earldom

The Earldom at its greatest extent

Nevertheless, the actual size of the Earldom of Ulster in the thirteenth century remained very small. It was confined to a coastal strip of no more than fifteen miles in width, which left out much of County Down and County Antrim.

King John in Ireland

When John first went to Ireland in 1185, the Irish annals referred to the fact that 'John Lackland, son of the king of the Saxons, came to Ireland'. John was not, of course, the son of a Saxon king, but he did lack a territory of his own, hence the name by which he was widely known. Matters had changed when he visited Ireland again in 1210 as king of England, with all the authority that the position carried. He came to deal with some turbulent behaviour by his nobles in Ireland, one of whom, Hugh de Lacy, the younger, was driven out of Ulster by John and not restored to the earldom until 1227. Particular royal anger, however, was reserved for William de Broase who was accused of spreading rumours that John had murdered his nephew, Arthur of Brittany (not without some evidence). So de Broase's lands in Limerick were confiscated by the Crown and his wife was allowed to starve in prison. All the Irish kings seem to have done homage to John in 1210, and the visit underlined the importance of regular visits to Ireland by English monarchs. John's visit was actually to be the last by an English king until Richard II went there nearly 200 years later. In the interim no native Irish king did homage to John's successors.

A pattern emerged, therefore, from the original Norman conquest which remained constant throughout the medieval period in Ireland. The rule of the English kings extended only so far as the areas controlled by their vassals. Outside these areas the native Irish did pretty much as they pleased, so that the term 'conquest' has to be used with caution. In theory the Anglo-Norman baronage had conquered three-quarters of Ireland in the thirteenth century; in practice the control they exercised could never be described as more than loose. Just how loose was shown as late as 1280 by a document in which the peasants of Saggart, near Dublin, complained that in the previous seven years the native Irish had stolen 30,000 sheep, 200 head of cattle and 200 pigs from them. And this right under the noses of the royal authorities in Dublin.

The Irish Reaction

What was the native Irish reaction to the Norman conquest? On one level it was cultural. Gerald of Wales discovered that old prophecies made in the names of various Irish saints and used against the Vikings were then being used against the Norman invaders. In 1214 one 'Aodh the Deliverer' claimed to be the embodiment of one of these prophecies. But he turned out to be a fraud, just like Perkin Warbeck (of whom more later) and the succession of false Dimitrys in Russia.

Nevertheless there is some surviving material which bears testimony to the bitterness of the Irish towards this latest wave of foreign invaders. One fragment is a poem from thirteenth-century Bréifne denouncing the murder of Tighearnán O'Rourke by de Lacy:

> Numerous will be their powerful wiles,
>> Their fetters and their manacles,
> Numerous their lies, and executions
>> And their stone houses
> Though great you deem the success of the foreigners
>> You noble men of Ireland;
>> The glorious Angel tells me
> That the Brefnians will avenge Tighearnán

The poem is revealing both in its references to the alien Anglo-Normans and 'their stone houses', and in the conviction that God would help the Irish seek their revenge. Throughout the depradations of successive invaders the native Irish retained their strong sense of cultural and religious identity.

There was also, as we have seen, a second physical reaction against Strongbow's invasion and such resistance went on into the second half of the thirteenth century. But it followed a period of false calm when a series of native Irish rulers, notable as the historian Kathleen Simms has pointed out for the length of their reigns, paid homage to the English king and were accordingly allowed to retain their lands as vassals of the Crown. Amongst these rulers were Cathal O'Connor of Connacht (1195–1224), Aodh Medith O'Neill of Tir Eoghain in Ulster (1198–1230), and Donaugh O'Brien of Thormond in North Munster (1210–42). By mid-century, however, Irish resentment against the new colonisers of their land overflowed. In 1257 Tadhaig O'Connor attacked colonists who were encroaching on his kingdom of Thormond, and in neighbouring Desmond Finghin MacCarthy burnt down the frontier castles which the Anglo-Normans were building around his dwindling kingdom. He followed this up by defeating John Fitz-Thomas and his son at the battle of Callan in 1261, though it was a short-lived victory because Finghin himself was killed in the same year, and replaced as king of Desmond by the more pliant Donal MacCarthy. Succession problems then put a temporary stop to the expansion of the Anglo-Norman baronage in the south-west.

The striking feature about the native Irish kingdoms in the thirteenth century was that so many of them survived at all. The O'Connors survived in Connacht and the O'Neills in Ulster, and in 1258 the Irish were even able to nominate a high king, Brian O'Neill. It did him little good. His reward for this piece of impertinence (as it was perceived in England) was to have his head cut off and sent to King Henry III (1216–72) for claiming the title of 'King of the kings of Ireland'. It followed O'Neill's defeat by Anglo-Norman colonists at the battle of Downpatrick in 1260. Significantly, no native Irishman ever claimed the title of high king of Tara again.

Yet Norman dominance was constantly under challenge in the last half of the century, with native Irish kings waiting to take advantage of any circumstance, such as a baronial minority which favoured them.

THE GERALDINES

The greatest Anglo-Norman baronial family in the thirteenth century were the Fitzgeralds, whose ancestors had come over with Strongbow in 1170. Maurice Fitzgerald, baron of Offaly, was royal justiciar (the secular representative of the Crown) between 1234 and 1245, and during this time he deliberately used Crown forces in Ireland to expand his own territorial base. He was so successful that the Geraldines controlled most of County Sligo and had extensive estates in Mayo, Galway and in Ulster (albeit with the agreement of the de Lacys). Maurice Fitzgerald even laid claim to the whole of County Fermanagh (Fir Manach) and built a castle at Beleek in 1252 while relatives held land in Limerick and Leinster. But when he died it was knocked down by the local Irish king Geoffrey O'Donnell. The town of Sligo, which Fitzgerald had built, was also destroyed by O'Donnell's men. So even the greatest magnates were vulnerable to native Irish revolts.

THE KERNS

In time the Anglo-Norman invaders began to become assimilated and to adopt Irish ways, just as the Vikings had done before them. This process first occurred in the sphere of warfare as the Anglo-Normans tried to adapt to the peculiarities of warfare in Ireland. Indeed, following the advice of Gerald of Wales in his *Expugnatio*, they began to wear lighter armour and even to ride horses bareback in the Irish style and fight on foot in the Irish bogs.

In similar fashion the Irish, who had hired Norman barons in the first place in Dermot MacMurrough's day, began to hire out their military prowess to their new rulers. Such mercenaries were known as 'kerns', small groups of about twenty men, lightly armed and swift of foot, who were recruited by the Anglo-Norman baronage to fight their wars. In peacetime they were a menace as they fell back on robbery and pillage to support themselves.

For their part the Normans had 'routes' or heavily armed foot-soldiers, known to the native Irish as 'seirsenaigh' (close to sergeants), who were also hired by Irish kings to fight in their wars. Gradually the two sides became virtually indistinguishable so that thirteenth-century illustrations show Irish chiefs also wearing chain-mail and tunics.

THE SCOTS

A further cosmopolitan dimension was brought to Irish wars by the appearance of Scots. These mercenaries were known as 'galloglass' (from gall ó glaigh or foreign warriors), and some of them became permanent fixtures in Ireland. Aodh nGall, for example, king of Leinster, was known as 'Aodh of the Foreigners' because in 1259 he married the daughter of Dougal MacRory, king of the Hebrides, who brought 160 galloglass with her to Ireland. It is interesting that the reference to 'Foreigners' here refers to the Scots, which suggests that the Anglo-Normans were coming to be accepted as part of the Irish scene. It would not be long before they would come to think of themselves as Anglo-Irish. Maurice Fitzgerald, the uncle of Gerald of Wales, is quoted as saying, 'To the English we are Irish, to the Irish we are English.' So the distinct identities of the Anglo-Normans and the native Irish were already starting to blur by the middle of the twelfth century.

The Structure of Ireland After the Conquest

By the end of the thirteenth century Ireland had a new political structure. The lands of the English Crown were subdivided into counties and run by royal officials. The history of these counties shows how Crown control spread out gradually from the east coast: Dublin (1199), Cork and Waterford (1207), Munster, Tipperary, Louth (1211), Kerry (1233), Connacht (1247), Roscommon (1292), Carlow (1306). Outside these counties the old Irish kingdoms remained virtually intact.

There were additional Crown territorial units known as 'Liberties'. These were comparable to English palatine earldoms and the most important were Ulster, Leinster and Meath. Initially the Liberties carried no formal title of hereditary earl: in the case of Ulster, for example, the hereditary title only came to Hugh de Burgh in 1263. But the Liberties were subject to English law, although this law was administered by the officials of the Liberty rather than those of the Crown, as was the case in the counties.

Gradually also the other English crown institutions spread to Ireland, such as the Exchequer in 1200, so that the administration in most of that country became distinctively 'English'.

THE CHURCH

The Anglo-Norman conquerors had little difficulty with the Church whose most influential figure, Lorcan O'Toole, archbishop of Dublin

A surviving archway from the Nun's Church at Clonmacnoise which is an excellent example of later Irish Romanesque

(1162–80), attempted to mediate between them and the native Irish. For this he has been attacked by some modern Irish historians, but he was in essence only doing what the native Irish rulers were doing, that is coming to terms with the power of the English Crown. O'Toole was the last archbishop of Dublin of Irish descent, and sufficiently saintly to be canonised by the Church in 1225.

A feature of John's reign was his attempt to ensure that all the bishops in Crown dioceses were Anglo-Norman but Pope Innocent III (1198–1216) prevented this, and by the time of the Fourth Lateran Council in 1215 only a quarter of the thirty-six Irish bishoprics were held by Anglo-Normans. John's own clash with the Papacy resulted in England being placed under a papal interdict, whereby no one was allowed to receive the sacraments and churches were locked. When John capitulated in 1213, Innocent III only agreed to remove the interdict if England and Ireland became papal fiefs. This effectively made King John a papal vassal, and gave Innocent and his successor far more scope for interference in Irish affairs.

In most respects, however, Anglo-Norman influence in the Irish Church increased. John Comyn succeeded O'Toole as archbishop of Dublin in 1181 and it was he who laid the foundation of St Patrick's Cathedral, while his successor Henry of London started the construction of Dublin Castle in 1212. Henry's ambition to secure the primacy of the archbishopric of Dublin over Armagh caused tensions within the Irish Church.

Among the lower clergy, the Anglo-Norman conquest had little immediate effect. Old Irish habits died hard, so clergy were still married and even had concubines. Many lived in separate houses with their families, and clerical livings became hereditary. Only orders like the Franciscans and Dominicans remained free of these native customs, with the former, however, showing considerable interest (like their founder St Francis) in vernacular poetry and music; they formed a close relationship with the Irish bardic musicians and poets. There were still, of course, great centres of monastic learning and piety like the Abbey of Holy Cross, the Cistercian house in County Tipperary.

CONCLUSION

The Anglo-Norman incursions into Ireland after 1169 were, therefore, far more important and influential than those of the Vikings, and they left their imprint on the country in a far more decisive manner. Yet Irish resilience and tenacity were actually to achieve a remarkable resurgence in the fourteenth century.

CHAPTER SIX

The Anglo-Scots War and the Statutes of Kilkenny, 1300–1366

Ireland at the beginning of the fourteenth century was as divided as ever. Ostensibly it was ruled by the English Crown from Dublin but large tracts of land (in western Ulster for example) were beyond the control of the English kings and their barons in Ireland. They could now be delineated as 'English', although intermarriage was to bring them still closer to the native Irish.

The Role of the Crown

Given that the royal justiciars in Dublin lacked the clout to control remote areas like Ulster, the most satisfactory solution was to allow powerful regional magnates like Richard de Burgh, the 'Red Earl' of Ulster, to administer most of that province while remaining formally the feudal vassal of the English king. At the turn of the century, de Burgh was busy strengthening his position in Ulster by taking control of the peninsula of Inishowen, seizing Derry from the Church, and building a castle for himself at Ballymote. The 'Red Earl' had, of course, got English vassals of his own, and his task was to keep them and the native Irish under control. This was no easy task.

Both Edward I (1272–1307) and Edward II (1307–27) seem to have regarded Ireland as a sort of milch-cow to finance their wars in Wales, Scotland and France. Indeed, by 1327 they had brought the Irish exchequer in Dublin near to bankruptcy, although neither monarch had personally set foot in Ireland. Military contributions were also expected. In 1296, for example, an Irish army of 3,000 followed Edward I in his war against the Scots, and 1,500 of these men were supplied by de Burgh.

ABSENTEEISM

When the regional magnate was powerful and, more importantly, *resident*, the system of government worked well enough. But economic factors worked against this in the early part of the fourteenth century. A fall in corn prices, combined with a decline in population growth, meant that many English magnates found more attractive land for themselves in England, and effectively became absentee lords. By 1327 about half of all the English barons in Ireland were absentee land-owners, and resident lords complained bitterly about how the absentees' castles were left in disrepair and the native Irish allowed to encroach into the area of English lordships. Having said this, it was common for barons not just to fight each other but also to encourage the Irish in a rival's lordship to revolt.

The Scottish Intervention

At least one major historian has written that the events which occurred in Ireland between 1315 and 1318 were the most significant there for 150 years. But they saw Ireland unusually involved in the political struggle on the neighbouring island.

Edward I was known as 'the Hammer of the Scots' and he dedicated much of his time to trying to conquer and pacify his troublesome northern neighbour. However, the Scots resolutely refused to accept English rule, and the Scottish war drained Edward's treasury.

Edward was at least a capable soldier, a sphere in which his son Edward II was a disaster. His inept attempts to subdue the Scots culminated in 1314 in a catastrophic defeat at Bannockburn at the hands of Robert the Bruce. This victory, however, which made Bruce a national hero, flew in the face of the realities of power, for inept and bungling though Edward II might be, his kingdom was greater in resources and population. There was an evident danger that the English could, and would, try and conquer Scotland again. This seems to have been the realisation behind Robert Bruce's decision to send his brother Edward to Ireland in 1315 (at that time there was no 'auld alliance' between Scotland and France). Stirring up trouble for the English in Ireland would divert their energies and resources away from Scotland.

EDWARD BRUCE IN IRELAND

Edward Bruce was actually the son-in-law of the earl of Ulster, but such kinship was forgotten when he was offered the support of Donal O'Neill, who asked him to become king of Ireland. O'Neill was probably motivated by dislike of the English, but he had also hoped that Bruce would marry into the native Irish aristocracy and that he would gain personally if Bruce were successful. It is clear that Donal O'Neill did not consult other Irish leaders about the invitation to Bruce, or have their agreement to it.

Nor, as the historian Michael Richter has pointed out, was Bruce's invasion any part of a 'Celtic alliance'. Bruce was descended from a Norman family which had gone to England late in the eleventh century, and then moved on to Scotland where the family became prominent in the fourteenth century. There is, though, a striking similarity between the circumstances surrounding Bruce's invitation to Ireland and that made to Strongbow by Dermot MacMurrough in 1169 (except that Strongbow proved to be much more successful).

Edward Bruce landed at Larne in County Antrim. He immediately defeated the forces of the 'Red Earl' at the Battle of Connor and advanced into Connacht, although the royal authorities in Dublin seem to have believed that he was in league with de Burgh. In Connacht Bruce defeated Roger Mortimer, lord of Trim, returned to Ulster, and was then crowned 'King of Ireland' at Faughart in May 1316. This was absurd, as Bruce had been nowhere near the westernmost province of Munster and had no support there. Bruce's invasion of Connacht also precipitated a native Irish uprising there against the English baronage which was crushed in a savage battle at Athenry in 1316; five Irish kings and many chieftains died in the battle.

In Thomond Richard de Clare, the descendant of Strongbow, was supported by Muirchetach O'Brien and they blocked the southward advance of Bruce and his brother Robert (who came to Ireland for a few weeks in 1317). Nevertheless the Scottish troops advanced up to the walls of Dublin before turning to the south-west and ravaging Tipperary and Limerick. By now, however, Edward Bruce had alienated the English colonists, who must have regarded him as a traitor to their common Norman heritage, and in October 1318, after three years of fire and pillage, he was defeated and killed at the Battle of Faughart. His progress throughout Ireland had merely destabilised the country even further, and thereafter the Scots were to rely on the French alliance as the most effective means of hitting back at the 'auld enemy'.

Meantime the tensions created by the Scottish intervention resulted in further fighting between de Clare and O'Brien when the English baron tried to seize O'Brien's territory. This ended with the defeat and death of de Clare at the Battle of Dysert O'Dea in May 1318. Dynastic problems then arose when de Clare's heir died without issue in 1321, so that claims to the title of king of Thomond were divided between various absentee lords. This left the native Irish O'Briens effectively to themselves for the rest of the Middle Ages.

ROGER MORTIMER

In 1317 Roger Mortimer, who had extensive holdings in Ireland as lord of Trim (Co. Meath), was appointed Lord Lieutenant of Ireland. He was responsible for organising baronial opposition to Edward Bruce and was also, as the ally and lover of Queen Isabella of England, to have extensive periods of influence there (1316–21, 1327–30). During these periods Anglo-Irish magnates increased their privileges, so that John Fitzgerald became earl of Kildare in 1316 and John de Berringham earl of Louth in 1319.

Mortimer's influence ended in Ireland and England because he connived (with Queen Isabella) at the torture and murder of King Edward II at Berkeley Castle in 1327. Mortimer was hanged as a common traitor in 1330 on the order of King Edward III who was outraged by what his mother and Mortimer had done. He even threatened to visit Ireland in person in 1331 (but never did), and ordered that all grants made by Mortimer in Ireland were to be set aside. Magnates were also to be restrained from quartering their private armies in the countryside, and the administration in Dublin was supposed to be purged. But before long Edward III was deeply engrossed in the question of the succession to the French Crown, after which Ireland came a bad second.

BARONIAL FEUDING

With the demise of Mortimer, the Anglo-Irish barons reverted to their normal pattern of squabbles and feuding. The greatest surviving magnate was Earl William de Burgh, grandson of the 'Red Earl', who for some reason was known as the 'Brown Earl'. He had been raised in England and was, therefore, ignorant of Irish conditions. He soon found himself involved in a complicated feud with the de Mandevilles and MacWilliams in Ulster. Temporary victory for the Brown Earl was followed by his death at the hands of the de Mandevilles in 1333, leaving only a baby daughter as heir. A female minority was the worst disaster that could befall a medieval baronial house, dealing a blow to the de Burgh earldom of Ulster from which it never recovered. Subsequently the de Burgh estates fell under direct royal administration though the lands west of the River Bann reverted to native Irish control. Such baronial turbulence was likely to encourage Irish uprisings, and in Connacht rebellious chieftains had to be crushed by a MacWilliam relative Eamonn, known as 'the Scotsman'.

The dangers of absenteeism were underlined by the events which followed the death of William de Burgh. For his daughter married Lionel of Clarence, the third son of Edward III, and their daughter Philippa then married Edmund Mortimer. This meant that the earldom of Ulster, the lordship of Connacht and the liberty of Trim were now all in the possession of one absentee landowner in England. Ultimately all reverted to the control of the Crown. Small wonder that, as Kathleen Simms tells us, the rest of the century was characterised by piteous wails from Dublin about the likelihood of Irish uprisings, assisted by 'Gaelicised Englishmen'.

THE SIGNIFICANCE OF BRUCE'S INVASION

As indicated above, O'Neill's invitation to Edward Bruce did not have the support of Irish kings and chieftains. Real Irish feelings about Bruce were demonstrated by the Irish Annals of 1318. It rejoiced that:

> Edward Bruce, the destroyer of Ireland in general, both foreigners and Gaidhi [Irish] was killed by foreigners in Ireland ... And there was not done from the beginning of the world a deed that was better for the men of

Ireland than that deed. For there came death and loss of people during his time in all Ireland in general for the space of three and a half years and undoubtedly people used to eat each other throughout Ireland.

This last sentence may suggest hyperbole but Bruce's invasion did take place in famine conditions, common to the whole of Europe after three successive harvest failures. In England, the Lanercost Chronicle for 1316 noted how

After Easter, the dearth of corn was much increased. Such a scarcity had not been seen in our time in England ... I have even heard it said that in Northumberland, dogs, horses, and other unclean things were eaten.

In Ireland Bruce's scorched-earth policy worsened an already bad situation.

The significance of Bruce's invasion lies mainly in the way that it showed up the limitations of English power in Ireland. County Roscommon, for example, fell out of English control after the Scottish war, and raids on Dublin by the native Irish of the Wicklow Mountains continued unabated. Yet throughout the disruption of the period, Dublin itself seemed to prosper as the fountainhead of English rule in Ireland. It is known that a new bridge was built over the Liffey in 1322, and that the archbishop of Dublin founded a short-lived university in the city. It seems, therefore, that Dublin had made a financial recovery by the 1320s, and had some status as a cultural centre which attracted scholars from other parts of the British Isles.

The Anglo-Irish Relationship

The relationship between the English baronage in Ireland and the native Irish was, by the fourteenth century, curiously ambivalent. In part this was because the English were becoming Gaelicised to such a degree that they can accurately be called 'Anglo-Irish'. As noted before, they had already adopted Irish ways of fighting and intermarried with them. Even Anglo-Irish castles had their distinct features, appropriate to Irish conditions as we have seen, and Irish chieftains began to build their own castles or 'tower houses'.

Normally the Irish Annals referred to the English as 'foreigners', even though by the 1320s they had been in Ireland for 150 years. But the tone of the comments begins to alter around the time of Edward Bruce's invasion, and some English knights and barons are being credited with good qualities. This probably had much to do with the fact that Irish and English had been united in the fight against Bruce.

THE IRISH REMONSTRANCE

Some Irishmen remained implacably hostile to 'the foreigners', and one such seems to have been Donal O'Neill. It was O'Neill who was responsible for sending the famous letter to Pope John XXII in 1317 which is generally known as 'the Irish Remonstrance'. In it he claimed that since the English had come to Ireland they had mistreated and abused the Irish, and that they were therefore justified in transferring their allegiance to Edward Bruce. He further claimed that, as the papal bull 'Laudabiliter' had been issued by the *English* Pope Adrian IV, it was biased against the Irish, and that the subsequent behaviour of the English in Ireland showed that they were not interested in safeguarding Christianity, the task which Adrian IV had set Henry II. The Ulster leader even went so far as to claim that English clerics said it was not sinful to eat Irishmen!

Claims like this have led some historians to dismiss the Remonstrance as a worthless piece of propaganda. But others see it as an early example of the acceptance of the idea that the bull 'Laudabiliter' was part of an English plot against Ireland. This then flowed into a nationalist tradition which saw England as the source of all Ireland's woes. When England itself ceased to be Catholic after the sixteenth-century Reformation, this Irish belief was strengthened. In the short run, however, the Remonstrance meant little and Edward Bruce had been killed in battle before Pope John XXII ever received it. Yet it did express in its way the ambivalence of Irish attitudes towards their conquerors, so that the Annals could describe Sir William Prendegast as 'a young knight of the best repute and liberality and disposition that was in Ireland', while O'Neill said they advocated cannibalism.

One fact was indisputable by the fourteenth century. The English baronage in Ireland was becoming more and more 'Irish' in its customs and manners, so that the two races were starting to become indistinguishable. Great Anglo-Norman families like the Fitzgeralds were rapidly becoming, to all intents and purposes, Irish.

The Church

Throughout the thirteenth and fourteenth centuries the process of attempting to anglicise the Irish Church went on. In some ways, with the arrival of the famous mendicant orders, the Dominicans (1224) and the Franciscans (1231), it did become more integrated into the European mainstream, but in others it remained obstinately Irish. Disputes continued about whether Irish bishops should be English or Irish, so that a rather unsatisfactory compromise was adopted whereby the incumbents at Armagh and Tuam were Irish, Dublin was an English see, while Cashel nominated clerics from both nationalities.

The situation changed in respect of Armagh after 1303 when all the archbishops were Anglo-Irish appointees, but this was a rare breakthrough for the English tradition in the thirteenth and fourteenth centuries. Even the Cistercians, seemingly the most successful of the European orders in Ireland, seem to have 'gone native' to some degree. An inspection ordered by the mother house at Clairvaux (whose name is associated with St Bernard) in 1228 resulted in the disestablishment of the great house at Mellifont and several others while more were put under the control of Cistercian houses outside Ireland. Such reorganisation left many houses with English superiors, which unsurprisingly caused bitter complaints from Irish monks. Mellifont was only reestablished in 1274.

Elsewhere English efforts to stamp out old Irish customs largely failed. Irish marriage laws, with marriages rather easily contracted and broken, continued to be operated (another feature was the lack of distinction between legitimate and illegitimate children which confused inheritance laws). So did the rather wayward lifestyle of Irish clergy involving marriage and concubinage, hereditary clerical positions, and links with native Irish poets and singers. Even the Cistercian and Augustinian monks in Ireland, historians tell us, abandoned their communal dormitories and lived in separate houses with their illicit families. In the remoter areas of western Ulster, beyond the pretence of

An abandoned monastic building

English rule, the pre-Norman reform movement of the twelfth century failed to make an impact. As late as 1256 one Irish bishop complained of lay people who were still worshipping idols!

The Statutes of Kilkenny

Like most English kings, Edward III intended to do something about Ireland, and then became preoccupied with other matters. He did though send his son Clarence to Ireland in 1361 to act as royal lieutenant, when a pause in the Hundred Years' War with France was temporarily imposed by the Treaty of Bretigny (1360). Warnings were also given to the English aristocracy about looking after their Irish lands properly; in 1360 no less than 80 per cent of English landholders were absentee landlords, which made the Anglo-Irish lords who *did* reside in Ireland quite a distinctive class.

During his stay in Ireland, Clarence considered moving some of the organs of government from Dublin to Carlow, but his first visit was a short one. He returned in 1364 and stayed for two years, and it was at his initiative that the so-called Statutes of Kilkenny of 1366 were promulgated.

On first sight these statutes appear to be a formalised version of colonial racism. The English in Ireland were to have no formal contact with the Irish through marriage, adoption or concubinage. There was to be no trading with the native Irish, and English names only were to be used. Above a certain level of income, horses were to be saddled (clearly aimed at the Anglo-Irish who had adopted the native habit of riding bareback). More significantly, the English Common Law was to replace the Irish Brehon Law. Other provisions seem quaint to a modern eye. There was to be no cursing or swearing at either race (reference was made to the use of expressions like 'Irish dog'). Hurling, a rather dangerous sport akin to hockey, was banned and to be replaced by training in the use of bow and lance (it was the longbowmen of England who had won the Welsh and Scots wars of Edward I and gave Edward III his victories over the French at Crécy and Poitiers). Lastly, there was to be no contact with Irish musicians, poets or singers for fear of espionage.

This was all highly optimistic legislation, given that the Crown was having considerable difficulty in hanging on to its Irish conquests, but it did reflect a genuine concern about the way resident English nobility in Ireland had shown a marked tendency to go native. In the two decades before the Statutes of Kilkenny there had been attempts to make English people get permission if they wished to marry Irish wives or husbands, and to make them use English laws only. Neither effort, it appears, made much impact on the process of Anglo-Irish fraternisation, but there is surviving documentary evidence about how concerned the Crown authorities in Dublin were. In 1367, for example, a document refers to 'Irish, enemies of our lord the king, or English rebels who are reputed and judged [our] enemies of Ireland'. The latter reference was to the Anglo-Irish lords who were perceived to be in alliance with the native Irish, either politically or because they had adopted Irish customs and culture.

The Plague

Ireland, like most of Europe, was affected by the plague of the mid-fourteenth century. It struck Ireland in 1348, presumably carried into the eastern ports by rats, who were the usual carriers of bubonic plague. The symptoms of the disease were hideous: foul-looking boils and fever led within a matter of days to delirium and death. In Kilkenny the

Franciscan friar John Flynn described how 'many died from boils and abscesses and from swellings under their armpits'; few houses, he noted, had only one victim as whole families were carried off by the pestilence. Flynn himself seems to have fallen victim to it. The fear of the plague in the population is also well expressed in another contemporary Irish extract:

> Hugh, son of Connor MacEgan, wrote this on his father's book, in the year of the great plague. It is just a year tonight since I wrote the lines on the margin below; and, if it be God's will, may I reach the anniversary of this great evening once more. Amen. Pater Noster.

The plague appears to have been most serious in urban areas rather than in the countryside where most of the Gaelic Irish lived, but it seems likely that, as elsewhere in Europe, one-third of the population died in the period of the 'Black Death' as it is commonly known.

CHAPTER SEVEN

The Gaelic Revival and The Wars of the Roses,
1366–1513

As English power waned in the course of the fourteenth century, there occurred that phenomenon known as 'The Gaelic Revival'. Its actual importance and extent remain a matter of controversy, but some facts are clear. One is that new areas of Ireland fell under native Irish control in this period. They covered broadly the peninsula of Inishowen, the town and lordship of Sligo, the coastline of County Clare from Ennis to Limerick, and other lands in Monaghan and Leinster. In addition, the Irish seized castles like Ballymote and Cloughoughter from the English colonists.

In large part this process was due to the decline of both baronial control and the power of the English Crown. Edward III, as we have seen, was preoccupied after 1337 with the French war, and only in 1394 was an English monarch to set foot on Irish soil again, the first since King John. But the collapse of baronial rule in certain areas meant that one strong family's rule was replaced by a series of rival lordships, some of them Irish and some of them English. Ulster, where the rule of the de Burghs had collapsed after the murder of William de Burgh in 1333, was a notable example. For although the O'Neills claimed to be lords of Ulster, they never controlled the whole province after the disappearance of the earldom. They even fought among themselves, this feuding often involving other powerful families as well, like the O'Donnell kings of Donegal (a constituent county of the province of Ulster).

What often seems to have happened is that, as the Gaelic Irish saw that English control had weakened, they began to dream great dreams of a past when foreigners had no say in Irish affairs. In 1374, for example, the royal administration is shown to have condemned O'Brien, king of Thomond, for falsely claiming the lordship of the whole of Ireland. This was plainly an inaccurate claim but reflected a hope that Gaelic Ireland was making a political comeback. The extent of this comeback was exaggerated by the native annals.

CULTURE

With a perceived political revival went a cultural revival as well, particularly among the bardic praise-poets who lauded the victories of their Irish patrons and their ancestors, reminding everyone of their noble lineage. Native historians were also used to underwrite the old territorial claims of Irish kings going back to pre-Norman times. One source frequently cited by historians is the Book of Ballymote, dating probably from the 1380s, but it was in many ways a throwback to the twelfth century. The style of the manuscript reflects that era with its leatherwork, wood-carvings and illuminations.

Other historians have noted a linguistic return to pre-Norman forms, although with some modification. Thus the term 'high king' reappears in Irish literature, but by the fourteenth century it was only applied to provincial kings and not to the whole island (the powerful O'Neills still found it impossible to dominate the whole of Ulster). Other terms like *tuath* and *ri* almost disappeared, to be replaced by others such as *taoiseach* (the modern word for prime minister in the Irish Republic) and *oirecht*, meaning a gathering or assembly. Another new term dating from this time was the 'clan', a word used by the Dublin administration to describe the small lordships set up in the vacuum created by local collapses of English power.

Alongside the so-called Gaelic revival went the increasing involvement of the Anglo-Irish baronage in native culture. Gerald Fitzgerald, earl of Desmond (1363–98), was the first great lyrical love poet in the Irish language, and de Berringham, earl of Louth, had the most famous Irish musician of the day, Mulrooney MacCarroll, in his employ. This merely underlines the points made in earlier chapters about the convergence of the two cultures. The Irish language had now also become the language of the Anglo-Irish baronage.

Political Division

Cultural convergence did not, however, coincide with political convergence. Irish kings may have thought they were going back to the good old days but this was not the reality of the time. What can be said is that English political control was a good deal *looser* during the period of the Resurgence. Indeed, the Dublin administration was commonly prepared to pay native Irish kings large sums of money for 'good behaviour', somewhat akin to the system of 'danegeld' in England when King Ethelred the Unready bought off the Danes. Curiously this royal bribery seems to have gone hand in hand with a blessing for the Irish ruler concerned. Thus in 1350 John O'Byrne was elected leader of the O'Byrnes in front of the royal justiciar, paid his money, and swore to keep the peace for two years! Confusingly though, in Ulster, where only the Savages remained as an English baronial power of substance, the English Crown still had a small toehold; Carrickfergus remained loyal to the Crown, as did those areas under the rule of the Savages and their allies, the Whites. Thus there was still a tripartite system operating in fourteenth-century Ireland

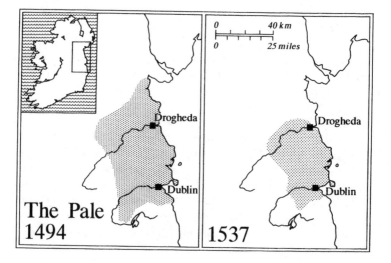

The Pale 1494

0   40 km
0   25 miles

Drogheda

Dublin

1537

Drogheda

Dublin

(Crown, Anglo-Irish baronage and Irish). But the goalposts had been moved.

What cannot be denied is that by the end of the century, and increasingly in the fifteenth century, the power and the influence of the English Crown in Ireland had waned substantially. In the second half of the latter century its control had effectively been reduced to the area known as the Pale (the origin of the saying 'beyond the pale'). This consisted of the four eastern counties of Kildare, Louth, Meath and Dublin, and was protected from Irish depradations by a fortified earthen rampant (although curiously half of Kildare and Meath was left on the other side of it).

Richard II's Intervention

In 1394 King Richard II (1377–99) sailed for Ireland, the first English monarch to visit that country since 1210. The English chronicler Walsingham described the event thus:

> In September, King Richard sailed for Ireland accompanied by the duke of Gloucester and the earls of March, Nottingham, and Rutland. The Irish were terrified by this huge force, and did not dare to risk an open battle; instead, they subjected the king's army to numerous ambushes. In the end, however, the English overcame them, and many of the Irish chieftains were compelled to submit to Richard, who kept several of them with him, lest they should stir up any more trouble. He remained in Ireland until after Easter 1395.

Walsingham showed a characteristic English disposition to assume that things were going better in Ireland than they really were. True, the native Irish were somewhat intimidated by the 'huge force' (actually 10,000 men and certainly the largest force sent by the English Crown to Ireland), and most of them appear to have sworn allegiance to Richard. In Leinster some of the chieftains did so with ropes around their necks (although the O'Donnells of the north-west refused their allegiance). However, this was something of a hollow victory because the 'rebel English' (i.e. the Anglo-Irish baronage) refused to show themselves, apparently for fear of losing their possessions should Richard cancel their titles.

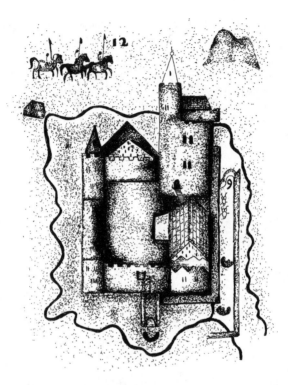

The Siege of Glin Castle. A contemporary drawing of a typical fortified castle as lived in by both the Gaelic and Anglo-Irish nobility

Richard, who saw himself as Lord of all the Irish and English, also tried to mediate between the O'Neills and Roger Mortimer, earl of March, earl of Ulster, and heir to the English throne. Mortimer's title meant little because he had no control over Ulster, but he took exception to the so-called 'Great O'Neill', Niall Mor, styling himself 'Prince' and 'Governor of the Irish in Ulster'. In reality O'Neill's claim was as meaningless as Mortimer's, but it did reflect a growing tendency of Irish leaders to adopt English titles as well as Irish ones.

That the Irish were never really in terror of the English Crown was soon demonstrated when Richard went home in 1395 and war immediately broke out between Mortimer and the O'Neills. Although he won the campaign with the help of the earls of Ormond and Desmond, Mortimer was to die in battle with the Leinster Irish in 1398. Richard himself returned to Ireland briefly in 1399 but the visit did him little good. While he was away, the usurper Henry Bolingbroke, earl of Lancaster (later Henry IV), landed in England and attracted widespread support from the English aristocracy. Ironically, therefore, one of the few English kings who took a personal interest in Irish affairs paid for this interest with the loss of his throne, and ultimately his life.

Ireland and the Wars of the Roses

The overthrow of Richard II in 1399 was the origin of the process which led to civil war in England, a struggle commonly known as the Wars of the Roses. In this struggle Ireland was generally a spectator, although not always an impartial one as the rival English factions found support there. The puzzle perhaps is that the lengthy struggle in England (1455–85) did not provide an opportunity for the Irish to free themselves of English rule permanently. That they did not was due to the power and influence of the Anglo-Irish earldoms which, however much they had imbibed Irish language and cultures, were not about to hand over control of Ireland to the O'Neills, O'Donnells and Mac-Carthys.

This did not mean that the Anglo-Irish were able to curb the marauding activities of the Irish chieftains in the early part of the fifteenth century. For the death of Mortimer in 1398 was followed by a period in Ulster when the O'Donnells formed a confederation of Irish chieftains which began to raid the Irish Midland counties of Meath and Louth. In 1423 such a raid forced Louth to agree to pay 'black rent', effectively protection money, to the Ulster chiefs.

This pattern continued into the second part of the century, as in 1466 when Conn O'Connor attacked along the borders of County Meath and actually succeeded in capturing the Great Earl of Desmond (leading figures in Ireland often acquired the title 'Great'), then Lord Deputy for the English Crown. This in turn allowed O'Brien of

**Late Fifteenth Century Ireland
with Lordship Boundaries**

Thormond in the south to invade Desmond and extract black rent from the city of Limerick.

The Domination of the Earls

What the Anglo-Irish did secure in the fourteenth century was a virtual monopoly of power in the Pale around Dublin because the English Crown was either preoccupied with the French war (renewed between 1415 and 1453) or the Wars of the Roses between the rival houses of York and Lancaster. This monopoly was held first by the Butler earls of Ormond, and then by the Fitzgerald earls of Desmond and Kildare. These great earls largely ignored feeble attempts by Henry VI (1422–61) and Edward IV (1461–83) to interfere with their activities in Ireland. There was one major period of exception when Richard of York, claimant to the English Crown, was Lord Lieutenant between 1447 and 1460, although he was only intermittently in the island. He won good opinions in Ireland, which did much to make the Anglo-Irish sympathetic to the white rose of York.

Generally, however, the country was dominated by the earls from about 1420 onwards. Firstly by James Butler, earl of Ormond, who maintained his influence by building up his support among royal officials in the Pale, and allegedly packing the Anglo-Irish parliament in Dublin even with his own servants. Whenever Ormond's political opponents seemed likely to get the top positions like treasurer or justiciar, he apparently incited the native Irish or 'rebel English' to rebel. His object was to secure permanent reappointment for himself as Lord Deputy, an ambition which he was kept from fulfilling entirely by Sir John Talbot, earl of Shrewsbury, and his brother Richard Talbot, archbishop of Dublin, both of whom used their influence to keep Ormond in check. James Butler, the 'White Earl' of Ormond, then died in 1452, but his sons made the mistake of backing the losing Lancastrian side in the English civil war, and the Butler earldom fell into abeyance. By contrast, the Geraldines (the Fitzgerald earls of Desmond and Kildare) backed the victorious Yorkists, and for the rest of the century the Lord Deputyship tended to alternate between the two rival branches of the family.

Only once was there serious meddling from England thereafter. This was between 1467 and 1470 when Edward IV unwisely appointed John Tiptoft, earl of Worcester, as Lord Deputy (he was already notorious for excesses in the Wars of the Roses). Tiptoft's efforts to assert royal authority resulted in the execution of the Great Earl of Desmond in 1468, which subsequently provoked a revolt by the Geraldines in Munster. When Tiptoft was recalled to assist Edward IV in the crisis of 1470–1 which almost cost him his throne, the earls of Kildare were left with a clear field. Starting with Thomas Fitzmaurice (1456–78), successive Fitzgerald earls of Kildare used the strategic position of their earldom, next to the Pale, to dominate the Anglo-Irish parliament and the King's Council in Dublin. The Palemen, as they became known, knew well enough that Kildare could annex the territory and had to bear with his exactions, which included billeting troops in their houses and forcing the householders to pay their expenses.

TWO PRETENDERS

The Anglo-Irish sympathy for the Yorkist cause remained after Henry VII (1485–1509) reversed the verdict of the main phase of the Wars of the Roses by defeating Richard III (1483–5) in 1485. This involved supporting the two Yorkist pretenders to the English throne, Lambert Simnel and Perkin Warbeck. Simnel (who was crowned in Dublin in 1487) claimed to be the earl of Warwick, Edward IV and Richard III's nephew, and Warbeck to be Edward V's younger brother Richard of York (the two brothers had probably been murdered in the Tower of London by Richard III). Both pretenders were defeated in England.

Poyning's Law

Henry VII was sufficiently irritated by the pretenders' support in Ireland to take some long overdue interest in Irish matters. He had been particularly angered by the Irish parliament's proclamations acknowledging both Simnel and Warbeck as true heirs, and sent Sir Edward Poyning to Ireland as Lord Deputy to curb its excesses. Poyning's Law of 1494 decreed that the Dublin parliament was to be subordinate to the English Crown Council. It also said that the great offices of chancellor and treasurer were no longer to be life appointments, nor were they to have the power to elect a new justiciar. No parliament was to be held in Ireland without the express permission of the English king.

As a punishment for his support for Simnel and Warbeck, Gerald Mór Fitzgerald, the 'Great Earl' of Kildare (1478–1513), had been dismissed from his position as Lord Deputy and imprisoned. But predictably, Kildare's arrest inspired a series of border raids by his native Irish allies against the Pale, and the Crown lacked the force to do anything about it. Living up to his reputation for meanness, Henry VII would not spend the money to reimpose English authority in Ireland effectively. Without such an effort Poyning's Law meant little, and this was soon shown by Kildare's return to the office of Lord Deputy in 1496, a position which he maintained until his death in 1513. In the absence of a deliberate policy of reconquest, the English Crown had little option but to rely on the support of the Kildares, however much it might dislike their pretensions.

CONCLUSION

Superficially, Ireland in the fifteenth century seemed to be in as chaotic a state as in the fourteenth. It was certainly true that the power of the English Crown had waned even further during the century, but under the Anglo-Irish earls, with their strong links with the native Irish, there was in fact a greater degree of stability. And from the point of view of the native Irish, the domination of an Ormond or a Kildare was infinitely preferable to strong rule from Dublin or London.

CHAPTER EIGHT

The Tudor Conquest, 1513–1607

The domination of Ireland by the earls of Kildare continued until the end of the first third of the sixteenth century. Again this dominance owed much to the preoccupation of the English Crown with other matters: Henry VII was anxious to secure the throne for the Tudor dynasty, and his successor Henry VIII (1509–47) fought wars with the French and the Scots before devoting his attention to the severance of England's allegiance to the Catholic Church.

The last issue was to have serious consequences for Ireland, as a Protestant England was to adopt an increasingly hostile attitude towards her neighbour. Either the Irish were labelled as obstinate 'Papists' (Catholics), or they were regarded as a security risk because their adherence to the old faith made them potential allies for Catholic powers like France and Spain. Certainly, as one historian has pointed out, Catholic Ireland always had the ear of Madrid or Paris for its grievances against the English. Conversely, Henry's decision to marry Anne Boleyn, his second wife, provoked a greater interest in Irish affairs, because the Boleyns had claims on the Butler earldom of Ormond and encouraged Henry to reassert his authority there.

The Fall of the Kildares

Until 1534, however, the Kildares were left to run Irish affairs much as they pleased, although large tracts of Gaelic Irish land were outside their effective control. The English Crown recognised that the Kildare earls Gerald Mór Fitzgerald (1478–1513) and Gerald Óg Fitzgerald (1513–34) were the only magnates in Ireland with the power and reputation to hold down the post of Lord Deputy of Ireland. Nor, as has been seen in the last chapter, was their influence much restricted by Poyning's Law.

It is important to note, none the less, that the authority of the Kildares was strictly limited, even if it was more extensive than that of the Crown authorities in the Pale (now so weak that it had been effectively devolved to the Kildares). The Tudor state papers for 1515 give a vivid picture of the rather anarchic state of Ireland, just six years after the accession of Henry VIII:

> More than sixty counties called regions inhabited with the King's enemies ... where reigneth more than sixty chief captains wherein some call themselves Kings, some Princes, some Dukes, some Archdukes that liveth only by the sword and obeyeth unto no other temporal person ... and every of the said captains maketh war and peace for himself ... Also there be thirty great captains of the English folk that follow the same Irish order ... and every of them maketh war and peace for himself without any licence of the King...

The collapse of royal authority in Ireland may have encouraged Gerald Óg Fitzgerald and his son, 'Silken' Thomas, to revolt against Henry VIII in 1534, and this gave Henry a chance to reorder Irish affairs. The elder Fitzgerald died in the Tower; 'Silken' Thomas perished on the scaffold in 1536 for his treason. But English attempts to reduce Ireland by force were no more successful than they had been in the past: royal artillery and the few troops available to be sent to Ireland could scatter Irish bowmen but they could then retreat into their pathless bogs and forests where only the foolhardy might follow them. Henry's problem was that nothing short of a large, well-paid army would suffice to conquer Ireland and he did not have one.

Henry VIII's Reforms

Plainly some alternative strategy had to be adopted. Henry had already, in 1537, enacted the same religious legislation for Ireland as for England (that is, laws creating him Supreme Head of the Church in England and severing the link with Rome), but it meant little when Crown authority carried such little clout. He therefore decided on a radically new approach. First of all the Crown declared its ownership of all lands in Ireland: all existing land was to be surrendered to it, and then regranted to the king's Irish subjects. The title 'Lord of Ireland' which successive English monarchs had taken was replaced by that of 'King of Ireland', which Henry now took.

At least one historian, Ciaran Brady, sees the 1541 Act proclaiming Ireland a kingdom on an equal footing with England (but, of course, under the Tudor monarchy) as a more significant watershed than the fall of the Kildares between 1534 and 1536. It also swept away the thinking behind the Statutes of Kilkenny, which had placed the native Irish outside English law. Instead English law, most importantly that applying to property, was to apply to Irish and English alike. Gaelic chieftains were offered secure land titles as tenants-in-chief of the English Crown, and also a share of monastic land which Henry intended to confiscate in Ireland as he did in England at the time of the Reformation. The same privileges were accorded to the Anglo-Irish baronage, whom the Tudor chroniclers had taken to referring to as 'the degenerate English'. In return the aristocracy, be they Irish or Anglo-Irish, were expected to attend parliament in Dublin, be available for military service, stop demanding black rent, and allow the English king to educate their sons. The last two provisions really only applied to the Irish, some of whom now became part of the Anglo-Irish aristocracy. Thus the O'Neills became earls of Tyrone, the O'Briens earls of Thomond, and the Mac William Burkes earls of Clanrickarde.

In the short term, the new policy seemed to be having some success. Irish kerns fought in Henry's army at the siege of Boulogne in 1544, and the new Lord Deputy, Saint Leger, wrote that if the new strategy could be followed 'but two descents' (i.e. two generations) it would succeed. But it did not. Superficially this failure appeared to have resulted from the efforts of Edward VI (1547–53) and his government to 'Protestantise' Ireland; this included such provocative behaviour as the burning of St Patrick's staff and other holy relics, and such behaviour was resented by the Catholic Irish. More easily forgotten is the fact that it was the fiercely Catholic Mary Tudor (1553–8) who confiscated the lands of the rebellious O'Mores and O'Connors, so beginning the much-resented policy of planting English settlers, by creating King's County (Co. Laois) and Queen's County (Co. Offaly).

The real reason for the failure of the reforms resulted from a misunderstanding of the nature of Irish society. A native Irish chieftain,

Sir Thomas Lee, English Captain General of the kern. A 1594 portrait which shows him dressed partly in conventional Elizabethan style and barefooted, carrying the lance of an Irish kern in keeping with alleged Gaelic 'barbarism'

unlike his Anglo-Irish counterpart, had never been a feudal lord; the land belonged not to him but to the clan, by means of the process known as gavelkind (arranging a periodic redistribution of land among the clan members). The chieftain was not selected by primogeniture but by election (normally the strongest available member from the male line was picked) as *tánaiste* or successor. Such a system of land ownership made the Henrican land reforms inoperable, because there was no consistent line of authority to enforce it. This problem was only to be addressed during the reign of Henry's daughter and successor Elizabeth I (1558–1603). Her reign too was to see the first comprehensive attempt to conquer the whole island of Ireland since the time of Strongbow, firstly by persuasion and then by force.

Ireland under Elizabeth I

Like her brother Edward, Elizabeth Tudor espoused the Protestant religion. She was, therefore, aware of the danger presented by an anarchic, still Catholic Ireland as a tempting base for hostile powers desiring her overthrow and that of the Protestant Reformation in England. Yet for much of her reign Ireland was in as chaotic a state as it was under her predecessors; nor did the queen show undue interest in her other realm. Just three parliaments met in Dublin in a period of forty-three years, and the lord deputies behaved no better than the native Irish whom they affected to despise. They were free in the use of kidnapping and assassination, and the coinage in the Pale was frequently debased to raise funds. Captains in the employ of the Crown were known to take pay for non-existent soldiers, while expatriate Englishmen sought opportunities to grab land in Ireland. This last development was a precursor of a much more systematic attempt to settle Englishmen in Ireland, particularly in Munster.

Wars raged throughout the later Elizabethan period, devastating the country. A foreign ambassador described the Irish wars as 'the Englishman's grave', as the wretched inmates of England's gaols were sent to fight, often without pay, against an enemy who melted away into misty bogs and whom, one Englishman wrote, 'hounds can scarce follow and much less men'. Thousands of English died of dysentery and scurvy. As for the Irish themselves, the English poet Edmund Spenser (himself a Munster colonist) wrote of how, in Munster,

> They were brought to such wretchedness as that any stony heart would have rued the same. Out of every corner of the woods and glens they came creeping forth upon their hands, for their legs would not bear them. They looked anatomies of death, they spake like ghosts crying out of their graves...

In the war for Munster there were contemporary accounts of cannibalism and bodies found with mouths green from eating nettles. Wolves returned to parts of the province and cattle reputedly disappeared from miles of countryside. Such terrible suffering was a consequence of desperate Irish resistance to the systematic conquest of Ireland in the later years of Elizabeth's reign.

SHANE O'NEILL

In the earlier decades of her reign Elizabeth had other problems, notably Mary Queen of Scots who had a claim to the English throne. This encouraged the ambitions of Shane O'Neill (1530–67), whose career demonstrated precisely why the Henrican reforms would not work.

O'Neill, often known as 'the Proud', was the son of Con, first earl of Tyrone, and was elected 'The O'Neill' (head of the clan) in 1559. This election had Queen Elizabeth's approval but it was withdrawn in 1560, whereupon O'Neill took up arms against the Crown and refused his allegiance. Summoned to London in 1562 to submit, O'Neill allegedly howled for forgiveness at the queen's feet and persuaded her to accept his rights and titles! Once back in Ireland, however, he continued his career as an opponent of the English Crown. He attacked the MacDonnells in Antrim, invaded the Pale, and burnt Armagh in 1566 before being ultimately defeated by Hugh Dubh O'Donnell at Lough Swilly in 1567. O'Neill then sought refuge in Cushendun with the MacDonnells, who murdered him and sent his head to the Lord Deputy Sidney in pickle. Historians have seen Shane O'Neill as the archetype of the old Gaelic chieftain; he never learnt English.

The Geraldine Revolt

The Geraldine revolt from 1569 to 1583, which represented a far more serious challenge to Crown authority than Shane O'Neill had done, was influenced by three major factors. One was jealousy of the new influence of Ormond, an anglicised favourite of Queen Elizabeth who was advising her on Irish policy. Another was the animosity between England and Catholic Spain, a country which Irish chieftains claimed as their motherland; in Munster especially there was, from the Crown viewpoint, an ominous falling away in loyalty. Most importantly, however, there was a new unity among the Irish, encouraged by opposition in an overwhelmingly Catholic country to the Protestant Reformation although the zealotry of later centuries was not a feature of Irish life at this time. This was not because the English government attempted to enforce oaths of acceptance of the new religion, but because, in many areas, religious observance itself was low. Certainly the state of the new Church of Ireland (Ireland's version of the Church of England) was parlous indeed. Even in County Meath, the most anglicised of the Irish counties, 105 out of 224 parishes had no parson, while in others curates were starving and few of them spoke English. Hundreds of churches were in ruins, and there were no service books in Irish until the end of the Elizabethan period. So bad had the situation become that in 1604, the year after Elizabeth I died, the Crown Attorney-General noted that in Ireland there was 'no more demonstration of religion than among Tartars or cannibals'.

The Geraldine revolt was spearheaded by James Fitzmaurice Fitzgerald (1530–79), cousin of the fifteenth earl of Desmond, who fought on the Continent before returning to Ireland in 1570 to lead opposition to the plantation of English settlers in Munster. Fitzgerald was unable, at this stage, to win support in the Spanish or French courts but was well received in Rome by Pope Pius V (1566–72) (who excommunicated Elizabeth I as a heretic). In July 1579 Fitzgerald landed with a small force at Dingle (Co. Kerry) and proclaimed a 'holy war' against the English heretics. Roy Foster points out that this religious crusade was unusual because 'Irishness' and Catholicism were not at that time synonymous. Typically, the Geraldine revolt was undone by that Irish vice of disunity, for as he prepared to march northwards to whip up support Fitzgerald was killed in a skirmish with a Burke cousin.

The Revolt of Hugh O'Neill

Hugh O'Neill (1540–1616), earl of Tyrone, was the antithesis of his ill-starred kinsman Shane O'Neill. He was in a real sense an English gentleman, brought up in the new religion in England, and serving in the English army in Ireland from 1568. He is known to have bewailed the Irish refusal to adopt English ways, yet it was he who was to lead what has been described as the 'last great Gaelic counter-attack'. Why was this? He seemed to be a protégé of Elizabeth I, who made him earl of Tyrone in 1585, but his Gaelic ancestry turned out to be the dominant factor. Had not the Uí Néills of the legendary past claimed the mythical high kingship of Tara? These bonds proved strong indeed. Another way of looking at it is to see Hugh O'Neill as a man who was loyal to the Crown when it suited his book to be so.

At first the rebel cause prospered. O'Neill allied himself to the neighbouring O'Donnells and in 1598 defeated an English force at the

The Earl of Tyrone, Hugh O'Neill

Yellow Ford (ironically the English commander was his own brother-in-law), so endangering the whole of English rule in Ireland. Queen Elizabeth was alarmed enough to send her own favourite, the earl of Essex, to Ireland to bring O'Neill to heel. Instead Essex was hoodwinked by O'Neill into a compromise peace while his angry mistress bombarded him with messages: 'O'Neill, my lord, is in the north. You are in the south. Why, my lord, why?' she demanded, while ignoring the fact that the wretched Essex had to put down rebels in Munster. Provoked into an ill-advised attempt to overthrow the queen himself Essex was beheaded and replaced by his own subordinate, Mountjoy, as Lord Deputy.

Mountjoy used draconian methods to reconquer Ireland, but the moment of crisis came in 1601 when a great Spanish fleet set sail to help O'Neill. It anchored in the harbour at Kinsale (Co. Cork), forcing Mountjoy to turn southwards and besiege the Spaniards there. Meanwhile O'Neill and Hugh O'Donnell were in Ulster when they received the news of the Spanish landing, but manoeuvring cleverly they evaded all Crown forces in a southward march. In his turn Mountjoy was besieged at Kinsale.

A decisive engagement now took place. But whereas at the Yellow Ford O'Neill had used the guerilla tactics at which the Irish were so skilled, at Kinsale he was forced to fight in the open. The Irish were routed by Mountjoy and O'Neill's army was broken up in confusion. The earl himself made his formal submission to the English Crown, apparently kneeling for a long time before Mountjoy in a gesture of humility before being taken to Dublin Castle. He obtained a pardon but his power was broken.

The traditional view of the Tudor Conquest in Ireland was that it was part of a long-term systematic attempt to conquer the country. Modern research does not support this view. Rather it was the last expedient of an English government which had hoped to win over the Anglo-Irish, and to a degree the Gaelic Irish, by persuasion and bribery. Bribery might mean giving the Butlers and Fitzgeralds their share of confiscated monastic land in Ireland (and it was accepted with gratitude). Nor was the 1537 Act of Supremacy forced down Irish throats, despite some provocations referred to already. Only late in the century were royal officials required to be Protestants.

So what went wrong? Various suggestions have been put forward, two of which have the most credibility. The first is that the absence of an Irish court meant that there was no natural focus for Anglo-Irish or Gaelic lords; London was too far away to be an adequate substitute. The other is that, despite the restoration of the Kildares and Desmonds to royal favour in the 1550s, political stability was not restored to Ireland thereafter. Whereas up to the 1530s the Kildares had been in alliance with families like the O'Neills who accepted their authority, they were never to hold such power again and were not replaced. Hence the O'Neill revolts of the 1560s and 1590s, in what had become a political vacuum. Crucially, too, the successive Lord Deputies failed to offer an adequate alternative. Earlier, like Saint Leger, they had showered the Irish with favours to win support; later, like Sir Henry Sidney, they left the Irish severely alone and bestowed no favours. Neither policy worked, and conquest was the last resort. It went hand in hand with the concept of plantation, which dominated the seventeenth century in Ireland. Disloyal Gaelic Irish and Anglo-Irish would be replaced by loyal English and Scots settlers.

The Conqueror's View

The Tudor wars in Ireland had devastated the country and became increasingly like a war between civilisations. The religious differences between England and Ireland were starting to become acute, but were not paramount in the sixteenth century. Instead it was the sense of English superiority over the Gaelic Irish which was uppermost in the minds of most of the conquerors.

Queen Elizabeth herself spoke of the need 'to bring that rude and barbarous nation to civility', and another English observer wrote of how 'the Irish live like beasts ... are more uncivil, more uncleanly, more barbarous in their customs and demeanours than in any part of the world that is known'. Since the Irish were deemed to be inferior and feckless, harsh measures were justified because, in the words of one of Elizabeth's officers in Ireland, 'A barbarous country must first be broken by a war before it will be capable of good government'.

There was still a disposition to believe wild stories about Ireland.

Amazingly, a map in 1610 repeated Gerald of Wales's claims that offshore islands were 'some full of angels, some full of devils'. The Gaelic Irish were regarded with the same suspicion as these wraiths, 'servile, crafty and inquisitive after news, the symptoms of a conquered nation'. But there was ambiguity. The poet Spenser wrote:

> And sure it is yet a most beautiful and sweet country as any under heaven, seamed throughout with many goodly rivers with all sorts of fish most abundantly sprinkled with many very sweet islands and goodly lakes like little inland seas.

He was not the only English settler to be attracted by the 'mists and mellow fruitfulness' of Ireland, but Elizabeth's administrators were

This drawing of *c.* 1575 shows the perceived contrast between a civilised woman from the Pale and a Gaelic Irishman

generally harsh in their appraisal of Gaelic society. There had to be order in an ocean of Gaelic disorder, and this justified both savage repression after other methods had failed and the planting of English, and later Scots, settlers in Gaelic lands. Mountjoy, for example, generally regarded by historians as a humane man, had no scruples about devastating Hugh O'Neill's home province of Ulster in 1601. English attitudes then were often colonial, and reminiscent of the 'white man's burden' philosophy of the nineteenth century: England's initial task was to civilise the barbaric Irish. Only later did the religious aspect, the struggle of the true faith against Popery, become predominant.

WOMEN

The attitude of the English administrators towards Irish women offers an interesting insight into the clash between Gaelic Irish and English culture (remembering that the Anglo-Irish had drifted slowly into Gaelic ways). English visitors were taken aback by the fact that Irish women greeted them with a kiss, drank alcohol and presided at feasts. This was taken as a sign of uncivilised behaviour, yet the Tudor Englishman was renowned throughout Europe for his rudeness and incivility to foreigners. In fact Irish women had more freedom than their English counterparts. They could keep their own names after marriage, and divorce was made easy under Brehon Law. The practices of trial marriages, so-called voluntary 'affiliation', whereby a father was 'named', also purportedly shocked the English. Irish marriage laws were not English ones, and one historian has noted that even in twentieth-century Donegal wives sometimes went on living in the parental home. It is also notable that sexual relations within degrees of affinity (cousin and cousin, etc.) were common, and that Jesuits in Ireland issued dispensations to allow this even though it was against Catholic practice.

English observers were divided about some aspects of Irish women's behaviour. Some thought them sexually promiscuous and wild, others found them chaste; most agreed that the Irish of both sexes were sensual and volatile. Clearly, too, some observers were looking for abhorrent sexual behaviour as proof that the Irish needed civilising. What was true is that the Gaelic Irish family system was far more flexible and durable. Englishmen were struck by the strength of the links between fostered children, even though the practice of fostering children was quite common in England itself.

THE ECONOMY

Life in Gaelic Ireland during the Tudor wars was still primitive. Clothing, for example, was very basic, with heavy woollen mantles and linen shirts being manufactured in the Gaelic areas for their inhabitants. Food was equally basic. Some grain was grown, but oats were the most common cereal crop, used to make oatmeal, sometimes for cakes and otherwise mixed with butter and other milk products. There was a striking absence of green vegetables and there seems to have been no systematic growth of them in Gaelic Ireland. Instead, people's diets were supplemented by watercress or other wild herbs mixed with butter. Gaelic feasts are described during this period when meat was eaten in large amounts, but this probably only applied to the chieftains and their families.

Pastoral Farming

Instead of systematic cultivation of the land, the Irish allowed great herds of cattle to roam in the areas under their control. Although these herds were reared for their wool and skins rather than for their meat, they did provide butter and cheese in abundance, and cattle blood was used to make blood pudding after being mixed with oatmeal. This system of pastoral farming was, of course, wasteful and a result of primitive methods which were primarily reliant on the spade. It did have the advantage of flexibility in troubled political times because the herds could be driven on to safer pastures, but it made the foundation of permanent settlements difficult. Towns were a rarity in the Gaelic areas.

The Anglo-Irish Areas

Agricultural practice was substantially different in areas under Anglo-Irish control, where systematic tillage was the norm. This was partly because the Anglo-Irish were conversant with such methods in southern England, but also because they had tended to colonise the areas with the best soil! This allowed them to grow a full range of crops, using ploughs, and to found permanent village settlements. Conversely, this very permanence made the Anglo-Irish communities more vulnerable to the disruption caused by the Tudor wars. Historians suggest that the Anglo-Irish in sixteenth-century Munster suffered most severely from such disruption.

Population

The primitive agricultural techniques available in the Gaelic areas, plus the disruption caused by wars, gave Irish demography a unique feature. For whereas in Europe as a whole the population doubled during the century, in Ireland it remained static at about 750,000. The population seems to have been fairly evenly distributed until the wars of the 1580s and 1590s which devastated the more fertile areas of Munster and Ulster.

TRADE

The attitude of Gaelic chieftaïns in the sixteenth century seems to have made economic development difficult. This was because of the financial exactions they imposed on merchants who tried to trade in Gaelic areas. Trade, therefore, within and without Ireland (never large) was the prerequisite of the Anglo-Irish. Tallow, skins, hides and linen yarn were exchanged for wine, salt and manufactured goods. Export trade with England was handled by Anglo-Irish merchants in ports like Dublin and Wexford.

CHAPTER NINE

From Rathmullan to the Boyne, 1607–1690

On 4 September 1607 a French ship called at the little port of Rathmullan on the western side of the long sea inlet called Lough Swilly. Two men boarded this ship with their families and followers. One was Hugh O'Neill, Earl of Tyrone, 'the O'Neill', the other was Rory O'Donnell, Earl of Tyrconnell and younger brother of Hugh O'Donnell. Thus took place the event known in modern Irish history as 'the flight of the earls'. Indeed some have seen it as the event which marks off modern Ireland from its ancient Gaelic past.

In one sense the flight of Tyrone and Tyrconnell was a surprise, and it certainly surprised the English officials in Dublin. This was because Hugh O'Neill, after many years of fighting, had made his submission to the Crown in 1603 and been allowed to keep his extensive estates in Ulster (this infuriated many of Mountjoy's former soldiers). His authority in Ulster was still unimpaired. In that same year the then Crown attorney-general noted that 'the better sort of the province of Ulster did refuse to accept the king's commission of the peace until they received warrant from the Earl of Tyrone to do so'.

Why then did Tyrone and Tyrconnell flee, leaving their lands open to confiscation by the English Crown? Their motives seem to have been mixed. Certainly they, and O'Neill in particular, were under more pressure from royal officials by 1607 and were losing some of their freedom of action in their native province. A more punitive religious policy was also taking shape under James I (1603–25) and Catholics, the overwhelming majority of the two earls' supporters, were being fined for recusancy (that is failure to attend Church of Ireland services on a set number of occasions each year). There were also stories about O'Neill being in league with the Spanish, probably spread by those who wanted to get their hands on his land, but not so outlandish perhaps after the events of Kinsale in 1601.

Whatever the relative importance of these factors, O'Neill and O'Donnell felt pressurised to a degree which decided them to flee the country (they both died in exile in Rome, in 1616 and 1608 respectively). This flight subsequently became a central mythical event in Irish history, and the victim of a degree of hyperbole. True, it did open up Ulster to the Anglo-Scots plantation of the seventeenth century, but modern research has shown that even O'Neill, the great Gaelic hero, was introducing English methods of subletting to tenants rather than using the free and easy Gaelic methods based on blood ties.

O'Neill himself was, of course, a sort of Anglo-Irish hybrid, Gaelic champion and protégé of Queen Elizabeth, but it is interesting that even traditional Gaelic poets were critical of the behaviour of native Irish lords. Modern research shows that in Ulster, then the most Gaelic of Ireland's provinces, poets like Lughaidh Ó Cleirigh and Eochaidh Ó hEodhasa attacked the vanity of the native lords and even accepted land grants when the new plantation got under way.

The Ulster Plantations

The flight of the earls left the English Crown with an urgent problem: what was to be done with the extensive holdings deserted by Tyrone and Tyrconnell in Ulster? Two years were spent in slow deliberation about their fate, before in 1610 the urgings of James I produced a result. This caution was a consequence of the dire results of the Munster plantations in the 1560s and 1580s, and even of a more modest attempt to plant settlers in Ulster in the 1570s. Rules were thus laid down for the regulation of the new plantation under the rather grand-sounding title of 'Orders and Conditions of the Ulster Plantation'. This new plantation of 1610 covered the former territories of the earls in Counties Donegal, Tyrone, Derry and Armagh, plus Counties Fermanagh and Cavan as well. It was, therefore, far larger than the earlier ones.

It was also far better organised, as an examination of the plantation in County Derry bears out. It was under the control of the so-called 'Irish

Society' in the city of Derry, soon to be rechristened Londonderry by the new settlers as a result of the prominent role played by the City of London in the plantation of County Derry: it gave out parcels of land to its various companies – drapers, salters, fishmongers, haberdashers and so on (County Londonderry still has a Draperstown and a Salterstown).

The settlement in County Derry was a catastrophic one as far as the Gaelic Irish were concerned. They were only to get 10 per cent of the existing land and pay double the rent asked for it from the new settlers. A further 5 per cent was to go to former English soldiers who had fought in the Irish wars. The rest was to go to English and Scots settlers, who got the best, most fertile land. But there were conditions. The new settlers had to impose English ways and the Protestant religion. Neither were they to have any Irish tenants.

The new plantation gave every sign of being a success. By 1630 there were 14,500 male settlers in Ulster which, when their families are added, suggests a figure of 24,000, an impressive transfer of population for those days. The settlers also appear to have been men of independent spirit, on the look-out for the fortunes which they had not obtained in England and Scotland.

Ireland, however, was Ireland, and native conditions produced a watering down of the original terms of settlement. Most importantly, the native Irish did go on living on the land, for the obvious reason that the new settlers needed both cheap labour and the rents which the Irish labourers would pay them. So although the Irish *landowners* were driven westwards to the wild fringes of the province, their former bondmen were not. It was an important weakness and deviation from the original scheme which meant that, instead of planting a totally loyal Protestant population throughout Ulster, the new settlers were surrounded by resentful, deprived Gaelic Irish (a situation akin to that facing the Pilgrim Fathers in the years immediately following their landing in New England in 1620). Small wonder that the English and Scots settlers felt apprehensive and worried for their own security.

THE EAST ULSTER PLANTATION

There was one broad exception to the general situation in Ulster after 1610, although outside Derry both ex-soldiers and Gaelic alike got more land. This was the East Ulster Scots Plantation. Here geography was a dominant factor, for Scots migrants had poured across the narrow channel to Ulster over the centuries (the MacDonnells being an example), and a crucial small settlement was made on the Ards peninsula in 1606. It was sponsored by two Protestant adventurers, Montgomery and Hamilton, who made a deal with the local Gaelic chieftain. The plantation then prospered and became a sort of bridgehead for Scots migration later in the century. These Scotsmen actually filled the gaps left by the main Crown-sponsored plantation in the province, and their success meant that most of the new settlers were Scots rather than English.

PRESBYTERIANISM

These Scots were Presbyterian not Anglican, which is a significant point essential to the understanding of modern Irish history, and especially the recent history of Northern Ireland. A faith based on the doctrines of the French theologian John Calvin, with its belief (then) in the concept of 'predestination' of the 'elect' for paradise and damnation for the rest of humanity, Presbyterianism gave the Scots settlers a fierce righteousness which their English counterparts could not match, particularly as they were persecuted by the Crown authorities in Ulster for practising their version of Protestantism.

There was, then, a situation of growing complexity in Ulster in the years after 1610, as the province gained a population of English and Scots settlers uneasily mixed with a downtrodden Gaelic population. Further danger was added by the known existence of some 5,000 former soldiers of Tyrone and Tyrconnell who, in Robert Kee's words, were 'still lurking resentfully in the bogs and woods'. It was perhaps a disaster waiting to happen.

The Uprising of 1641

Disaster duly arrived in October 1641, but it was not confined just to Ulster because the oppression of the Gaelic Irish was felt throughout the island. And many members of the old Anglo-Irish gentry, sometimes known as the 'Old English', also felt that their positions were endangered by the flood of new settlers. Hence it was not surprising to find representatives of this class, like Sir Phelim O'Neill and Rory O'More, as leaders of the great Irish uprising of 1641.

There was, too, a complicating factor. This was because the rebels of 1641 thought they had the blessing of King Charles I (1625–49), following his disputes with the English House of Commons since the 1620s and the anti-Scots policy followed in Ireland by the Lord Deputy Thomas Wentworth, earl of Strafford. Strafford had plans for further confiscations in Wicklow and Clare, but royal policy was being perceived as sympathetic to the Catholics. His recall in 1640, and subsequent execution at the behest of the Commons, may have been seen as evidence of a weakening of the king's position. Clearly the Irish rebels of 1641 regarded Charles as a potential ally. He, with a degree of cynicism, was prepared to use an Irish army to fight his rebellious parliament. But the priority of the Irish rebels was to smash the Protestant ascendancy in Ireland which had been the consequence of the 1610 settlement.

This woodcut illustrates some of the atrocities suffered by the Protestant settlers

The events of 1641 have remained a matter of controversy ever since. There is no doubt that hideous massacres of Protestant settlers by the Gaelic Irish *did* take place, notably at Portadown (Co. Armagh) where some hundred men, women and children were thrown from the bridge after being abducted from their homes by the rebels. Those who managed to swim to the shore were shot or knocked on the head, while some of the Irish allegedly took to boats and bashed victims on the head as they struggled in the waters of the Bann.

The debate has been about the number of victims, particularly as thirty-two volumes of evidence were lodged in the Library of Trinity College, Dublin, about the massacres. A flavour of much of this testimony is given in the case of one Elizabeth Price of Armagh, whose five children were taken from her and pushed off the bridge at Portadown:

> And for this deponent and many others that were stayed behind, diverse tortures were used upon them ... and this deponent for her part was thrice hanged up to confess to money, and afterwards let down, and had the soles of her feet fried and burnt at the fire and was often scourged and whipt....

Modern historians like Roy Foster, however, have no doubt that much of the 'evidence' is hearsay and wildly exaggerated. Foster himself suggests a figure of 4,000 dead, which would still have been about 20 per cent of the 1630 population figure (population growth would make the percentage lower).

More important perhaps than the actual numbers killed was the myth of 1641, and its place in the history of the Protestant community in Ulster. The slogan 'Remember 1641' was burned into the collective Protestant consciousness and into the annual pattern of life in the province. In 1662, for example, the Irish Parliament declared that 23 October, the day that the rebellion was discovered, 'shall be kept, and celebrated as an anniversary holy day in this kingdom for ever'. And well into the nineteenth century there were commemorative demonstrations and Protestant church services to remind the minority community of those dark days. So began an unhealthy pattern in Ulster of remembering and institutionalising events by and large best forgotten.

After 1641 events in Ireland fitted into what became known as 'the war of the Three Kingdoms', as Scots and English armies intervened in Ireland and an Irish force was sent to help King Charles. In 1642 two events of significance took place: the English Civil War between the king and parliament broke out; and the Irish rebels found a fine military commander in Owen Roe O'Neill (1590–1649), nephew of the great Hugh, who had gained considerable fighting experience in the Spanish army. He was one of the Irish leaders who opposed atrocities, and historians take the view that the ones which did take place were the result of indiscipline rather than any co-ordinated plan to wipe out the Protestant population. It has to be remembered too that a portion of the Anglo-Irish aristocracy remained loyal to the English cause. Their forces were commanded by James Butler, earl of Ormond (1610–88), later to be made Lord Lieutenant in 1644.

This apparently curious paradox came about because Charles I, anxious to avoid the charge of concerting with Papists (he already had a Catholic wife), dissociated himself from the Irish rebels, although secretly he had hopes of using an Irish Catholic army against his parliamentary enemies. In the 1640s, then, Catholic Ireland was divided between those in open revolt against Crown authority and those loyal to it, just as Protestant Ireland was to be divided between those loyal to King Charles and those wanting a victory for Parliament. To make the situation even more complicated, a Scots army of 10,000 men under Monro was also raised to fight for Ulster Protestantism. King Charles had alienated the Scots by trying to impose Anglican practice on them rather than the Presbyterianism which was the norm in the Lowlands (the Highlands remaining Catholic).

The Confederacy

The Catholic rebels in Ireland after 1641 are usually referred to as 'the Confederates'. But they were a house divided. On the one hand were Owen Roe O'Neill and the Gaelic Irish, determined to protect their Catholic religion and to destroy the plantation system (a determination made sharper by the news that the English parliament planned a further massive confiscation in Ireland worth one million pounds). Even here there were differences of emphasis, for O'Neill was a product of the

Counter-Reformation in Spain, that force which would have no truck with Protestantism at all, rather than a rebel anxious to seize back lost lands as the Gaelic Irish were.

On the other were the Anglo-Irish aristocracy, excepting Ormond's supporters, who believed rather naively that under the English Crown their Catholicism would be tolerated. This might perhaps have been the case had Charles I, and not Parliament, won the English Civil War. Certainly O'Neill regarded such a view as absurdly unrealistic; he was used to the savage religious wars of the Continent on which the Thirty Years' War (1618–48) was then raging.

In the long run O'Neill was proved right, and in the short run he became the effective commander of the forces of the Confederacy. His talents were shown by his victory over Monro's Scots army at Benburb in 1646 and the Leinster lords needed O'Neill's help to drive the Crown forces out of the Pale. Such victories proved to be illusory, and even during a period of relative success the Confederacy demonstrated the sharp tensions within it. Amongst other complaints it was said that the mainly Anglo-Irish leaders of the rebellion would not allow the Gaelic Irish access to muskets and ammunition.

Cromwell's Intervention

The fate of Catholic Ireland was in fact sealed by events in England between 1642 and 1649, which culminated in the defeat, deposition and execution of Charles I and the rise to power of Oliver Cromwell, who became Lord Protector of the newly established Commonwealth or republic. Having disposed of a challenge from the Scots, in August 1649 Cromwell turned his attention to Ireland. The nuances of Irish politics meant little to him, and he cared not one jot that Ormond or other Anglo-Irish lords had been loyal to the English Crown. In Cromwell's eyes Papists were Papists, and his task was to impose Protestantism on the whole of Ireland and restore order. He also, like all Protestants, remembered the massacres of 1641 and regarded himself as the agent of a wrathful god. Catholic Irish iniquity was only worsened by the fact that they had sided with Charles Stuart, 'that man of blood', in the English Civil War.

To wreak vengeance Cromwell had an army of 20,000 men, then just about the best fighting troops in Europe. This army was to cut such a bloody swathe across Ireland that Cromwell's passage has never been forgotten, or to a large degree forgiven, in that country.

DROGHEDA

Cromwell's evil reputation in Ireland owes much to the brutal sack of the town of Drogheda, just to the north of Dublin. It was surrounded by Cromwell's army in September 1649 and he demanded that the garrison surrender to avoid 'the effusion of blood'. It refused and the English army therefore stormed the town, and made a breach in its formidable walls but could not break through the defenders at this point, and suffered heavy casualties.

This setback seems to have infuriated Cromwell and his men. On the second attempt they broke into the town, slaughtering some thousand men, women and children (including babies) in the street. The Catholic friars and priests were slaughtered in a church, while other defenders of Drogheda were burnt to death in another church. In an infamous letter to the English parliament, Cromwell wrote that 'I am persuaded that this is a righteous judgement of God upon these barbarous wretches'.

It is difficult to defend Cromwell's behaviour at Drogheda and his biographer, Antonia Fraser, makes little effort to do so. Her judgement is that 'the conclusion cannot be escaped that Cromwell lost all self-control at Drogheda, literally saw red – the red of his comrades' blood – after the failure of the first assaults'. She does, though, make the point that such behaviour was unusual for Cromwell, who was usually merciful to enemies, but he may have been influenced by his perceived role as the avenger of 1641. He also seems to have convinced himself that the inhabitants of Drogheda had been involved in the massacres of that year. This was nonsense, as Drogheda was inside the Pale, but more pertinently there were former royalist officers in the Drogheda garrison. Legend has it that Ashton, the English commander of the garrison, was battered to death with his wooden leg. He was a longstanding foe of Cromwell.

In one sense the bloodshed at Drogheda achieved its purpose, as the news of the massacre of its inhabitants spread throughout Ireland. Ormond wrote to the future King Charles II:

> It is not to be imagined how great the Terror is that those successes and the power of the rebels [the English as Ormond was loyal to the Crown and not Parliament] have struck into this people.

Fortress after fortress surrendered to Cromwell's army without a blow being struck because of the fear of another Drogheda. Wexford was an exception; Cromwell's troops sacked the town while its surrender was in the process of negotiation, killing 2,000 people including 200 women and children. When this death toll is added to that of towns like Clonmel which managed to hold out for some time, the account for 1641 was more than rendered.

There is little, therefore, to be said in defence of Cromwell's Irish campaign, but one point is worth remembering. The seventeenth century in Europe was a period of extreme religious intolerance (the terrible sack of the city of Magdeburg in Germany took place only a year before the massacres in Drogheda and Wexford) and Cromwell's behaviour has to be seen in that context. He was sufficiently tolerant to allow Jews to resettle in England, but such tolerance did not extend to Catholics, whether Irish or English.

Cromwellian Ireland

Traditionally little attention has been paid by historians to Cromwellian Ireland. Given the Irish nationalist tradition of the 'curse of Cromwell' this is not perhaps surprising, although one or two British historians, like J.A. Froude in the nineteenth century, have tried to present Commonwealth rule in Ireland as a model of enlightenment. The major count against it has been the new punitive plantations which followed Cromwell's victory. Its basic feature was the transplantation of Catholic Irish *landowners* to the westernmost province of Connacht, where they were resettled on land that was both stony and inferior. Catholic tenants were left behind to serve their new Protestant masters, but the Cromwellian plantations were a symbolic humiliation of the whole of Catholic Gaelic Ireland and much of the old Anglo-Irish aristocracy. Even Ormond had been deposed by Cromwell, in his case precisely because he was loyal to the English Crown.

The Catholic landowners were to be replaced by so-called 'adventurers' whose purchase of Irish land would, it was hoped, defray the costs of £3 million involved in putting down the revolt of 1641. In fact, the money raised never approached this sum even though the English parliament brought in settlers from as far away as Holland. In other respects, the Cromwellian resettlement was a failure. It had been hoped, for example, that Catholics could be totally excluded from towns in Ireland, but they were not – despiste implausible ideas like selling off the whole of Galway to the City of Gloucester.

ANTI-CATHOLICISM

A marked feature of the Commonwealth period was an attack on the Catholic Church. Significantly the parliamentary commissioners appointed by Cromwell to rule in Ireland made little effort to convert the Gaelic Irish, perhaps reasoning that they were beyond redemption. But priests were ruthlessly hunted down, and considerable efforts were made to prevent the celebration of the Catholic mass. Thus arose the tradition of the 'mass-rock', a fixed point in the wilderness where mass was celebrated in the open air.

The problem of conversion continued to perplex Irish Protestantism, but it was never addressed. Increasingly, after Cromwell, Ireland became 'two nations', an ascendant Protestant minority ruling a deprived and resentful Catholic majority.

IRELAND UNDER CHARLES II

When Charles II (1660–85) was restored to the English throne, Irish Catholics were hopeful of change. He, after all, was married to a Portuguese Catholic and Irish Catholics had fought and suffered in his father's cause. Such hopes proved to be illusory for Charles, renowned for his desire never to go on his 'travels again', was too canny to alienate English Protestant opinion by improving conditions for Irish Catholics.

Just how vehement was anti-Catholic feeling in England was made clear yet again during the time of the alleged 'Popish Plot' in 1678, when the renegade Titus Oates invented a Catholic conspiracy against the English government. This extract from a contemporary preacher, whose passion would certainly have been duplicated among Irish Presbyterians, gives a flavour of the time. Protestants were warned by this divine that their wives would be in danger of being

> prostituted to the lust of every savage bog-trotter, your daughters ravished by goatish monks, your smaller children tossed upon pikes, and torn limb from limb, whilst you have your own bowels ripped out ... or else murdered with some other exquisite torture and holy candles made of your grease which was done within our memory [a clear reference to 1641].

In Ireland, the most prominent victim of the anti-Catholic hysteria surrounding Oates' allegations was Oliver Plunkett (1629–81), the Catholic archbishop of Dublin, who was brought to London and, after what one historian has called 'a travesty of a trial', hung, drawn and quartered at Tyburn. (Plunkett was canonised by Pope Paul VI in 1975.)

James II and the Revival of Catholic Hopes

There seemed briefly to be real hope for Catholic Ireland when Charles II's brother James II (1685–8) became king. James was certainly committed to the rehabilitation of Catholicism in England, and he sent Richard Talbot, earl of Tyrconnell, to Ireland as Lord Lieutenant. Tactlessly, and far too speedily, Tyrconnell began to place Catholics in important public offices. He also began to mobilise a Catholic army for possible use by his royal master, and to plan the packing of the Irish parliament in Dublin with Catholics who would duly undo the Cromwellian land settlement.

This policy, and the equivalent one pursued by James himself in England, was asking for trouble, which duly arrived in 1688 in the shape of his own son-in-law, William of Orange. William was invited to take the English throne by a rebellious Lords and Commons, and James was forced to invoke French aid and seek the help of his Catholic Irish subjects who remained loyal to the House of Stuart.

THE SIEGE OF DERRY

James's landing in Ireland aroused severe anxiety in the Protestant community and there was talk of the massacres of 1641 once more.

Particularly in Derry, when news came that James was sending a Catholic regiment under the earl of Antrim, nicknamed 'Redshanks', to garrison the city.

The Protestants in Derry were divided about what to do. The Anglicans, including the bishop of Londonderry, as the Protestants called it, thought that there was no way they could reasonably exclude a royal garrison, whereas the Presbyterians were convinced of the need to protect themselves from a Papist force. The city authorities decided to admit the Redshanks but were circumvented by thirteen apprentice boys who on 7 December 1688 took matters into their own hands by seizing the gates of the city and slamming them shut in the faces of Antrim's men. This is a date which is burnt deep into the Ulster Protestant psyche, and religiously commemorated every year in cere-monies which often seem bizarre to outsiders.

The siege of Derry did not start in earnest until April 1689 and, despite all the symbolism surrounding it, was severely pressed only in June, this phase lasting only six weeks. James II did appear in person before the city walls but his army was woefully ill-equipped for a siege (it only had one real cannon). Even so the Protestant commander Robert Lundy favoured surrender to the Jacobite army, but the citizens would not allow him to. Instead Lundy was ignominiously forced out of Derry disguised as a common soldier carrying matchwood. Even to this day 'Lundy' is a term of abuse for an Ulster Protestant deemed to be less than zealous in the cause.

As the siege progressed, the 30,000 Protestants inside Derry's walls began to suffer severely. They were soon reduced to eating mice, rats, dogs, candles and even leather. According to one surviving story, a particularly fat Derry citizen dared not come out of his house during the siege because his neighbours were eyeing his bulk enviously! On the Catholic side, the siege was made more difficult by the army's deficiencies. Some howitzers were brought up to supplement the one gun capable of breaching walls, but many of the soldiers only had pikes or sharpened sticks for weapons.

The besiegers had placed a boom across the River Foyle to keep out relieving ships, and the Williamite forces seemingly lacked the nerve to break it. On two occasions English ships failed to break through and

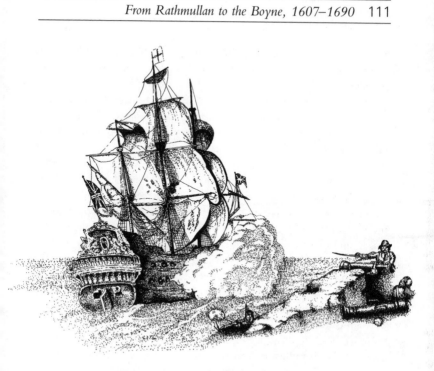

Ships going to the relief of Londonderry

sailed off before, on 28 July 1689, they did do so and raised the siege. This event also entered Protestant mythology, as did a tendency to think that the English could not be relied on (although it was they who had rescued Derry in the end). 'No surrender' went straight into the lexicon of Protestant slogans.

THE BOYNE

William of Orange, William III (1689–1702), landed at Carrickfergus in 1690 to secure the Irish part of his kingdom. Soon afterwards, on 12 July, he defeated the army of King James at the battle of the River Boyne, another name which came to have great symbolic importance for Protestants. In fact the battle was not decisive, because William had to fight another serious campaign in 1691, and the most serious Catholic resistance came west of the Shannon where the Catholic landholdings were concentrated and needed to be defended. There was desperate resistance at Athlone, on the battlefield of Aughrim, and in two separate sieges of Limerick, but all to no avail. In 1691 the Jacobite Catholic army under Patrick Sarsfield, earl of Lucan, was finally forced to surrender at Limerick. Surprisingly perhaps, the officers were allowed by the Treaty of Limerick to take service under King Louis XIV of France. So began the tradition of the 'Wild Geese', those Catholic Irishmen who served with distinction in the armies of France; at least one of their descendants was to become a marshal of France in the nineteenth century.

Whatever the relative importance of the Battle of the Boyne itself, the Williamite campaign of 1690–1 did seal the fate of Catholic Ireland and ensure that the eighteenth century would be the century of Protestant ascendancy. But by a profound historical irony the Boyne did not stand for that titanic clash between Protestantism and Catholicism on which Protestant mythology has insisted. It is an inconvenient fact that, when the battle was fought, the Pope was siding *with* Protestant William of Orange in his desperate struggle with Louis XIV of France (as indeed did the Catholic Austrian Habsburgs). The religious 'black and white' of Irish history never extended to the rest of Europe, which may be part of the reason why the religious question outside Ireland has not been so divisive. A whole Protestant vocabulary about 'Popery and wooden shoes' and 'Remember 1690' stretches back in an unbroken line to the events at Derry and on the banks of the Boyne.

For Catholics the events of 1690–1 could mean only one thing, further discrimination and repression. Neither the English parliament nor the Irish Protestants were in any mood for clemency. Legislation passed in Westminster excluded Irish Catholics from office and parliament. But the Irish parliament in Dublin, again packed with Protestants, extended religious discrimination: priests and bishops were banished, Catholics forbidden to teach, to carry arms, to marry Protestants, or to take action in the courts over land settlements. Irish Catholics then paid as dearly for the failure of James II as he, now an exile in France, did himself. In retrospect, however, it is hard to see how James, denuded of support in England as he was, could have triumphed in Ireland.

Culture

The losing fight by Irish Catholics to preserve their religion and the Jacobite cause was paralleled by the unsuccessful attempt to resist English cultural imperialism. As the seventeenth century wore on, so the use of English began to spread inexorably in Ireland. It became the language of business, a fact made evident by the use of the Gaelic word Béarla, originally meaning technical jargon, for the English language. Interestingly 'Sasanach' (more associated with Scots Gaelic) was the Gaelic word used for 'Protestant' as well as 'Englishman'.

There was no specific government policy to stamp out the use of Irish Gaelic, but the penetration of English settlers and English ways into Ireland's outermost fringes made its demise almost inevitable. Gaelic, after all, was the language of the oppressed and defeated. As in earlier centuries, though, the Gaelic lived on in myth, poetry and oral history, and as a sort of propaganda against English accusations of Irish barbarism. Several Gaelic poets, notably Piras Feiritéir (Pierce Ferrier, 1600–53), had fought in the Confederate Wars, and took as the theme of their work the lost Gaelic world which had been destroyed by the Cromwellian plantations.

On the other side there was a vigorous settler intellectual life in the seventeenth century. Some was centred on the Church of Ireland archbishop Ussher in Dublin, notably the Dutch brothers Arnold and Gerard Boate (the latter wrote the significant scientific study *The Natural History of Ireland*). In mainstream planter society there was the important physicist Robert Boyle (1627–91), a founder of the English Royal Society and proponent of the well-known 'Boyle's Law' on the relationship between elasticity and pressure. Another formidable figure was Sir William Petty (1623–87) who produced a survey of the whole of Ireland to ease the problems associated with land settlement. Ireland thus had the rather dubious privilege of being the best surveyed land in Europe, even if the survey's main purpose was to assist Protestant land confiscations. But from areas like the natural sciences, the Gaelic Irish were excluded, thus encouraging the myth that all they were interested in was legends and whimsy.

Ireland in 1700

According to Petty's calculations, Ireland at the beginning of the eighteenth century had a population of about 1.3 million, making it one of the most densely populated countries in Western Europe. It was also a society which had been traumatised by the constant land resettlement and plantation of the previous century. Striking backing for this assessment is given by the following statistics. In 1641 the Catholic Irish owned 59 per cent of Ireland's land, a figure which had dropped to 22 per cent in 1660 after the Cromwellian settlement. In 1695, after the victory of William of Orange, the figure was 14 per cent, and by the time the Hanoverian George I came to the throne in 1714 it had fallen to a mere 7 per cent. In less than a century, therefore, the Gaelic and Anglo-Irish had seen their land holdings drop from almost two-thirds of the island of Ireland to virtually nothing, and that a miserable, stony remnant in Connacht (or County Clare, the other area chosen by the Cromwellian parliament). This had been the overwhelming reality of seventeenth-century Ireland.

Attempts to bring the two societies together thereafter were almost bound to be doomed as 'winners' and 'losers' rubbed shoulders in uneasy co-existence. It may have been true that the changed balance of power ruled out another 1641 for the foreseeable future, but the Protestant minority was to be frequently reminded of the seething discontent over which they presided. The mass of the Irish people continued to live on the land, and to be engaged in tillage and raising cattle. Some supplemented their incomes by spinning and weaving woollen and linen cloth. Ireland's exports, therefore, consisted largely of textiles and animal by-products, sent out through Dublin, Cork and Waterford. But they did little or nothing to raise the miserable standard of living of the average Irish peasant.

The lords and masters of the peasantry had begun to demonstrate their wealth by building capacious country houses, or possibly town houses in Dublin, by now growing into a significant metropolis of 50,000 people. With its two ancient cathedrals and vigorous intellectual life, the Irish capital was fit now to be compared with other major European cities. Its export trade was certainly enhanced by the building of an inland waterway which brought most of Leinster, north-east Ulster and part of eastern Connacht into the metropolitan hinterland.

Yet Ireland, as the historian Nicholas Canny has pointed out, remained a subordinated society even among its élite. They might complain about the circumscribed powers of the Dublin parliament, but the landowners still preferred to educate their children in England and marry them off to the English aristocracy rather than their peers in Ireland (if the former would have them). And just as medieval English monarchs showed scant interest in events across the Irish Sea, so only two of their successors visited the sister kingdom between 1500 and 1689.

'Irishness', though, refused to disappear, and a dispossessed Catholic peasantry and landowning class remained convinced that 'they were the dispossessed who would one day recover that of which they had been so unjustly deprived'. How far off that day was to be in 1700 no Catholic Irishman could tell.

CHAPTER TEN

The Protestant Ascendancy, 1690–1800

The events of 1690–1 in Ireland had ensured that the Catholic counter-revolution of James II would fail, and led directly to that period of Irish history known as 'the Ascendancy'. This is the term used to denote the eighteenth-century heyday of Irish Protestantism, which was of course built on Catholic inferiority.

The Penal Laws

The Irish Protestant parliament in Dublin did, in fact, go back on the terms of the 1691 Treaty of Limerick enforced by a Dutch general of William III, as William of Orange had become, who now ruled England and Ireland jointly with his wife Mary (James II's daughter). Instead Catholic Irishmen and women were systematically excluded from whole areas of Irish life. Under the penal legislation enacted by the Dublin parliament after the defeat of James II, Catholics were banned from holding any offices of state, deprived of the vote, prohibited from practising at the bar, buying land, holding a lease for more than thirty-one years and bequeathing land to Catholic relatives. Only if one of them became a Protestant could land revert to him, and then he would be entitled to the share of other Catholic members of the family as well.

The penal laws did not actually prohibit the practice of the Catholic religion in Ireland after 1691, but they made it as difficult as possible. Thus Catholic priests were forced to register with the authorities, and the Catholic Church could only exist at a parish level. Religious orders, such as the Benedictines, were banned, and there were to be no bishops or archbishops. The intention, therefore, was to kill off the Catholic Church altogether, because without bishops no new priests could be ordained in Ireland.

But this was theory. The reality was that the overwhelming mass of the Irish people were Catholic and that penal legislation could not be enforced. As early as the 1720s, indeed, Catholic churches were being built in Ireland's major towns, even if they tended to be hidden in the back streets. Seeing that Catholicism could not be stamped out, the local authorities connived at its continued existence – albeit with the encouragement of the odd judicious bribe! In Galway, for example, the accounts for a Dominican house (technically illegal) in 1731 contained the following entry: 'for claret to treat ye Sheriffs in their search . . . two shillings and twopence'. It seems that 'ye Sheriffs' organised the odd raid on known Catholic religious houses but were easily bought off, and then the status quo was continued as before. As long as Benedictine, Dominican and Augustinian friars did not advertise their existence they were tolerated. So were Catholic bishops and archbishops, although they could not live with the pomp and style associated with their continental counterparts.

In the long run, official attempts to suppress Catholicism, however half-hearted, merely strengthened the links between the Church and most Irish people. Catholicism and Irish nationalism tended to become synonymous because the Catholic Irish had no other means of expressing themselves in political terms. Other than through the secret agrarian societies known as the 'Whiteboys' (so called because they wore white shirts over their heads to try and disguise themselves) which were set up in the eighteenth century to protect Catholic tenants from rapacious landlords, but they had no national political ambitions.

A Protestant Nation

Conscious Catholic nationalism was to be largely a product of the nineteenth century in Ireland. The paradox of the eighteenth century was that such nationalism as there was was associated with Protestantism – seemingly a bizarre situation because it was the Protestant minority, fiercely loyal to the British Crown, which ruled Ireland and

Russborough House, Co. Wicklow in the Palladian style

maintained a gracious and wealthy lifestyle. Evidence for this remains today in Dublin's Georgian squares, and in lavish country houses such as Russborough House in County Wicklow, built in 1742 for the earl of Milltown.

The roots of this Protestant nationalism, centred on the Parliament building in Dublin (now the Bank of Ireland), can be traced back to that old Anglo-Irish mentality which was condemned for being 'unEnglish' in London. But it differed from it in its Protestantism, and the belief propounded by men like the famous writer and propagandist, Jonathan Swift, that there could be a separate 'Protestant nation' in Ireland which would be independent of Westminster and separate from Gaelic, Catholic Ireland. The Irish parliament in Dublin was to be for many Protestants a body which must claim the right to legislate separately for Ireland. For such Protestant 'Patriots' England and Ireland were separate, but equal, kingdoms united by their loyalty to the English Crown.

Resentment at Ireland's colonial status also lay behind the movement for legislative equality. Swift remarked that although he did not doubt that the English government always appointed good and righteous men to Irish positions, he believed that they were always waylaid and killed by bandits somewhere near Chester on their way to take up such appointments. The bandits then took up their jobs in Ireland!

There was a widespread belief amongst the Irish Protestant community that Irish trade was hindered by English legislation, and this thinking was behind Swift's 1720 campaign against English exports to Ireland.

WOOD'S HALF PENCE

The most memorable example of this anti-English feeling among Irish Protestants was the affair of Wood's half pence in 1725. It arose from the Crown decision to award William Wood the patent to mint Irish half pence, which sparked off a bitter campaign of protest. The so-called 'Patriot' party objected, firstly because they believed that this was merely a device to permit debasement of the Irish coinage and 'brass money', and secondly because the Irish Privy Council in Dublin had not been consulted first. So great was the uproar that Wood's patent was withdrawn even though, as one historian has pointed out, Ireland needed more coin and Wood's half pence were up to the mint's standard. Trivial though the issue may seem in retrospect, it was not to the Patriots, among whom Swift thundered, 'Government without the consent of the governed is the very definition of slavery.'

Ultimately the whole Irish Protestant case skated on very thin constitutional ice. Irish patronage was in the control of the Crown ministers in London, and the Dublin parliament really had no right to complain about Crown appointments in Ireland. Neither did Irish Protestants want real separation and reform which would allow Catholics to sit as MPs and hold positions of state. What they wanted was to wriggle free of those parts of English rule which were deemed to be irksome, while retaining their ascendancy over the Catholic Irish (some of whom, it must be noted, converted to Protestantism to further their careers).

Grattan's Parliament

Circumstances in the last decades of the eighteenth century seemed to favour Irish Protestant separatism. Particularly significant was the out-break of the American War of Independence in 1776, which stretched the resources of a British Crown and government anxious to put down the rebellion in the New World. This gave the Patriots the opportunity to form a force of 'Volunteers', ostensibly to replace English regiments drafted to fight in the American colonies, but really to put pressure on Westminster to give in to Irish demands.

The leader of the movement demanding the right for Dublin to legislate separately was Henry Grattan (1746–1820), a lawyer and Irish MP who had already been associated with demands for free trade (1779) and an unsuccessful bid for Irish legislative independence in 1780–1. In 1782 Grattan and his supporters were successful in winning the right to legislate separately, and a grateful parliament voted him £50,000 (Grattan consistently refused all office).

Significantly, however (in the context of later Irish history), Grattan's campaign was backed by the threat of force. The 'Volunteers' had taken their cue from the Boston Tea Party (when American colonists had poured English tea into the harbour) with their slogan 'Free Trade or else', and the mouths of their cannon bore the legend 'O Lord open thou our lips, and our mouths shall sound forth their praise'. Given, too, the American emergency which forced the British to concede to Grattan in 1782, there remained the question of what would happen when the American War ended, as it did in 1783. What would the independence of the Irish parliament be worth when the British Empire had regained its strength?

Catholic Irishmen, at least the majority of them, could not be so enthusiastic about Grattan's success. They, as Thomas Pakenham has pointed out, could see the new legislative independence only as giving Protestants 'new power to persecute them with tithes and taxes and Acts against sedition and insurrection'.

The United Irishmen

More important ultimately for Ireland was the outbreak of the French Revolution in 1789. This encouraged a new breed of radicalism centred on Belfast and led to the formation of the 'United Irishmen'. Significantly its founding members were Presbyterians rather than Catholics, for they too had been excluded from privileged Irish society in the eighteenth century. Unlike the 'Protestant nation' advocates of the earlier part of the century, the United Irishmen wanted both to reform parliament and to unite the separate Protestant and Catholic communities. One of the society's earliest members was Wolfe Tone (1763–98), a Dublin Protestant who dreamed of substituting the word

Irish for Catholic and Protestant. But sadly for Tone and others like him, religious sectarianism had already begun to raise its ugly head in Ulster, and the United Irishmen's peaceful lobbying had no success with the majority of Protestants or with the British government.

This forced it underground in 1796, and Tone himself to take refuge in Revolutionary France where he was an able and respected (even by Napoleon Bonaparte) advocate of the Irish nationalist cause. Tone had come to believe that Ireland, like France, must become an independent republic and, although his journals reveal a mordant wit, he became a dedicated revolutionary.

THE FRENCH INTERVENTION

Britain was at war with France from 1793 onwards, and the French naturally saw a rebellious Ireland as a potential base for an attack on England itself. A golden opportunity seemed to present itself in the winter of 1796 when a great fleet of thirty-six warships evaded the blockading British fleet in the Channel and appeared in Bantry Bay off County Cork. The only part of the operation to go wrong was the disappearance of the fleet's flagship, which became detached from the rest of the fleet during the voyage. This was crucial because on it was General Hoche, the commander of the 15,000 men the French planned to put ashore and who would (hopefully) link up with the United Irishmen.

So throughout that first day, 21 December 1796, the French ships waited for Hoche in the magnificent natural waterway which comprises Bantry Bay. So close were they to the shore, noted Wolfe Tone who had made the voyage with them, that he could have thrown a biscuit on to it from his ship. Worse still, from the British point of view, there were only a few hundred local militia in the neighbourhood of Bantry Bay to contest a French landing.

Then nature played a cruel trick on Tone and his French allies. Waiting on that first day for Hoche (who never did arrive), the invaders had been favoured by the wind. Now it turned round to the east. Ironically this very same east wind had allowed the French to slip past the blockading Royal Navy on their outward journey, but now it prevented them from making the last tantalising few yards to the Irish shore. Faced with a persistent easterly wind, some of the warships cut their cables and made out to sea. Others, including the *Indomitable* with Tone aboard, waited vainly for the wind to turn. But this 'Protestant wind', as the historian Thomas Pakenham has called it, did not turn. Instead, by 27 December it had become a howling gale and the remaining French vessels, Tone's last of all, were forced to make for the open sea.

There can be no doubt that at Bantry Bay the British authorities had an amazing stroke of luck. For who can tell what might have happened if Hoche's well-disciplined veterans had landed in 1796? His Majesty's Government were to be just as fortunate the following year when mutinies in the Royal Navy at Spithead and the Nore opened England to the danger of direct invasion. Although this crisis was weathered it had direct relevance to the Irish situation, for, paranoid in their fears about the threat from France, the British authorities instituted massive searches for United Irishmen arms caches both in Ulster and Midland counties like Kilkenny, Carlow and Kildare. The main danger facing them was another French landing combined with a national uprising by the United Irishmen.

Driven on by this fear, the authorities reacted ruthlessly and to some effect. Early in 1798 the National Directory of the United Irishmen was betrayed by informers and arrested. Only Lord Edward Fitzgerald, a romantic if somewhat desperate figure, escaped among the leadership and this reprieve was short-lived. Soon afterwards he was fatally wounded while resisting arrest when his hiding place was discovered. However, instead of deducing that they had broken the back of the conspiracy, the British authorities led by the Viceroy, Lord Camden, in Dublin became panic-stricken about its extent (Fitzgerald, for example, was a leading member of the Anglo-Irish establishment).

REPRESSION

This was the background to the horrors which followed in Ireland's Midland counties, as the army and militia were let loose on the Catholic population in an effort to extract information about United Irishmen cells. What followed was really a legalising of torture. The first device used by the British army was the notorious 'triangles', whereby

A brutal flogging carried out by the British army

victims were tied to triangles of wood and flogged unmercifully. As many as 500 lashes were administered on occasion, as quite innocent civilians were flogged in an effort to get information about arms caches and the organisation of the United Irishmen. The diary of a Quaker woman recorded that troops

> set fire to some cabins near the village – took P. Murphy the father of a family, who kept a shop of spirits in the house where B. Wills had lived – apparently an inoffensive man – tied him to a cart opposite his own door – and those above-mentioned officers degraded themselves so far as to scourge him with their own hands.

Another method of questioning, the infamous 'pitch-capping', was if anything even more barbarous. A brown paper cap was set on the victim's head, and after the pitch had begun to set a little it was set on fire. The unfortunate victim would then attempt to try and tear off the cap, which would cause the pitch to fall into his eyes. The cap could only ultimately be removed with the loss of hair and scalp as well. A ghastly triumvirate was completed by the process known as 'half hanging', in which a rope was pulled around the victim's neck and slackened every time the victim lost consciousness. One particular army sergeant who applied this method was nicknamed 'the Walking Gallows'; one of the heroines of the 1798 uprisings, Anne Devlin, was half hanged to make her talk (she was the subject of a 1980s Irish film).

The Wexford Rising

Although many arms were found in counties like Kildare, the savage methods employed by the authorities proved in the long run to be counterproductive, because the terror sparked off by the rumours about the floggings actually brought about a serious uprising by the Catholic peasantry in the south-eastern county of Wexford, hitherto not one of the strongholds of the United Irishmen. But the authorities, discovering some evidence of United Irish activity in Wexford (they had infiltrated a peasant secret society called 'the Defenders'), let loose the local Protestant yeomanry upon them (Wexford Protestants were known to be among the most sectarian in the whole island). Matters were made even worse by the use of the North Cork militia, largely Catholic in its rank and file, but ill-disciplined and anxious to prove its loyalty to the Crown. Thus the combination of terror stories from Kildare, sectarianism, and a turbulent militia proved to be too much for the Catholic peasantry of Wexford.

They rose up in June 1798, albeit sometimes with Protestant United Irish leadership, but more intriguingly led at a crucial stage by two Catholic priests named Murphy. This was unusual because the Catholic clergy generally tried to prevent their people from taking up arms. As it was, a ramshackle army of rebels armed with pikes, blunderbusses, pistols, scythes and other ill-assorted weapons was welded by Father John Murphy into a remarkably effective fighting force.

At Aulart over a hundred militiamen were piked and hacked to death, leaving only three survivors. At New Ross the rebels were repulsed, even after a remarkable episode when an old rebel stuck his hand in a militia cannon, crying 'she stop'd boys, she stop'd' before being blown sky high. But they continued to be a threat.

VINEGAR HILL

Outside the town of Enniscorthy today a large white cross (one of many in the Irish countryside which mark the sites of battles and massacres) denotes the site of the decisive engagement of the 1798 uprising. It was here that on a pudding-shaped hill Father John Murphy's force, together with women, children and assorted stragglers from other rebel forces, made their last stand against the British army and Irish militias on 21 June 1798.

Vinegar Hill did not, in fact, have any notable advantages as a defensive position and had been chosen primarily as a rendezvous point for rebel forces. So it was entirely open to General Lake's bombarding howitzers, which the gallant pikemen stood for an hour before breaking and fleeing down the Wexford road. The vengeance of the Crown forces was then let loose on the town of Enniscorthy. Once again, as in several other instances in 1798, innocent Protestant loyalists were slaughtered along with rebels. The latter were also guilty of piking and massacring Protestant gentry and their families, notably at Scullabogue.

Ulster

The United Irishmen had also made a desperate attempt at rebellion in the province of Ulster where the movement had started. There the chief rebel leader was Henry McCracken, whose nationalism embraced a hatred of privilege as well as of English domination. McCracken's motto was 'the Rich always betray the Poor' but he was really betrayed by his fellow Protestants, who regarded the United Irishmen as a threat to the Protestant ascendancy. It was from this period that the so-called 'Orange Lodges', named after William of Orange and devoted to protecting Protestantism and the union with England, date. Partly because of this factor McCracken, with 6,000 men, was defeated at Antrim, and with that setback the Ulster revolt fizzled out. A surprising feature was the refusal of the Catholic peasantry, perhaps intimidated by the horror stories from the south, to support McCracken. His men were Presbyterian and working class, those who had done least well in the Protestant community during the Ascendancy. As events turned out, this was the last hurrah of Protestant nationalism in the republican mould, a point underlined by the fate of the unfortunate Wolfe Tone.

THE FRENCH AGAIN

Throughout 1798 the United Irishmen had waited vainly for a decisive French intervention on the scale of 1796. When it did come it was too

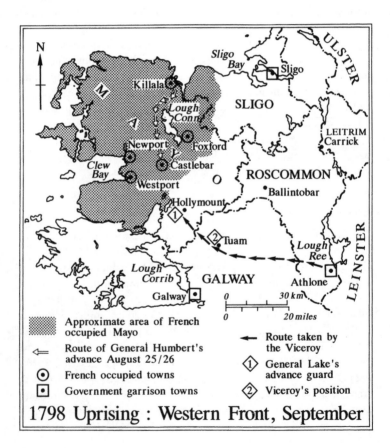

Legend:

- Approximate area of French occupied Mayo
- ⇐ Route of General Humbert's advance August 25/26
- ⊙ French occupied towns
- ▣ Government garrison towns
- ← Route taken by the Viceroy
- ①◇ General Lake's advance guard
- ②◇ Viceroy's position

1798 Uprising : Western Front, September

late, for the Wexford revolt had been crushed and other uprisings failed to materialise. The intervention was also on a minute scale for just 1,099 men landed with General Humbert in County Mayo in August, although another 5,000 were supposed to follow later.

Humbert's expedition had a short but colourful life. His grizzled veterans were unimpressed by native Irish support, although a 'Republic of Connaught' was duly proclaimed, but did rout the Irish militia, again led by Lake, at Castlebar. So swiftly did the militia take to their heels that the battle has gone down into history as 'the Races of Castlebar'.

Humbert soon realised that his position was hopeless, but resolved to go down fighting in the face of superior British forces (the second, larger expedition failed to arrive in time). The end duly came at the village of Ballinamuck, followed for Humbert and his men by imprisonment in Dublin where they became sought-after celebrities. By contrast their native Irish allies, though few in number, were butchered and hanged. (All these events were well portrayed in a 1983 French/British/Irish TV production, *The Year of the French*, based on Thomas Flanagan's novel.)

A rather pathetic sequel followed. First Wolfe Tone arrived in Lough Swilly in September with the second expedition, only to be taken prisoner after refusing to escape in the face of superior British forces. 'Shall it be said,' Tone reportedly told a French officer, 'that I fled while the French were fighting the battles of my country?' In prison Tone botched an attempt to slit his throat but died of his wound a week later. Then Tone's arch-rival, the unlikely named Napper Tandy, put ashore from a single ship in north-west Ireland, spent the night carousing with the local postmaster, and then returned to France.

The Significance of 1798

The events of 1798 were motivated by the assumption, in the words of the nationalist slogan, that 'England's difficulty was Ireland's opportunity'. In the event it was an opportunity missed, but were the hopes of the United Irishmen ever justified?

Perhaps they would have been a year earlier, but by 1798 their movement was under the severest pressure from the authorities. Sectarianism had also become a significant factor, although the religious nuances of the revolts can still confuse. In Ulster, for example, the Protestant McCracken was let down by his co-religionists, but also by the Catholic peasantry who stayed at home. In Wexford, too, we face the paradox of *Catholic* militiamen vainly waving their missals at the rebellious Catholic army of Father John Murphy in a doomed attempt to save their lives. Sectarian Protestantism had helped to incite the Wexford revolt, but the Protestants Bagenal Harvey and John Moore were hanged for supporting it.

Historians have reflected this ambivalence in their reaction to the events of 1798. A socialist historian like P. Beresford Ellis sees the '98 as a movement betrayed by muddle, government spies and, in the words of McCracken, the one thing that can always be relied upon, that 'the Rich always betray the Poor'. Thomas Pakenham has expressed the more traditional view that 1798 led directly to closer union with England, but Roy Foster, while recognising the special circumstances of the 1790s, believes that such a union was being contemplated earlier because of the separatist behaviour of the Irish parliament in the 1780s.

There were other more obscure long-term results of 1798. One was that rebels who were not executed were transported to the penal colony in Botany Bay, Australia, where by 1802 a quarter of the colonists were Irish (one of the prison governors thereabouts was Captain Bligh of *Bounty* fame). So began a long historic connection between the two countries. Other survivors of 1798 ended up in New York City.

For Irish republicans 1798 became symbolic. It centred on the person of Wolfe Tone, although for some decades after his death he appeared to be forgotten by his fellow countrymen. But today Tone's alleged burial place at Bodenstown in County Kildare is a sacred shrine for Irish republicans and nationalists because he is regarded as a martyr for the cause which eventually brought independence in 1921.

Culture

The Protestant ascendancy in the eighteenth century was linked with a remarkable flowering of literary talent. Jonathan Swift (1667–1745) was its most significant figure. A clergyman of the Church of Ireland who became Dean of Saint Patrick's Cathedral in 1713, Swift's work epitomised much of the ambivalence of the Protestant minority in Ireland about the relationship with England. Some of it was just polemical like his *Proposal for the Universal Use of Irish Manufactures* (1720), but he also produced the celebrated *Gulliver's Travels* (1726), although even this contained coded references to Ireland's inferior status. Swift himself always believed that his support for the Tory party during the reign of Queen Anne (1702–14) prevented him from getting the promotion to an English living which he deserved. He therefore resented both his 'exile' in Dublin and the arrogance of Westminster which prevented him from getting his just deserts. The strength of this resentment comes across in the following extract from one of his poems:

> Remove me from this land of slaves,
> Where all are fools, and all are knaves;
> Where every knave and fool is brought,
> Yet kindly sells himself for naught;
> Where Whig and Tory fiercely fight
> Who's in the wrong, who in the right;
> And when their country lies at stake
> They only fight for fighting's sake.

Oliver Goldsmith (1728–74) was the son of a poor Church of Ireland clergyman. His literary talents only really began to assert themselves after his return to London in 1756. Thereafter he became a considerable figure in literary circles there. Among his most notable works were the play *She Stoops to Conquer* (1773), his long poems *The Traveller* and *The Deserted Village*, and his novel *The Vicar of Wakefield* (1766). Goldsmith seems to have completely sublimated his Irishness and no links with the Protestant 'Patriots' are recorded. Nevertheless he was in a great tradition of Irish writers and playwrights whose literary achievement came only when they went abroad.

Richard Brinsley Sheridan (1751–1816) was born into a leading Irish literary family and, like Goldsmith, sought fame and fortune in England where he wrote numerous comedies for the London stage. Among the best known are *The Rivals* (1775) and *The School for Scandal* (1777). But Sheridan also had political ambitions, became a Westminster MP in 1780, and subsequently a friend of the Prince of Wales and the great

The writer Maria Edgeworth

radical, Charles James Fox. Although as a politician he supported conciliatory policies towards Ireland, Sheridan was otherwise, according to one historian, 'unique in his ability to jettison Irishness'.

Maria Edgeworth (1767–1849) was Irish only by adoption, being born in Oxfordshire but settling in Edgeworthstown (Co. Longford). She wrote improving tales for small children and the first real Anglo-Irish novel *Castle Rackrent* (1800). Her diary contains interesting references to the events of 1798 in her locality.

Edmund Burke (1729–97) was born in Dublin to parents of mixed religion (his father was a Protestant and his mother a Catholic). Like so many of his compatriots Burke pursued a career in England, although he never apparently lost a distinctive Irish accent. This seems to have hindered political advancement although he was elected to the House of Commons in 1765. Although the greatest constitutional theorist and political thinker of his day (as shown by his famous *Reflections on the French Revolution*, 1790), Burke was never to obtain major office of any kind.

CHAPTER ELEVEN

The Rise of Catholic Nationalism and the Famine, 1800–1868

The Act of Union

Whether it was a consequence of 1798 or the behaviour of Grattan's parliament, the Act of Union of 1800 marked a clear watershed in Irish history. It abolished the separate Irish parliament in Dublin and from 1 January 1801 united the kingdoms of England and Ireland, supposedly 'forever'. Irish MPs, all Protestant of course, were to take their seats in Westminster.

At the time the Irish reactions to the Act reflected the paradoxes of eighteenth-century politics in the country. Thus members of the old Protestant 'Patriot' party opposed the Union for being an interference with perceived Irish rights. Whereas Catholics tended to support the Union because the rule of Protestant Englishmen was thought likely to be milder than that of their more sectarian Irish brothers. This reaction, it should be added, was to be short-lived for, as the nineteenth century drew on, Protestantism would increasingly be identified with the Union, while Catholics wanted the Act repealed. A theme with very modern echoes was also highlighted: was Ireland to have a devolved parliament of its own, or was it to be ruled directly from Westminster?

EMMET'S REVOLT

The revolutionary fervour of 1798 did not in any case disappear altogether in the years following the failure of the revolts. There were uprisings in Galway and even by unemployed Protestant yeomanry in County Wexford itself. But there was a definitive end to the United

Irishmen movement with the failure of Robert Emmet's uprising in 1803.

Emmet (1778–1803) had been a member of the society and was enthused with its revolutionary doctrines. Such a man was unlikely to accept the Act of Union, and Emmet began to create an organisation which would seize power and set up an Irish Republic. But his planned rising was hopelessly bungled. First there was an explosion at an arms dump which gave away his intentions a week before the planned revolt, and then the authorities seized all the conspirators' pamphlets as they came off the presses. Emmet hoped to recruit 2,000 men for an uprising in Dublin; in the event he had just ninety with which to seize Dublin Castle.

On their way to the castle, Emmet's adherents seized the Lord Chief Justice of Ireland in his coach, piked him to death and began to riot in the streets. Needless to say, this tiny band of revolutionaries never got anywhere near the castle and Emmet, by now thoroughly disillusioned by his followers' indiscipline, went into hiding. Weeks later, he was arrested, tried and condemned to death.

Like many Irish republican martyrs, Robert Emmet was far more powerful in death than he was in life. This is mainly because of the statement he made on the scaffold:

> Let no man write my epitaph ... When my country takes her place among the nations of the earth, then, and not till then let my epitaph be written.

Even though his attempted uprising was a fiasco, Emmet immediately entered the martyrology of Irish republicanism.

The 'Liberator'

Throughout modern Irish history, the twin themes of constitutional nationalism and bloody revolt have run side by side. At times one has predominated but the other has always been there in the background. So it was after 1803, when a man who had turned out to fight Emmet's rebels deduced that if Ireland were to secure any sort of independence, she must do so by peaceful means. This man was Daniel O'Connell (1775–1847), nicknamed the 'Liberator', arguably the greatest political personality in nineteenth-century Ireland.

O'Connell was a fascinating figure. Born into a well-off landed Catholic family which had survived the penal laws and held its property, O'Connell grew up in Derrynane Abbey in the wilds of County Kerry in the south-west (a tree planted by the youthful O'Connell can still be seen in the grounds of the house). He was, therefore, a patrician, an indulgent landlord, but someone who had little sympathy with urban nineteenth-century forces like trade unionism. He was also a skilful barrister and a great orator, so much so that an admirer said of his voice, 'You'd hear it a mile off as if it were coming through honey.'

One historian has commented on his love of the trappings of Irishness – wolfhounds, shamrocks, bands, uniforms and round towers. Strangely, too, for an Irish nationalist, O'Connell loved the monarchy, later calling Queen Victoria his 'darling little Queen'. Yet O'Connell advocated a union of the two kingdoms separate but equal under the British Crown, just as Grattan had done. The difference was that O'Connell intended that the majority in an Irish parliament would be Catholic, just as the majority of Irish people were Catholics. He did not disregard the importance of winning Protestant support, but when this support was not forthcoming he became intolerant. Partly because of his background he knew nothing of Ulster, and always tended to underestimate the importance of sectarian differences.

There were two great causes in Daniel O'Connell's career, Catholic Emancipation and Repeal of the Union. One was achieved, and the other brought him to ruin before it was subsumed in an infinitely greater tragedy. In both causes, however, his gifts as a political organiser were evident. A great 'Catholic Association' was formed which the peasantry could join for a monthly payment of a penny; well organised by middle-class Catholic supporters, it crucially got the support of the Catholic clergy for the cause of emancipation (they were less enthusiastic about severing the Union).

From 1826 onwards the pressure on Westminster to concede Catholic emancipation grew apace, and O'Connell was especially adept at organising so-called 'Monster Meetings'. Vast crowds, disciplined by an almost military precision, were assembled and, although O'Connell always stressed his opposition to violence, the sight of such big crowds was bound to alarm the authorities. Historians have naturally speculated about the extent to which, despite O'Connell's protestations of non-violence, the *threat* of it was present. Here, O'Connell seemed to be saying, is a great mass of my well-disciplined aupporters, but what if my iron control and leadership were removed?

Proof of O'Connell's undoubted charisma was presented in 1828 by his victory at the East Clare by-election over another Catholic, but anti-emancipation, candidate. It was this which forced the hand of the then British prime minister, the Duke of Wellington, and his home secretary, Sir Robert Peel. The Catholic Emancipation Act was duly passed in 1829, whereby Catholics could become Westminster MPs even if restrictions remained on their entry into other spheres of public life.

Successful then in his first great campaign, O'Connell moved on to launch another against the Act of Union. Again 'Monster Meetings' assembled with all the panoply of Irishness (such as wolfhound flags) which O'Connell so much enjoyed. The campaign reached its peak in 1843 at a huge meeting on the old royal hill of Tara when some half a million of O'Connell's supporters gathered (he claimed there were one and a half million). With characteristic flamboyance O'Connell stated: 'We are at Tara of the Kings – the spot from which emanated the social power, the legal authority, the rights to dominion over the furthest extremes of the land.' (This was historically inaccurate because no high king of Tara had obtained such authority.) More significantly, O'Connell said: 'Step by step we are approaching the great goal of Repeal of the Union, but it is at length with the strides of a giant.'

The British authorities called O'Connell's bluff. They cancelled another monster meeting at Clontarf, and arrested him and some of his leading colleagues on a charge of conspiracy. O'Connell only actually served five months in the Richmond Bridewell, but he was now nearly seventy and his star had waned. He died in Genoa in 1847, an exile despite his achievement.

'THE ENEMY WITHIN'?

The socialist historian P. Beresford Ellis is among those who have attacked O'Connell as a betrayer of the Irish nationalist cause. Ellis has gone so far as to call him 'the enemy within'. Such a denunciation derives from O'Connell's lack of interest in the language issue for, although a fluent Irish speaker, he deliberately spoke English in Irish-speaking areas and said, 'I am sufficiently utilitarian not to regret its abandonment.' This, when according to one estimate there were as many as four million native Irish speakers in 1831, was regarded later as a betrayal by supporters of the Gaelic revival.

O'Connell's opposition to trade unionism has already been referred to (he was embarrassed by the activities of the Dublin Trades Union Political Union founded in 1831), and he also opposed agrarian campaigns when they involved violence. His monarchism and even his pacifism (he had after all fought against Emmet in 1803) have also been attacked or questioned. Even the effectiveness of Catholic emancipation has been questioned because it did little for Ireland's poor masses.

The alternative view put forward by Robert Kee is that O'Connell gave concrete shape to the political demands of the Catholic peasantry, which hitherto had been unheard. In Kee's view this makes him greater than Tone or Emmet, and it is one which again highlights the difference between those who admire non-violent constitutional nationalism and those (like Beresford Ellis and his English colleague, E.P. Thompson) who regard republican violence as inevitable, and a consequence of centuries of English oppression.

THE CHURCH

A key role in O'Connell's emancipation campaign was played, as has been noted, by the Catholic Church. It was also heavily involved in a third subsidiary campaign waged by O'Connell, generally known as 'the Tithe War'. It took its name from the system whereby tithes were imposed on the Catholic peasantry by the Anglican Church, an absurd situation when that Church represented only a tiny proportion of the Irish population. However, the existing law in Ireland allowed the Anglican clergy (or strictly speaking the Church of Ireland clergy) to confiscate the crops of the peasantry if they could not pay tithes, even if this left the peasants near to starvation.

O'Connell began a campaign against tithes, but there was also a state of virtual civil war in the Irish countryside in the 1830s between peasant, church and landlord. The military were often called in to intervene. Ultimately the British authorities recognised the absurdity of the situation and abolished tithes by means of the Tithe Commutation Act of 1838 (although the Church of Ireland maintained its inappropriately privileged position in other areas). Some historians have argued that this development owed more to the pressure from the Irish peasantry than anything Daniel O'Connell ever did.

EDUCATION

In the early part of the nineteenth century in Ireland 'Hedge Schools' were a common phenomenon. These were outdoor schools taught by itinerant schoolteachers in the absence of a proper school system for the Catholic Irish people. The medium of instruction was Irish, although a good deal of time was spent reading English, Latin and even Greek. For this reason the 'Hedge Schools' did not have the approval of the United Irishmen who (in an example of extreme political utopianism) wanted the English language to be abolished.

When in 1831 a national system of primary schools was introduced in Ireland, it too was subsequently criticised (notably by Daniel Corkery in *The Hidden Ireland*) for ignoring the existence of the Irish language. But the attitude of the British authorities was hardly surprising, for as far as they were concerned English not Irish was to be the language of the classroom, just as it was the language of business and administration.

ULSTER

One area of Ireland not receptive to O'Connell's ideas was the province of Ulster, which was largely Protestant and opposed emancipation, and more prosperous than the rest of the country because of the flourishing linen trade. Repeal of the Union, which in Ulster was seen as responsible for its prosperity, had no appeal therefore. And Ulster continued to boom, nowhere more so than its leading city Belfast, which grew faster in the second half of the nineteenth century than any other city in the British Isles. As early as 1842 the English novelist Thackeray wrote admiringly of Belfast's bustle as 'hearty, thriving, and prosperous, as if it had money in its pocket and roast beef for dinner'.

In religious terms, too, this prosperity was significant in the province because Anglican ascendancy was challenged by the rise of the Presbyterian merchant class, just as the rise of the propertied Catholic middle class elsewhere fuelled O'Connell's campaigns.

The Famine

Everything that happened in Ireland in the nineteenth century, and indeed since, has been overshadowed by the catastrophe which overtook the country between 1845 and 1849. It was a disaster which poisoned Anglo-Irish relations for generations afterwards, and had the most profound effects in Ireland itself. This was the Potato Famine.

Nineteenth-century Ireland was the most densely populated country in Europe. In 1800 its population was 4½ million but by 1841, when the first official census took place, it had risen to 8 million. Yet much of this population existed in conditions of misery which were a byword

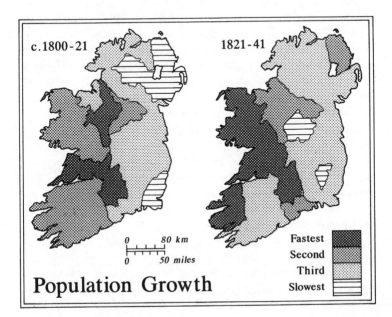

c.1800-21   1821-41

0   80 km
0   50 miles

Fastest
Second
Third
Slowest

Population Growth

and shocked foreign visitors. The root of this misery lay in the dependence of the peasantry on just one staple crop, the potato; in western counties like Mayo and Galway nine-tenths of the people ate nothing else. Here was a disaster waiting to happen, made worse by the rapid rise in population in the first half of the century which forced the peasants to subsist on smaller plots of land. Crops other than potatoes had to be sold to pay the rent.

The authorities in Ireland were not blind to the peril, for there had been a serious blight of the potato as far back as 1817 when thousands had died, and in 1824 a government commission had identified chronic overdependence on the potato crop as a potential menace to the population. In 1844, too, there had been another serious blight when half the potato crop had been lost, so that only the special hardiness of Irish peasants had allowed many to survive.

Hopes were high in the summer of 1845, however, when there was every sign of a fine, healthy crop of potatoes. But the weather that summer was curious, and in retrospect sinister. Summer heat was mingled with thunderstorms, mists, and big variations in temperature unusual in Ireland. So a superstitious peasantry wondered what lay in store for them. The first rumours of blight came from Cork in June, but as late as August peasants and farmers still expected a bumper crop of what they called 'praties'. Reports from Galway, for example, still spoke of potatoes of 'the most luxuriant character'. By mid-September all this had changed. On 11 September the *Freeman's Journal* reported a case where a man had been digging in a fine field of potatoes on the previous Monday, but on the Tuesday he found 'the tubers all blasted, and unfit for the use of man or beast'. In fact, the whole potato plant was changed into a filthy, odorous black mush, all the more appalling because the crop had seemed so healthy. Desperate people, seeing a year's food supply disappearing before their eyes, cast about for an explanation, and came up with bizarre ones which (alternatively) made the moon, fog, frost, easterly winds, and even the electricity from the summer storms responsible. What had happened?

The villain in this tragedy was a humble fungus called *Phytophthora infestans*, brought to Ireland by ship from America, which unknown to the peasantry infested first the soil and then the potato plants. And because they did not, and could not in the state of existing scientific knowledge, know this, the peasants attempted to save their crops by hauling them out of the ground to dry or cutting away seemingly healthy bits to eat. In their ignorance this was understandable, because the leaves of the plant had black spots with a whitish mould underneath, and they could not know that once the fungus established itself, both potato and stalk were doomed. Equally incomprehensible was the sinister speed with which the blight spread, so that by early 1846 every county in Ireland was affected. In fact wind, rain and insects carried the fungus spores to other potato plants.

THE IRISH REACTION

The impact of the total blight of the potato crop on the Irish population was devastating, and well conveyed in Thomas Gallagher's recent study *Paddy's Lament*. Gallagher notes that the first premonition of disaster came with a hideous smell

> that was sulphurous, sewerlike ... carried by the wind from the rotting plants in the first-struck places. Farmers who had gone to bed imbued with the image of their lush potato gardens were awakened by this awful smell and by the dogs howling their disapproval of it.

After the stench of blight came despair, as a Catholic priest noted at the time:

> In many places, the wretched people were seated on the fences of their decaying gardens wringing their hands and wailing bitterly the destruction that had left them foodless.

Then in desperation people tried to find other things to eat. Mussels and other sea food were seized on around the coast (frequently poisoning the wretched peasants who did not know what was safe to eat), and sheep-stealing increased markedly. Some lucky folk caught wild game; others tried eating plants. But nothing could fill the gap left by the stricken potato. In Ireland's dire emergency, the Catholic archbishop of Dublin called for prayers in all Catholic churches 'that God in His mercy would vouchsafe to avert the calamity which seems impending over us'.

THE BRITISH REACTION

The British authorities were not, as we have seen, unaware of the extent of the problem in Ireland, even if there was a tendency to think that the Irish exaggerated everything. However, from the outset the British government was completely unprepared for the scale of the disaster. The prime minister, Sir Robert Peel, was not a heartless man, and he ordered a scientific commission to enquire immediately into the causes of the blight. This produced useless advice for the starving Irish. In County Limerick people tried 'making large holes in the sides of the pits to admit air and by scarcely putting any covering on top of the pits but the dry stalks', but nothing worked.

Then Peel tried more practical measures, but ones which were hopelessly entrapped in the bleak economic theory of the day. This was called 'political economy' and was the most extreme form imaginable of market economics, often associated with the phrase 'laissez-faire'. It meant that in no circumstances might the government interfere with the market, and no doctrine could have been less suited to the Irish

The total failure of the potato crop spelt starvation for the Irish community

crisis of the 1840s. Laissez-faire forbade the giving of food to the starving Irish because such an action would be an interference with natural market laws, and interfere with prices so that merchants would hold back from the market. None the less Peel knew that by the beginning of 1846 a quarter of the Irish population was on the verge of starvation, and that something had to be done. Everything that was done, however, had to fall in with the orthodoxies of political economy and laissez-faire.

Three separate measures were put in train. Firstly Peel ordered from the USA a large supply of maize, popularly known as 'Indian corn', which was sent to Ireland to be sold at low cost. It mattered not that the Irish had never eaten maize and did not know how to prepare it for consumption. What did matter was that never before had there been a market for maize in Ireland, so the principles of political economy were not infringed. Peel's second measure was to appoint a relief commission to supervise the maize depots. It was also supposed to liaise with local magistrates and landlords' committees, which were meant to provide employment for the starving peasants so that they could buy the maize. Lastly, in 1846 Peel repealed the Corn Laws, in existence since 1815, so removing all protectionist duties on grain imported into Britain and Ireland. This measure lowered the price of bread but was also almost totally irrelevant in Ireland (repeal was a major issue in the rest of Britain) where much of the population could not afford to buy bread anyway.

The imperatives of political economy were also underlined by the decision, extraordinary to modern eyes, to keep the Indian corn depots closed until general food prices had gone too high, by which time most of the Irish were driven desperate with hunger. But this, of course, was all part of political economy, because Peel's task was not to feed the people (a secondary issue) but to give market forces free rein. This inflexible economic theory was then disastrously combined with a most unfortunate appointment. The man put in charge of Irish Famine Relief, Charles Edward Trevelyan (1807–86), was a distinguished civil servant and an upright man, but he could scarcely have been less sympathetic to Ireland's predicament. Indeed, some of his statements have a touch of racism about them. Thus he described the practice of

Charles Trevelyan

subletting parts of a tenant's holding as 'barbarous' when, in fact, it was forced on the peasants by economic necessity. More notoriously, Trevelyan pronounced his view that 'Ireland must be left to the operation of natural causes'. His correspondence is full of references like 'idle', 'feckless' and 'improvident'.

By 1847 matters were so desperate that even Trevelyan was forced to accept a Soup Kitchens Act which provided for the feeding of the starving in Ireland, this after the poor relief system based on the concept of the able-bodied poor being obliged to work (enshrined in the 1834 Poor Law) had been shown to be hopelessly inappropriate there. By then, in any case, dysentery and typhus, the dreaded 'travelling sickness', were rife anyway. And yet it would be wrong to suggest that the English people turned their backs on Ireland's distress. Queen Victoria gave generously to Irish famine relief and titled ladies set up committees to raise funds. But their efforts were dwarfed by the scale of the calamity.

THE COST

Contrary to what Trevelyan, knighted for his services, claimed, the Famine did not end in 1847 but stretched on into 1848 and 1849, when the potato crop was again blighted. In many respects too 1849 was the worst year of all, with an eyewitness writing from the village of Ballinrobe in County Galway of how 'the streets are daily thronged with moving skeletons. The fields are strewn with dead ... the curse of Russell, more terrible that the curse of Cromwell, is upon us' (Lord John Russell had succeeded Peel as prime minister in 1846). All over Ireland starving peasants walled themselves up in their cabins awaiting death.

Some tried to flee abroad. Liverpool's streets were full of some 100,000 starving and destitute Irish. Others sailed for the New World in the notorious 'coffin ships', so called because many died en route or arrived half dead in the USA or Canada. To take but one example, from the month of July 1847, it is known that 804 out of 4,227 persons sailing from Cork and Liverpool to Canada were dead on arrival. There were similar stories on the routes to the United States.

How many died? Given the immense loss of life between 1845 and 1849 such estimates are bound to be speculative, but there are some fairly reliable statistics calculated on the basis of the 1841 census figure of 8 million. Such calculations indicate that, had the Irish population maintained its previous rate of increase, it would have reached a figure of over 9 million in 1851. The census for 1851 actually gave a figure of 6,552,385; if about 1.5 million are added to this for the number of famine emigrants, we are left with a figure of some 8 million. As many as a million Irish people *may*, therefore, have died of starvation and disease between 1845 and 1849. The problem with this figure is that it is calculated on the basis of what the population increase between 1841 and 1851 would have been *without* the Famine. Roy Foster prefers a lower figure of 775,000, and other Irish historians estimate a figure of 800,000 (and they are now extremely objective about this emotive issue). However, even these figures only refer to the dead, and not to the miserable fate awaiting countless Irish migrants in their new homes where they were the despised and ostracised newcomers in societies built on migrant labour. Truly the 'wretched of the earth'.

THE ISSUE OF RESPONSIBILITY

As the horror of the Famine years passed into history, a myth grew in Ireland that the deaths of hundreds of thousands of Irish people had been part of a deliberate English plot to murder them. Nothing less, in fact, than genocide by wilful neglect. So the Famine joined those other dark pages in Irish history about Cromwell and 1798, and its countless dead were added to the list of Irish martyrs.

There is no proof, and never has been, that the British government's policy was to allow the Irish population to starve to death. Even highly critical studies of British policy at the time, like Cecil Woodham Smith's *The Great Hunger* and Thomas Gallagher's *Paddy's Lament*, do not attempt to suggest that such an intention existed. Having said this, however, it must immediately be conceded that statements by the British government at the time did little to discourage the emergence of such a myth. When Lord John Russell could say (at a time when exports of grain continued to pour out of Ireland), 'I do not believe it is in the power of this House to prevent the dreadful scenes of suffering and death now occurring in Ireland,' his protestations seemed like the purest hypocrisy. Or at best a whitewash over the pronouncements of Charles Trevelyan who believed that 'if the Irish once find out there are any circumstances in which they can get free government grants, we shall have a system of mendicancy such as the world never knew'.

The Irish could hardly be expected to see that, had there been a similar calamity in England, the rules of political economy and laissez-faire would almost certainly have brought the same result. Ireland's suffering was multiplied by that dependence on the potato for which undoubtedly the British government must bear some responsibility. But the workings of mid-Victorian government were not designed to cope with the Irish horror, any more than it could cope with the cholera epidemic which carried off the Prince Consort a decade later.

That there was sometimes scant sympathy for the Irish in their plight has to be conceded (Protestant preachers in England decreed that it was a judgement of God on Popery), but it was not universal in England and not a consequence of deliberate English malice.

THE SIGNIFICANCE OF THE FAMINE

There can be little doubt that the Famine experience sharpened the attractiveness of that element in Irish nationalism which preferred violence to the peaceful redress of grievances. But the reaction of the suffering masses was, in general, amazingly peaceful; even at the Famine's height a skeletal crowd which petitioned for help outside the house of the Marquess of Sligo in Westport, County Mayo (one of many landowners who tried to help), was careful not to tread on his grass. So the trauma of the Famine did not destroy the social fabric. What it did do was create a well of bitterness and hatred, not only in Ireland but also across the Atlantic, where a great emigrant Irish community was to grow up in the United States and thus strengthen the links between America and Ireland, where the Quaker Famine Relief Committee acknowledged the 'munificent bounty' of US citizens in aiding Famine victims.

Generation after generation then preserved the legend of the Famine horror, just as the ruined and deserted villages in Mayo and Galway were a permanent physical reminder of the disaster. Sometimes these ghastly dwellings were a left-over from a brutal eviction, deliberately wrecked by callous landlords who had ousted the wretched tenants because, with no potatoes, they had no money for rent. It cannot be a matter for surprise, therefore, that the Irish people found it hard to forget:

> For nothing would ever be able to efface the memory of this monstrous thing that had happened in these years to Irish men, women and children in their own country, in the name of the British government in Ireland.

Such was the nature of what Robert Kee calls 'this monstrous thing' that many Irish people, not always fairly, have felt forced to agree with the Englishman Sydney Smith who said:

The moment the very name of Ireland is mentioned, the English seem to bid adieu to common feeling, common prudence and common sense, and to act with the barbarity of tyrants and the fatuity of idiots.

And there was the silence of the countryside, 'the land that is so desolate', depopulated and tinged with sadness for the lost thousands. It was memorably summed up by Hugh Dorian in *Donegal Sixty Years Ago*:

In a very short time there was nothing but stillness, a mournful silence in the villages, in the cottages grim poverty and emaciated faces ... The tinkers ... fled to the cities, the musicians ... disappeared and never returned. Many of the residents too made their escape at once, finding employment or early graves elsewhere ... There were no more friendly meetings at the neighbours' houses in the afternoons, no gatherings on the hillsides on Sundays, no song, no merry laugh of the maidens. Not only were the human beings silent and lonely, but the brute creation also, for not even the bark of the dog, or the crowing of a cock was to be heard ...

Young Ireland

Even while the Famine raged the revolutionary tradition of 1798 reasserted itself, albeit feebly. It did so through the mechanism of the 'Young Ireland' organisation, itself a copy of continental radicalism personified by the great Italian patriot Mazzini's 'Young Italy'. 'Young Ireland', however, remained distinctively Irish and retained many of the characteristics of the 1798 movement. Protestants still played a leading part, notably Thomas Davis (1814–45), the main inspiration behind the organisation, a ballad writer responsible for the nationalist 'A Nation Once Again', as did the 'Wolfe Tone' of the movement John Mitchel (1815–75), who was the publisher of the nationalist newspaper *The United Irishman*.

Ironically, the central figure in the 'Young Ireland' revolt of 1848 was its most conservative. William Smith O'Brien (1803–64) was a late convert even to O'Connell-style nationalism, and only joined 'Young Ireland' under the impact of the Famine tragedy. For years he had been a Westminster MP, and was a product of both Harrow and Cambridge. Before the Young Irelanders had concerted their plans, however,

Mitchel was arrested, and only O'Brien became involved in the tragicomedy known as 'The Battle of Widow MacCormack's Cabbage Patch'. O'Brien and twenty ill-armed peasants were routed by the local constabulary at Ballingarry in County Tipperary, and the leader was later arrested at a local railway station while attempting to flee. The Young Ireland rising in 1848, the great year of revolutions in Europe, was therefore a fiasco, but one which pointed the way to the future.

The Economy

The Irish economic historian L.M. Cullen has shown that over-dependence on the potato before 1845 was not the only significant factor in pre-Famine Ireland. He pointed out that the last general famine in Ireland was as far back as 1740–1, that of 1817 being only partial, and also detected a difference between the sufferings of the peasant or labouring class and the more wealthy farmers who could afford a richer diet. The main thrust of Cullen's work, however, was in highlighting the importance of the decline in the domestic weaving and linen industries outside the north-east (devastating, for example, the formerly prosperous weaving centre of Westport, Co. Mayo), which deprived many of any real alternative to subsistence potato-growing. He concluded: 'The background to the Famine, through the crisis in domestic industry, is as much an industrial as an agrarian one.' His conclusion that the effect of the Famine was patchy, and related to the impoverishment of outlying areas in Munster and Connaught, has been endorsed by other historians.

What of the massive population rise between 1800 and 1845? Contrary to older interpretations, the evidence does not support the view that this growth was abnormal, or that it was linked to early marriage in Ireland. Both the birth rate and the marriage rate at the time of the 1841 census seem to have been in line with that in other European countries. While it is true that the Irish population did rise by 105 per cent between 1785 and 1841, this was a period of sharp population increase throughout Europe. Perversely, too, medical improvements may have made the impoverished peasants more vulnerable to the potato blight, precisely because smallpox inoculation seems to have brought down the levels of child mortality. Roy Foster has contributed to this debate by pointing out that the *rate* of growth in the Irish population had actually begun to fall off in the 1820s. In part this was because many young men had started to emigrate (a phenomenon, therefore, not wholly associated with the Famine), and, it has been suggested, because women began to marry later in the 1830s.

CONCLUSION

The debate about the Famine has been a crucial one in Irish history. In its earlier manifestations it demonstrated the power of myth in history. What, therefore, can be said about it from the vantage point of the twenty-first century? Firstly, the 'genocide theory' is untenable. Deplorable though the attitude of the British government towards Ireland may have been in many respects, there was no genocidal plot as nationalists from 'Young Ireland' onwards have attempted to suggest. Secondly, recent research by economic historians has shown that pre-Famine factors contributed considerably to the disaster, and that its effects were most catastrophic for the poorest segment of the population. Lastly, the Famine did undoubtedly give an impetus to the physical force variant of Irish nationalism identified with Tone, Emmet and Davis.

CHAPTER TWELVE

Parnell and Home Rule,
1868–1891

When W.E. Gladstone made his celebrated promise to 'pacify Ireland', he did so in the context of a turbulent and unstable island. The catastrophe of the Potato Famine, and the bitterness which followed it, had resulted in 1858 in the formation by James Stephens of the Fenian movement (taking its name from the ancient Irish warriors, the Fianna) which pledged itself to sever the English link for ever.

In 1867 several Fenian uprisings had failed, leaders had been arrested, and three executed in Manchester for a raid on a police van in which a warder had been killed. Successive British governments had ignored the kernel of the Irish problem, the land, for it was this rather than desperate republicanism of the Fenian sort which concerned most Irishmen. It was therefore to Gladstone's credit that he set about this problem with some vigour shortly after forming his first government in 1868. He seemed, indeed, to encourage Irish aspirations by high-lighting the unfair nature of the land settlement. In this area he said the 'old Irish ideas were never supplanted except by the rude hand of violence – by laws written on the Statute Book – but never entering into the heart of the Irish people'.

Statements of this type from the British prime minister naturally tended to encourage Irish nationalists, like the former Fenian Michael Davitt (1846–1906) who denounced 'the landlord garrison established by England in this country centuries ago' (a reference to the Anglo-Irish landlord class, often called the 'West Britons', many of whom chose to live in England). The difference was that Davitt wished to put an end to English rule in Ireland, while Gladstone wished to preserve it.

The Disestablishment of the Irish Church

An even more glaring anomaly, as Gladstone fully recognised, was the position of the Church of Ireland. The equivalent of the Church of England on the other side of the Irish Sea, it enjoyed all the latter's privileges but none of its support. The Catholic Irish were forced to hear Mass in the countryside in the years before 1829 while Church of Ireland ministers preached in empty churches.

In 1868 Gladstone declared that the Church of Ireland 'must cease to exist' as a state Church, but he was surprised by the reaction. Irate Irish clerics denounced the Liberal leader's 'sacrilegious assault' although they could not stop it. In 1869 Article 5 of the Act of Union of 1800 was repealed by the House of Commons. This broke the link between the Church of Ireland and the Church of England and put it on the same level as the Catholic Church in Ireland. It was, Gladstone wrote to Lord Glanville, the end of 'this woeful huckstering affair'.

The 1870 Land Act

The disestablishment of the Irish Church went some way to meeting Irish grievances, but it was the Land Act which followed it which was intended to bring about the 'pacification' which Gladstone had talked about in 1868. In the event the Act was a modest measure: tenant farmers were protected against eviction, but they had no security of tenure and nothing was done to ensure that rents were fair (this had to wait until the 1881 Act). The result, one historian tells us, was that the tenant farmers were 'left to face the long years of agricultural depression after 1875, with no provision for downward adjustments of rents'. If Gladstone hoped for a settlement of the Irish Question by these means he was soon to be disillusioned.

JOHN BULL'S OTHER ISLAND

It was perhaps a mark of English ignorance about Ireland that Gladstone, the most concerned of their statesmen on the Irish Question, should have been so naive. He himself felt the need to visit the country only once (in 1877 when he was in opposition), and planted a tree in memory of his stay at Enniskerry! Although Liberal leaders like Gladstone and John Bright believed that enlightened policies could redress Ireland's grievances, which they acknowledged to be just, others were less charitable in their opinions. Queen Victoria felt justified in stating that 'these Irish are really shocking, abominable people – not like any other civilised nation'. Her favourite prime minister, Benjamin Disraeli, by contrast expressed the bewilderment of English statesmen when confronted with the intractable nature of Ireland's problems: 'I want to see a public man come forward and say what the Irish Question is ... It is the Pope one day; potatoes the next.'

Learned government commissions were in fact just as patronising and hostile in their conclusions as the monarch. In 1836 the *Report on the State of the Irish Poor in Great Britain* stated:

> The Irish emigration into Britain is an example of a less civilised population spreading themselves, as a kind of substratum, beneath a more civilised community; and without excelling in any branch of industry, obtaining possession of all the lowest departments of manual labour.

Yet as E.P. Thompson has pointed out, the Irish were 'neither stupid nor barbarians'; rather they 'adhered to a different value-system than that of the English artisan'. Whether, however, in the midst of English society or being their turbulent selves across the sea, they were seen to be different. *Punch* was full of cartoons of wicked-looking Irish brigands, armed to the teeth, awaiting their chance to disturb the peace of John Bull's empire. They were reckless, lazy, lawless and, worst of all in English eyes, Catholic. Matthew Arnold could only hope piously that English 'good nature' would ultimately 'solve the problem posed by "Irishness"'.

Contempt and irritation on one side were paralleled by hatred on the other. *The United Irishman* reminded its readers that 'Saxon was the name for fiend', and the nationalist leader William Redmond told a meeting in Fermoy that in his opinion 'there was not a single man from Parnell down to himself who did not hate the government of England with all the intensity of his heart'. Seven hundred years of injustice and foreign oppression lent moral weight to the Irish cause, but it did nothing to ease the solution of the country's economic and political problems. It was Ireland's misfortune, as Patrick O'Farrell has pointed out, that the general English attitude to her was reflected by 'the low quality, incompetence, and irresponsibility of English politicians'. There were honourable exceptions, like Gladstone and John Morley, but the verdict is a just one.

The Rise of the Home Rule Party, 1872–6

The violent tactics of the Fenians in the 1860s failed to achieve their aim, but so did Gladstone's attempts to coerce the Irish in the latter stages of his first administration (1868–74). Nevertheless, the early 1870s was an important period because it marked the emergence of a distinctive Irish Home Rule party. It was prepared to achieve its object by constitutional means and was led by Isaac Butt (1813–79). He had defended Fenian prisoners in 1867 and as a result became an opponent of the Union between Great Britain and Ireland. He wanted 'the restoration to Ireland of that right of domestic legislation, without which Ireland can never enjoy real prosperity or peace', and in 1872 he helped found a Home Government Association (which was replaced by the Home Rule League in November 1873). Such moves were greeted with suspicion in nationalist circles, and the *Dublin Evening Post* described the League as a 'vile sham'. In the context of the whole Irish problem, though, it represented movement and Gladstone had little to offer. His scheme for a desegregated university in Ireland was rejected by the Irish bishops, and Queen Victoria was outraged by his suggestion that the Prince of Wales should become a permanent viceroy in Dublin. Dreadful though 'Bertie' might be she would not exile him to Ireland, and told Gladstone in an audience in June 1871 that Scotland and England deserved the royal presence 'much more'.

The election of 1874 did little to improve matters for it gave Disraeli and the Conservatives a majority of 100 over the Liberals. The new prime minister had never shown much sympathy for the Irish; as his biographer Robert Blake acknowledges, 'he never did or said anything helpful to them'. This negative attitude in Westminster meant that any initiatives would have to come from the fifty-seven Irish Home Rulers who had been returned under Butt's leadership in 1874. Butt himself was in any case rapidly losing influence to the rising star, Charles Stuart Parnell (1846–91), the MP for West Meath. In his maiden speech in 1875 Parnell had objected to the description of Ireland as 'a geographical fragment', and in 1876 he shocked English sensitivities by denying that any crime had been committed at Manchester in 1867.

Parnell's background

The new Irish leader was unusual in two respects: he was a Protestant, though by no means the first to serve the Irish nationalist cause; and he was a landlord in his own right, and might have found himself on the side of the British ascendancy. But his mother's father had been an American admiral in the war of 1812, and the Parnells had been involved in the short-lived attempt to get Ireland a separate parliament

Charles Parnell, after the *Vanity Fair* cartoon

in the 1780s. His radical background, combined with a fiery temper (which had resulted in his expulsion from Cambridge University), made Parnell a natural leader of the Home Rule party. He was, in Michael Davitt's famous phrase, 'an Englishman of the strongest sort moulded for an Irish purpose'.

THE ORIGINS OF PARNELLISM

Parnell was to provide the Irish nationalist cause with the dynamic leadership it craved, but he was only the fountain-head of new forces in nineteenth-century Irish society. Without them his leadership could not have been as effective as it was.

One striking development was the decline in the number of land-less labourers in Ireland in the years after the Famine, as these figures show:

1841	16.1%
1871	13.8%
1881	9.1%

This meant, as D. George Boyce has pointed out in his excellent study *Nationalism in Ireland*, that

> landless labourers were a decreasingly important factor in the development of a political movement based upon people who got their livelihood from the land; and the tension between labourers and farmers, which was such an important aspect of agrarian violence before the famine, became less commonplace.

Parnell's Home Rule party was therefore to be largely a party of tenant farmers, and attempts to exploit the grievances of the landless labourers did not break the impetus of the Home Rule movement.

This drive was helped too by the electoral changes which had taken place earlier in the century, in particular the Irish Franchise Act (1850) which granted the vote to those of a poor law valuation of £12 in counties and £8 in the boroughs. This meant that by 1853 88.7 per cent of the Irish electorate was registered for voting, although of course the poorer sections of the electorate were still excluded.

LITERACY AND THE PRESS

Boyce's study also lays emphasis on the importance of literacy and newspapers in the rise of Parnellism. In 1851 53 per cent of the Irish population over the age of five were literate, but by 1911 the figure was 88 per cent. This growth in literacy went hand in hand with an expansion of the popular press, so that by 1913 there were 230 local papers in Ireland. Journalists like Tim Harrington of the *Kerry Sentinel* and James Daly of the *Connaught Telegraph* had important political roles in their local areas.

The Influence of the Catholic Church

No analysis of Parnellism would be complete without a discussion of the relationship between the Home Rulers and the Catholic Church. The Catholic bishops wielded great power and influence as Parnell realised, and he went out of his way to court them. They in turn responded by giving the seal of Church approval to Parnell and his followers. Walsh and Croke, the leaders of the Catholic hierarchy in the 1880s, sympathised with nationalist aspirations, and local clergy played an important part in the organisation of Parnell's party.

FENIANISM

The Catholic Archbishop McHale made a fierce attack on the Fenians in 1879, but Parnell was always aware that an alliance with these 'hillside men' would be very valuable. He avoided public encouragement of violence but his early career owed much to the backing of former Fenians like Davitt. In this context the change in tactics by the Fenians in the early 1870s was vital for Parnell. By 1873 they had decided to support Home Rulers at the next election, and rejected the view put forward by Stephens that only Fenianism could save the nation. This decision meant that the years up to 1890 were to be dominated by Parnell's attempt to achieve Home Rule by constitutional means.

THE LAND WAR, 1879–82

It was from this base then that Parnell and his Fenian allies were able to launch what is known as the 'land war' in the years after 1879. This campaign was in itself a response to the crisis in the Irish countryside in the 1870s, brought about by foreign competition and further failures of the potato crop. Fortunately a great charity organisation set up by the Duchess of Marlborough prevented a repetition of the terrible suffering between 1845 and 1849. Nevertheless there were real fears that the bad days of the 1840s might come again, and Parnell was able to utilise such feelings.

In the summer of 1879 he made a great speech at Westport, County Mayo, in which he challenged the existing system of land rents, stating that

> a fair rent is a rent the tenant can reasonably afford to pay according to the times, but in bad times a tenant cannot be expected to pay as much as he did in good times . . .

It was an appeal that aroused an immediate response from a more literate, and politically aware, class of tenant farmers. They flocked to join Parnell and Davitt's campaign against those farmers who took over properties after their owners had been evicted because they could not pay the rent. Such men, Parnell demanded, should be sent to a kind of 'moral Coventry', ignored in public and treated as if they were lepers.

This campaign was to run head on into a rejuvenated Gladstone, who returned to office in 1880 even more determined to solve the Irish Question. His natural allies in the Liberal Cabinet were the radicals Sir Charles Dilke and Joseph Chamberlain, but Gladstone felt obliged to win over those Liberals who wished the rule of law to be restored in Ireland. For with or without Parnell's agreement, his Fenian supporters were shooting landlords in the countryside.

The 1881 Land Act

The solution was a compromise, a Land Act combined with a Coercion Act, which gave considerable powers to the Lord Lieutenant (who represented the Crown in Ireland). The Land Act, however, was a significant measure which went some way towards completing the process Gladstone had started in 1870. Rents were to be fixed for fifteen years by public tribunals, which were to prevent eviction of the tenants. The tenants were also to have the right of sale, thus granting what came to be known as the 'three Fs', fair rents, free sale and fixity of tenure. But the Act had important gaps, leaving out for example the 130,000 tenants who were behind in their rent payments, and did not satisfy nationalist opinion in Ireland.

Parnell openly opposed the Coercion Act, and he and thirty-five MPs were suspended from the Westminster parliament. He had already angered the Liberal government by visiting the USA in 1880 and renewing links with the Fenian organisation there. In one speech he went so far as to state his desire to 'destroy the last link which keeps Ireland bound to England'. This was too much for the embattled Gladstone, who fiercely attacked him in a speech in Leeds:

> If there is still to be fought in Ireland a final conflict between law on one side and sheer lawlessness on the other, then I say, gentlemen, without hesitation, the resources of civilisation are not yet exhausted.

In October 1881 Parnell was arrested and imprisoned in Kilmainham jail in Dublin.

It was not a particularly unpleasant experience, and in many respects imprisonment was a distinct advantage for Parnell. As Robert Kee points out,

> He had the best of all worlds: he was a martyr to the cause of extremism on the land, from which he wanted to withdraw in any case. At the same time he was absolved of all responsibility for the continuing violence.

His stay in Kilmainham though advantageous was brief and he was anxious to get out. The Fenian campaign against the landlords had failed, and Parnell had become involved with the great love of his life, Katherine O'Shea, 'his own darling Queenie' as he called her. She was the wife of William O'Shea, MP for County Clare, who turned a blind eye to her relationship in the hope that it would further his political career. It was she, in fact, who acted as a contact between Parnell and Gladstone, thereby securing his release.

This so-called 'Kilmainham Treaty' of May 1882 had two provisions, although it did not take a written form. Parnell was to use his influence to stop the agrarian violence in Ireland, and Gladstone was to

look favourably at Ireland's Home Rule aspirations. The cause of
Home Rule seemed ready to advance once more when it received
another shattering setback.

The Phoenix Park Murders

It came from an unexpected quarter when W.E. Forster, the Chief
Secretary for Ireland, resigned in protest against the Kilmainham
agreement. He was replaced by Lord Frederick Cavendish, a nephew of
Gladstone's by marriage, who went to Dublin. On his very first evening
in his new post, Cavendish and his Under-Secretary Thomas Burke
were stabbed to death by members of a group calling themselves 'the
Invincibles'. These murders, which took place in Phoenix Park, made
any immediate co-operation between Parnell and the Liberals impossible, especially when it became known that members of his Land
League had been involved.

A grisly period was to follow when violence and murder in the Irish
countryside resulted in the passage of another Coercion Act by Gladstone's government. But this time Parnell identified himself clearly
with the constitutional path and made his grip on Irish seats even more
secure.

The Struggle for Home Rule, 1885–6

At this stage the tactics of the Irish party were still flexible enough
not to rely on an alliance with Gladstone. In 1885, however, his
government fell and was replaced by a Conservative administration
under Lord Salisbury which was in a minority, and thus dependent
on Irish help. Parnell clearly believed that the Conservatives might
be persuaded to pass a Home Rule Bill, and in some senses the Irish
party would have preferred this because they feared the radical
Liberals. They were perhaps somewhat naive in their analysis of
Conservative intentions and encouraged by misleading statements by
Lord Randolph Churchill, then at the height of his brief, glittering
career. Nicholas Mansergh has no doubt that Churchill was to blame
for Irish illusions.

He was at all times opposed to Home Rule: yet no man with the possible and honourable exception of the Viceroy, Lord Carnarvon, did more to persuade the Irish leaders that co-operation with the Tories might bring them to their cherished goal.

Yet the same illusions were apparently shared by Gladstone who hoped that, with Irish support in the Commons, Salisbury could be induced to pass Home Rule.

He calculated that such a strategy would get the legislation past the Tory majority in the Lords, which the Liberals could never hope to do. In the event it was Gladstone's own son Herbert who ruined his father's plans by prematurely disclosing his conversion to Home Rule (December 1885). This had a twofold effect, neither helpful to Gladstone's ambition to get Home Rule for Ireland. Firstly, Lord Salisbury became aware of Gladstone's desire for Home Rule (his Cabinet had already decided to break off their negotiations with Parnell). Secondly, it brought Gladstone's conviction to the attention of Joseph Chamberlain, the Radical leader, who was completely opposed to it.

Gladstone, and indeed Parnell, were convinced that Chamberlain was a friend to Irish aspirations but they were both wrong. Chamberlain had opposed coercion, and even pressed for the Irish leader's release from Kilmainham, but he would never contemplate a reduction in the authority of the Imperial parliament. As far back as 1880 he had made known his view that 'national independence cannot be given to Ireland', and that the 'necessity for destroying the constitution in Ireland is not proved ...' He and Dilke were disliked in nationalist circles as leaders of the Non-Conformist Radical wing of the Liberal party, and on matters of social policy they had little in common with Parnell and the Irish.

The drama that followed then was based on a series of misunderstandings. Gladstone and Parnell thought that the Tories could be used for an Irish purpose, and equally wrongly they saw Joe Chamberlain as an ally in the struggle for Home Rule. The first miscalculation explains Parnell's public support for the Tories in the December 1885 election; the second was to bring about the failure of Gladstone's first Home Rule Bill in June 1886.

This was to be the linchpin of Gladstone's third administration, formed in February 1886, but the measure was doomed from the start. The Liberal anti-Home Rulers were implacably opposed, and Chamberlain would only serve until he could see the shape of the Home Rule Bill. It provided for the withdrawal of Irish MPs from Westminster, and the setting up of a single-chamber Irish parliament to control everything except foreign policy, defence and trade. This represented the very reduction of Imperial authority to which Chamberlain objected, and in March 1886 he resigned. When the Bill came to the vote in June, 93 Liberals led by Chamberlain opposed it and it was defeated in the Commons. The Irish members shouted 'Judas' and 'Traitor' at him but the decision was endorsed in the election that followed in July: 316 Conservatives and 78 Liberal

Kitty O'Shea

Unionists (those opposed to Home Rule) were returned against 191 Liberals and 85 Irish Nationalists.

Another factor was the vehement opposition to Home Rule in Ulster, where Lord Randolph Churchill had played his famous 'Orange Card', so underlining Parnell's misjudgement of him. Churchill encouraged the Ulster Protestants to fight against Home Rule by portraying it as the divider of the empire, and they needed little encouragement. The unity between Catholic and Protestant which had been such a feature of the Irish rising of 1798 had long since disappeared.

In retrospect it is difficult to disagree with the verdict of Nicholas Mansergh on the 1886 defeat:

> The more closely the political scene of 1886 is examined, the stronger grows the conviction that even the most skilful use of the Irish votes could not ensure the repeal of the Union.

Gladstone's attempt to force Home Rule through by sheer will power had foundered both in his mistaken analysis of feeling within his own party, and in the general unreadiness of the electorate to accept the principle. One issue, however, was definitely settled, for if Home Rule was ever to come it could only be by means of a Liberal-Nationalist alliance. Its achievement was Gladstone's remaining political ambition.

The Fall of Parnell

Before Home Rule was put to the test again at Westminster, it had lost its greatest champion in bizarre circumstances. Parnell had fallen in 1890, the victim of Victorian double standards and his long affair with Katherine O'Shea. He fell, in fact, after one of his greatest triumphs, when an attempt had been made through a series of forged letters to link him to the Phoenix Park murders. The forger Piggott killed himself, *The Times* which had published the letters had to retract, and Parnell was cheered in the Commons. Yet within two years he was a ruined man, as his name and that of Mrs O'Shea were dragged through the divorce courts. O'Shea, long a willing accomplice in the affair, had given the game away after failing to get his share of a family legacy.

Parnell fought back with typical courage, but his enemies were too strong. The Catholic Church denounced him as an adulterer and most of his supporters dared not stand against it. He had also offended Gladstone's sense of morality, which proved to be stronger than his commitment to Home Rule, and he told the Irish that he could not remain leader of the Liberal party if Parnell retained his post. The rest of the story was a personal tragedy, as Parnell tried to resist the strongest traditions of Irish society. His attempt to revive the earlier alliance with 'the hill-side' men failed, as Catholic clergy denounced him from their pulpits.

A series of by-elections in which Parnell tried to re-establish his leadership of the Irish party resulted in violent incidents, and on one occasion lime was thrown in his face. Finally, in 1891 he caught a chill while on a speaking engagement and died in Mrs O'Shea's arms. He was, said Gladstone, 'the most remarkable man I have ever met', and his impact on Irish history was enormous. The attempt to achieve a constitutional solution to the Irish problem, as opposed to a violent one, did not die with him, although he defined the issue in perhaps his most famous statement:

> No man has a right to fix the boundary to the march of a nation. No man has a right to say to his country: thus far shalt thou go and no further. We have never attempted to fix the ne plus ultra to the progress of Ireland's nationhood and we never shall.

Historians will argue about whether Parnell was a 'separatist' in the truest sense (some like Dr Boyce dispute that he was), but he had made Ireland the central issue in Westminster politics during his lifetime.

CHAPTER THIRTEEN

Orange Revolt and Republican Sacrifice, 1891–1916

After Parnell's death unseemly wrangling continued in his party, between those whose Catholicism had made them reject 'the Chief' and the fervent Parnellites who believed that Ireland was 'a priest-ridden country'. Even in death Parnell continued to be attacked by the Catholic clergy, one of whom told his flock that 'Parnellism is a simple love of adultery and all those who profess Parnellism profess to love and admire adultery'.

The depth of bitterness on the issue was well conveyed in a memorable passage from James Joyce's *Portrait of the Artist as a Young Man* when young Stephen Dedalus listens in on a family row about Parnell's fall:

> O he'll remember all this when he grows up, said Dante hotly – the language he heard against God and religion and priests in his own home.
>
> – Let him remember too, cried Mr Casey to her from across the table, the language with which the priests and the priests' pawns broke Parnell's heart and hounded him into his grave. Let him remember that too when he grows up.
>
> – Sons of bitches! cried Mr Dedalus. When he was down they turned on him to betray him and rend him like rats in a sewer. Lowlived dogs! And they look it! By Christ they look it!
>
> – They behaved rightly, cried Dante. They obeyed their bishops and their priests. Honour to them!

There is no doubt where Joyce's sympathies lie in this debate, but it proved to be a sterile one as far as the cause of Irish nationalism was concerned. The real effect of Parnell's fall was to set back the Home Rule cause for a generation.

The Gaelic Revival

Disgust with the feuding in the Home Rule Party also encouraged a turning back to Ireland's cultural roots. In 1893 the Gaelic League was founded with the brief of encouraging and developing every aspect of Ireland's heritage be it in language, poetry, music or dance. Its sister organisation, the Gaelic Athletic Association, played the same role in encouraging the growth of those distinctively Irish games of hurling and Gaelic football. To a degree this interest turned the attention of Irish people away from Home Rule, now seemingly a lost cause (particularly after Gladstone had failed yet again to get a Home Rule Bill through the House of Lords in 1893). But the interest in the cultural revival was largely middle class, for the peasantry were too absorbed in making a living.

A small group involved in the Gaelic revival and led by the poet and teacher Padraig (Patrick) Pearse (1879–1916) did see political potential behind the revival. Pearse ultimately joined the Irish Republican Brotherhood, a small splinter organisation which attracted some support after 1900 and was led by the old Fenian Tom Clarke.

Sinn Féin

Another significant figure in this period was the journalist Arthur Griffith (1872–1922), actually born in Edinburgh, who edited both *The United Irishman* and *Sinn Féin*, the newspaper of the new nationalist party Sinn Féin (Ourselves Alone) which he founded in 1905. Sinn Féin revived the old Grattan concept of a separate Irish parliament in Dublin and a boycott of Westminster by Irish MPs. It did not have much popular appeal, but Irish opinion hereabouts was somewhat ambivalent. There was considerable pleasure when the British suffered defeats in the Boer War, but popular enthusiasm when Queen Victoria visited Dublin in 1900. Even *The United Irishman* had to admit that she had been 'cheered frantically'.

TRADE UNIONISM

The period before 1914 was most significant perhaps because of the development of Irish trade unionism. The leading figures here were Jim

Larkin (1876–1947) and James Connolly (1868–1916), soon to be a leading personality in the struggle for Irish independence. Dublin, as Ireland's major city (the same urgencies did not exist in the more prosperous Belfast), was the centre of activity not least because it had the worst slums in Europe. Larkin founded the Irish Transport Union, which was involved in 1913 in a bitter confrontation with the Dublin trams employer; although the workers gained nothing from the strike, the employer was unable to break the union.

Connolly was to move later into the mainstream republican movement because the experience of industrial disputes before 1914 highlighted the fact that members of the old Parnellite party actually owned some of the worst slum properties; the owner of the tramways too was supposedly a strong supporter of Home Rule. Connolly was one of those who started the tradition of genuinely socialist politics in Ireland, even if its influence remained comparatively small.

The Orange Revolt

Between 1891 and 1910 Irish Home Rule seemed to be a dead issue. Its death was certainly devoutly desired by the Liberal Party, which had been seriously split over the issue and had little desire (even if it continued to pay lip service to the ideal) to reawaken the controversy about it. But the Liberals found themselves pre-empted by the two British elections of 1910, which left the Irish Nationalist party, now led by John Redmond (1856–1918), holding the balance of power in the House of Commons. The Liberal prime minister, Asquith, was then forced to introduce another Home Rule Bill or face the prospect of losing power to the Conservatives. At the same time the Liberals faced the likelihood of arousing Protestant feeling in Ulster which, as in 1886, was completely opposed to Home Rule.

Much of the Protestant dissent was expressed through the Orange Society, founded in 1795 as a sort of development of the secret agrarian society, the 'Peep O'Day Boys', who used to terrorise Catholics, as their name suggests, at dawn. From the society developed Orange Lodges which served as a focus for opposition to Home Rule and the great struggle to retain the Union between 1912 and 1914.

The Unionists, or 'Orangemen' as they are sometimes called, had two other important advantages. They had the support of the British Conservative Party led by Bonar Law, even if it was somewhat cynical, and a charismatic leader in Sir Edward Carson (1854–1935), a Dublin-born Protestant lawyer whose devotion to the Union was as rigorous as that of any Ulsterman. On the other side, a lukewarm Liberal Party was cajoled into reluctant support for Home Rule by Redmond's Nationalists, in a situation where even British army officers in Ireland refused to accept Home Rule.

The Campaign against Home Rule

The high point of the anti-Home Rule campaign came on 28 September 1912 when almost three-quarters of all Ulster Protestants over the age of fifteen (rather more women than men) signed a covenant or pledge that they would use 'all means which may be found necessary to defeat Home Rule'. This defiance was followed by the formation early in 1913 of an 'Ulster Volunteer Force' some 90,000 strong; it was well armed and organised, partly at least because of a well-run gun-running campaign which brought German Mauser guns into the port of Larne. By comparison, the rival Nationalist 'Irish Volunteers' were poorly equipped and drilled with wooden rifles. (Contemporary photographs show the UVF with armed motor-cycle units, far more sophisticated than anything Redmond's supporters could aspire to.)

In the end the Unionist campaign succeeded because, although a Home Act Rule was passed in 1914, the Liberal government was not prepared to coerce the Protestant minority. It could hardly do so with the army unreliable and the Tories encouraging Ulster resistance in a partisan and irresponsible manner. The talk was then of 'excluding' four Ulster counties with a Protestant majority from the provisions of the Home Rule Act, which would only, in fact, have given a separate Irish parliament control over most domestic matters while leaving defence, foreign affairs, most taxation imposition and even the running of the Royal Irish Constabulary under the Westminster parliament. Redmond resolutely opposed any such division of Ireland suggested by exclusion proposals, but by the summer of 1914 he was in a weak position because Liberals and Tories were clearly willing to do a deal about Ulster. In the meantime, the Irish Volunteers had tried to strengthen their weak military position by using the yacht of their English sympathiser Erskine Childers (1870–1922), author of the famous *Riddle of the Sands*, to run German arms into Howth harbour near Dublin.

Then, when civil war in Ireland seemed a real possibility, war in Europe switched everyone's attention from, in Winston Churchill's words, 'the dreary steeples of Fermanagh and Tyrone' to Belgium and Serbia. In this emergency Redmond magnanimously allowed the operation of the Home Rule Act to be suspended for a year, or until the war ended, whichever proved the longer. An Amending Bill would then be introduced to deal with Ulster, although it was still not clear how many of the province's nine counties would be excluded from the operation of the Home Rule Act. Redmond also pledged the loyalty of the Irish Nationalists to the British cause. And so matters rested while the great conflict in Europe raged.

Was Home Rule for the whole of Ireland ever a realistic outcome in the 1912–14 crisis? Almost certainly not, for as Roy Foster observes, 'Despite nationalist incredulity, there seems no good reason to doubt that Home Rule would have been greeted in Ulster with armed rebellion.' Another historian has pointed out that the original exclusion deal offered to Redmond was actually superior to the one offered to Irish nationalists when Ireland was partitioned in 1921.

The Easter Rebellion

Many thousands of nationalist Irishmen fought gallantly and well for Britain in the First World War, although no individual unit suffered as grievously as did the Ulster Division in the Battle of the Somme in 1916. It was true, too, that most Irish people were behind the war effort against Germany. However, this was not the position adopted by the hardline republicans for whom England's difficulty was always Ireland's opportunity. This attitude was epitomised in Padraig Pearse's famous statement that the Irish cause needed 'a blood sacrifice' before independence could he achieved.

An allegorical poster showing the birth of the Irish Republic in 1916

The background to the events of Easter 1916 was confused. The leader of the Irish Volunteers had actually called off the uprising, and attempts to enlist German help had failed. An arms supply ship *The Aud* was sent from Germany but it was intercepted, and Sir Roger Casement (1864–1916), seeking to prevent a rising which he deemed premature, was arrested by the British as he landed from a German submarine on Banna Strand in County Kerry. Casement had been a distinguished British colonial civil servant before he took up the cause of Irish independence and was hanged as a traitor. His reputation was sullied by the infamous 'Black Diaries' (still actually classified under the British Official Secrets Act).

But Pearse and his supporters in the Irish Republican Brotherhood (IRB) were determined to go ahead with an uprising, although they recognised that it was doomed to fail. More surprisingly James Connolly, a convinced socialist, also allowed himself to be persuaded by Pearse's physical force argument, which he had formerly opposed, and joined the IRB. Connolly allegedly told a supporter who asked him about prospects of success that there were 'none whatever'. Even then he had misgivings about the objectives of some of his new comrades, and many other republicans doubted the wisdom of the uprising.

The actual events are still surrounded by controversy. Why, for example, did the rebels not seize the British government centre at Dublin Castle (instead of just shooting dead the sentry on duty outside it)? According to the historian David Fitzpatrick, this was because the military council of the IRB took a conscious decision to seize central Dublin rather than the Castle, because this would cause the maximum damage to property and so to British imperialism. P. Beresford Ellis disagrees, citing Connolly's explanation that the Castle could not have been held against British counter-attack.

Certain facts are beyond dispute; one is that the British authorities were taken by surprise. Once Casement had been arrested, it seems a decision was made to round up the rest of the republican activists on Easter Monday. This was the very day chosen by Pearse and Connolly to strike; most of the British garrison were at Faireyhouse Races and only about 400 troops were available to the authorities when the uprising began.

The rebel headquarters was the Dublin Post Office and other strongpoints were set up inside the Central Dublin area. It was in the Post Office building that Pearse made his famous proclamation of an Irish Republic:

In the name of God and of the dead generations from which she receives her old tradition of nationhood Ireland through us summons her children to her flag and strikes for her freedom.

THE BRITISH REACTION

Once the British authorities had recovered from their initial surprise they reacted decisively. Reinforcements were brought in from England and the Post Office was shelled. In several instances quite innocent civilians were killed, partly no doubt because of the frustration experienced by the troops in reducing rebel strongpoints. The British were certainly surprised by the quality of rebel resistance, notably at Mount Street Bridge where withering fire made them think they were facing 200 men instead of just seventeen.

Nevertheless weight of numbers was bound to prevail in the end, and with the Post Office building evacuated and on fire Pearse made the decision to surrender on the Saturday. Despite his talk of the blood sacrifice, it is suggested that he himself was appalled by the bloodshed in Dublin. In all 64 rebels, 130 British soldiers and some 300 civilians died. There were isolated responses to Pearse's call for revolt elsewhere, most notably in County Meath where sixteen RIC constables were killed, and in Wexford where the town of Enniscorthy (so closely associated with 1798) was briefly held by Irish Volunteers.

THE IRISH REACTION

The initial Irish reaction was hostile. Dubliners were outraged by the destruction of their city and women pelted surrendered rebels with tomatoes. Even as the rebels were taking up their positions at the start of the rising, they were accused of being 'slackers' who would be better off doing their fighting against the Germans in France (it needs to be remembered that 25,000 Irishmen died in the First World War). Poorer people took advantage of the chaos in Central Dublin to engage in some profitable looting, and women were seen fleeing from the scene with fur coats while their husbands helped themselves to suits. But in no sense were Dubliners generally sympathetic to the rebels.

All this changed between 3 and 10 May 1916. The execution of Padraig Pearse might have been expected as he was the rebel leader, but

Willie Pearse was executed merely because he was Padraig's brother. Worst of all was the execution of James Connolly, already wounded in the legs and with gangrene setting in, who was carried out tied to a chair and then shot. In all, fifteen rebels were executed in batches, which prolonged the agony and changed the mood in Ireland. Within days this draconian action created a sympathy for the rebel cause which had never been there on Easter Monday.

Why did the British react in this way? In part, it was because Britain was engaged in a bitter and bloody war with Germany, and Pearse's men were regarded as traitors as well as rebels. But other short-term factors also prevailed, the most important of which was the catastrophic decision to hand Dublin over to martial law. This followed the resignation of the Irish Secretary, Birrell, when the revolt broke out, after he had had, by using ridicule rather than force, a good deal of success in defusing the republican threat. No successor was appointed for some months.

The Legacy of Easter 1916

What would have happened if the British had followed a more moderate policy must remain one of the big 'ifs' of modern Irish history. As it was, they made a minority and rather desperate movement into one with national appeal. The Irish poet, W.B. Yeats, was to write that 'a terrible beauty' was born in 1916, and there is no doubt that the symbolic deaths of Pearse and the others did create a nationalist myth which has survived ever since. Pearse's wilder pronouncements about bloodshed being 'a cleansing and sanctifying thing' have left a desperate and bloody legacy in the Irish body politic because violence has been seen to pay. The tragedy of 1916 was that a more intelligent British response *might* (it can be put no higher than that) have allowed a more peaceful evolutionary approach to prevail. Five years later such an approach was to be impossible.

James Connolly felt that an Irish revolution could have been the precursor of Europe-wide socialist revolutions, but Lenin regarded it as premature, and by throwing in his lot with the Catholic nationalists like Pearse, Connolly may have contributed to the ultimate marginalisation of the Irish Left. It was never to attract more than minority support after independence.

A significant feature of the 1916 uprising was the role played by Irish women. Although Constance Markievicz (1868–1927) was the only woman who actually fought with the insurgents (she was granted the rank of lieutenant, and was sentenced to death by the British but subsequently reprieved), others like Helena Moloney did take part, and the republican women's movement Cumann na mBan was called out to offer support in other non-violent ways. This female activism was to become a marked feature of militant Irish republicanism.

CHAPTER FOURTEEN

Independence and Civil War, 1916–1923

The Easter Rising of 1916, although ultimately attracting public sympathy, did not result in an immediate change in the political situation. For it was Redmond's Irish Nationalists who were still regarded as Ireland's political representatives, and Home Rule as the aspiration of Catholic Irishmen.

This began to change in 1917. An important factor was the discovery in Michael Collins (1890–1922) of a supremely able organiser for the IRB, and one who saw the futility of mounting armed uprisings which had virtually no chance of success. Collins was a militant republican, but he was supported by the non-violent members of Sinn Féin, like Arthur Griffith, who had not been involved in the events of 1916. These men were united in the view that Home Rule was now not enough to satisfy Irish aspirations, and that a 32-county republic must be conceded by the British. They therefore decided to challenge Redmond's party in a series of by-elections. The first, in County Roscommon, resulted in a massive republican victory, which was followed soon afterwards by another in County Longford. Such victories inevitably influenced the gradual movement of Irish public opinion away from Redmond and the Nationalists.

The British unwittingly assisted this process by releasing all surviving prisoners from the Easter Rising in July 1917 (they had been imprisoned in England). In marked contrast to 1916 they were greeted as heroes on their return to Dublin, and amongst them were key figures in the struggle for Irish independence, who would have no truck with constitutional nationalism so making a compromise solution difficult to negotiate.

De Valera

Éamon de Valera (1882–1975), the son of a Spanish father and an Irish mother, was born in the USA. He had 'been out' in 1916 (the popular phrase in Ireland for taking part in anti-British revolts), and had commanded one of the strongpoints during the events of Easter week. His American birth may well have saved him from execution. As it was he survived to become the most distinguished statesman of independent Ireland.

In 1917, using Collins' well-oiled political machine, de Valera won the most famous of by-elections in East Clare. Cannily he secured the support of the Catholic Church by saying that his programme combined 'religion and patriotism'. Thereafter de Valera became the leader of a united republican movement still called Sinn Féin, but containing

De Valera, the leader of the Sinn Féin movement

the IRB, the old Irish Volunteers of pre-war days and Griffith's original Sinn Féin. By the end of 1917 Sinn Féin had some 250,000 members in 1,250 clubs throughout Ireland.

The future of the old Nationalist party seemed bleak (the republicans even claimed that they were the true heirs of Parnell) but it still had some local support. In Waterford, for example, Redmond's son stood against the Sinn Féiners when his father died, and despite ostentatiously wearing his British army uniform beat them. Nevertheless the movement away from the old Home Rule party was unstoppable.

CONSCRIPTION

Britain's decision to release the Easter Rising prisoners, which might have made all the difference in the atmosphere of 1916, was unfortunately nullified by another major blunder. Once again it was because the needs of the German war were allowed to blot out Irish considerations, and in 1917 that war was going badly. Thus a decision was made to extend conscription, already introduced in the rest of Britain in 1916, to Ireland. Nothing could have inflamed an already volatile situation more, for the announcement united all shades of Irish opinion (save the Unionists) against the British authorities. This included Sinn Féin, the trade unions, the Redmondites and, crucially, the Catholic Church. Great public meetings were held throughout Ireland in 1917 at which people signed an anti-conscription pledge. The British government responded by dropping the scheme, but by then it was too late.

THE AMERICAN DIMENSION

Throughout 1916–17 the attitude of the United States was an important factor in what was happening in Ireland, particularly after President Woodrow Wilson took America into the war in April 1917 to make the world 'safe for democracy'. Irish republicans hoped (vainly as it turned out) that Wilson would be sympathetic to the cause of Irish independence at the peace treaty after the war.

But there was more direct American involvement through the large Irish-American community, which had been outraged by the executions after the Easter Rising. Sinn Féin was adept at using this sympathy to raise funds for the republican cause in the USA, so adept in fact that Jim Larkin, then living in America, was outraged by their behaviour, writing:

> The Sinn Fein movement here is anti-Labour and as for the Socialists they think they are anti-Christs. They have tried to impress the American public that the Revolution was a Catholic revolution, in fact they have done the cause incalculable harm. They are the most violent American jingoes always boasting how loyal they are to and how many Irish have fought and died for this Free Republic ... They make me sick to the soul. They held a meeting in Chicago sometime back and they spent 2,600 dollars on the meeting, 1,700 dollars to erect a special star spangled flag, electrically arrayed which flashed all thru the meeting. They are in a word super fine patriots and the most consummate tricksters of politicians.

Of course, Larkin was critical of what he regarded as the wilder excesses of Irish Catholic nationalism, but the passage does convey how powerful the Sinn Féin movement had become in the USA. This is doubly significant because evidence suggests that after Easter 1916 Irish-American Sinn Féiners, led by John Devoy, were in touch with the Germans who were naturally still interested in the possibility of revolution in Ireland. There is one recorded case of a Sinn Féiner being arrested in Galway after being landed from a German U-boat after the uprising.

This in turn provoked the British authorities, actually looking for an excuse to round up the leaders of the anti-conscription movement, to claim that Sinn Féin was involved in a 'German plot'. There is in fact no evidence that the Sinn Féin leadership in Ireland, influenced by Collins as it was, was involved in wild attempts to forge an alliance with Germany in 1917. Such an alliance would in any case have hindered the Irish cause in the USA, now fiercely anti-German, so the scheming of the American Sinn Féiners was counter-productive. Nevertheless, the US dimension remained an important one and may well have influenced the British decision to release the surviving Easter rebels. Historically, Irish-American republicans have been amongst the fiercest of that breed.

The 1918 Election

The event which really marked the break with Britain was the election of December 1918. It followed the abortive constitutional conference of 1917 when the Redmond Nationalists had conceded the principle of a 26-county Ireland, excluding six Ulster counties, in their desperation to get an agreement of some sort with Britain and steal the Sinn Féiners' thunder.

It availed them little. In the election Sinn Féin swept the board winning seventy-three seats nationwide to the Nationalists' miserly six. Only in Ulster where the Unionists won sixteen seats were they pushed into second place. How was this sensational victory achieved? Obviously it was partly due to the legacy of 1916, but there were other major factors as well.

One was that the election was fought on an entirely new electoral register, three times bigger than that of 1910, with women over thirty and all men over twenty-one voting for the first time. Another was that many Irish soldiers serving in the British army, who would presumably have voted for the Nationalist ticket, did not get their postal-ballot forms; in the event only about one-third of them voted. Lastly, there was plenty of evidence in the 1918 election of what had become an Irish tradition: 'impersonation'. This involved zealous study of the electoral register to discover who had died and been left on it, and then impersonating them at the polling booth. The Sinn Féiners were very good at this, and some claimed to have done it six times in 1918. There were even stories about people doing it twenty times!

However, when all these factors are considered, together with the Nationalist decline which left them with no candidate in a quarter of Irish constituencies, we are left with Roy Foster's judgement, shared by most historians, that 'a powerful Sinn Féin showing had been perceived as inevitable from the start'. Powerful it certainly was, and victorious Sinn Féin demanded the severance of the British link with a separate Irish parliament in Dublin. So although Sinn Féin had by far the largest number of Irish seats at Westminster, they were not taken up; one of the absentees was Constance Markievicz, the first woman to be elected to the House of Commons.

In place of Westminster, Sinn Féin set up its own Dáil Éireann (Irish Assembly) with Éamon de Valera as President. This, of course, was regarded by the British as an illegal act and was the genesis of the War of Independence which was to last until 1921.

ULSTER

In what seemed like the remorseless drive towards independence from Britain, one factor was generally forgotten by the Republicans. This was Ulster with its Protestant majority and implacable hostility (although there was a sizeable Catholic minority) to Home Rule, let alone an All-Ireland republic. For in all the propaganda about Pearse and 1916 (there were even accounts of people *praying* to Pearse and his colleagues) the strength of feeling of the Ulster Protestants about the proposed break with Britain was badly underestimated. And this only underlines the degree of myopia indulged in by Pearse particularly. There was never any chance that the Orangemen of Ulster would march peacefully into a united, Catholic-dominated Ireland when one of their slogans was still 'No Popery'. To imagine otherwise was to live in a republican and nationalist cloud-cuckoo-land.

The War of Independence

As the Dáil met in Dublin in January 1919, the first shots of what became known as the War of Independence rang out in Tipperary. The targets were two constables of the Royal Irish Constabulary who were gunned down by Volunteers, without orders from Collins or anyone else. But the deaths of these two men merely pre-empted what was already in Collins' mind. For within weeks he was telling colleagues that the

> sooner the fighting is forced and a general state of disorder created throughout the country, the better it will be for the country. Ireland is likely to get more out of a general state of disorder than from a continuance of the situation as it now stands.

Having proved himself as a political and financial organiser, Collins now displayed his talents as a guerilla fighter as he unleashed a deliberate assault on the RIC, most of whom of course were Irish themselves. His chosen instrument was the newly established Irish Republican Army, and the object of the campaign was to provoke the British authorities into harsh reprisals which would further alienate the Irish population. Within a year fourteen RIC constables were dead, and the Constabulary's ranks thinned out by early retirement and a falling off in recruitment.

Meantime Collins himself, 'the Big Fellow' as he was popularly known in republican circles, led an extraordinary double life. In one incarnation he was Finance Minister in the Dáil and busy organising a loan for the new Republic, and in another the carefree outlaw chief who bicycled around Dublin and even went into police stations to talk to RIC informers. But with that apparent carelessness went a deadly intent. The same man who arm-wrestled with IRB colleagues on the floor would ruthlessly order the execution of RIC political intelligence officers if they did not heed warnings and remained in their posts.

THE BLACK AND TANS

In March 1920 an unusual assassination took place in Cork City. Tómas Mac Curtain, the Lord Mayor, was shot down and killed by what was presumed to be an RIC reprisal gang, but the assassins were heard to speak with English accents. Who were they? The mystery was deepened by the fact that, instead of the familiar bottle-green RIC uniforms, these men had khaki trousers as part of their uniforms. They were, in fact, members of that notorious auxiliary RIC force, the 'Black and Tans', whose excesses are commemorated to this day in Ireland by a series of white crosses in the countryside.

Contrary to nationalist legend, the Black and Tans were not the dregs of British society, jailbirds and the like, but men who, disoriented by their demobilisation at the end of the First World War, had been recruited to help fill the depleted ranks of the RIC. For such ex-army drifters the war in Ireland offered the chance of pay and excitement in the guise of preserving law and order. The Black and Tans got their name from a famous pack of hounds in County Tipperary where they were first spotted wearing their curious mixture of khaki and green, and the name stuck. They owed their crossbreed appearance to the simple fact that there weren't enough RIC uniforms to go around. Some thousands of them had been recruited by 1920.

THE 'AUXIES'

Hand in hand with the Black and Tans were 'the Auxies', former British army officers who got a pound a day (more than the 'Tans'), a smaller force which earned, if anything, an even more ferocious reputation. Roaring around rural areas in the dead of night in their Crossley tenders (made up of a motor-car chassis fitted with the body of a lorry and holding up to ten men), the Auxies were feared opponents and generally regarded as the toughest the IRA had. When added to the RIC, the Black and Tans, and the British regular army, the Auxies gave the Crown forces in Ireland a fighting strength of about 40,000 men. Opposed to them were some 15,000 IRA men and women, with perhaps only 5,000 on active service although Collins himself only put the figure at 3,000.

TERROR AND COUNTER-TERROR

The IRA regarded all members of the Crown forces as legitimate targets in their drive to get the British out of Ireland. Their most effective unit

The Custom House in Dublin on fire

was the 'flying column', twenty to thirty men moving rapidly across country, merging into it when need be, and reliant on the aid of a generally sympathetic population. There were also sizeable units in cities like Dublin, Cork and Limerick which were more vulnerable to Crown counter-attack, but at no stage did the war involve the whole country. Most of the fighting was confined to the western and southern counties.

While big operations were mounted in the cities, like the burning of the Custom House in Dublin (actually a disaster for the IRA), most of the action consisted of well-planned ambushes of Auxie and Black and Tan columns, together with disruption of the rail system and attacks on Crown buildings. Perhaps the most famous was the ambush and killing of eighteen Auxies at Kilmichael in the south-west by a flying column led by the former British soldier, Tom Barry. In this instance the Auxies feigned surrender and shot two IRA dead, before being mowed down. Other episodes involving the IRA, like the shooting of a seventy-year-old lady who warned the authorities about one of their ambushes, and the massacre of a party of innocent tennis players in Country Galway, were a disgrace.

The worst single day of violence was in November 1920 on the first of several 'Bloody Sundays' in modern Irish history. It began with the clinical execution of fourteen British officers in Dublin (most of them in intelligence), some of them in front of their wives, by assassins who, in some instances, had just been to Mass. The British retaliated in kind: later that afternoon twelve people (including one of the players) were machine-gunned to death by Black and Tans at the All-Ireland football final in Croke Park. Even then the massacre wasn't over, for in the evening two more IRA men were killed in the guard-room of Dublin Castle together with a totally innocent Sinn Féin supporter who had mysteriously been brought in for questioning.

As the Black and Tans and Auxies grew more frustrated dealing with an enemy who remained elusive and fast-moving, atrocities on the British side grew worse. The worst was in Cork where they burnt down the city centre and cut the hoses of firemen attempting to put out the blaze. The government, then confident that it had (in Lloyd George's phrase) 'murder by the throat', made matters worse when the Irish Chief Secretary tried to claim that the citizens of Cork had deliberately burnt down their own city. Another terrible outrage was in Balbriggan, County Dublin, where the Black and Tans, having looted a local public house, burnt down the town including several creameries. The latter were a vital part of the local economy and burning of creameries became a common Black and Tan tactic.

When all this is conceded, however, it has to be put on the record that these outrages were invariably retaliatory. In Cork the Auxies had been infuriated by an ambush in which eleven of their colleagues had died, and in Balbriggan an RIC officer had died from appalling wounds from expanding bullets which then sparked off the Black and Tan rampage. Provocation is not, of course, an excuse for murder and arson, but one historian has highlighted the significant fact that, in most cases, after years in the trenches the nerves of the Auxies and the Black and Tans were stretched taut by the apparent ease with which the IRA could eliminate their colleagues.

By the lights of British officers, too, the war in Ireland was no war at all, but a justification for behaviour which drove the Auxie commander to resign in disgust. All in all it was a vicious, squalid and ruthless war in which any tactics became legitimate. And in the middle of it were the Irish people themselves, sometimes outraged by IRA tactics but often regarded by Crown forces as IRA supporters in the absence of any proof to the contrary. Many had Black and Tan or regular officers billeted in their houses while other civilians were forced to hide IRA men or did so for reasons of family loyalty.

Between 1919 and 1921, 752 Irish civilians and IRA men were killed and this seems a small figure compared with other conflicts, but great damage was also inflicted on the economic fabric of the country. No one was safe from the midnight knock on the door and the posse of Black and Tans that might follow it. By 1921 Irish people were weary of conflict, and sympathetic to the peace process which had already begun in a tentative way at the time of 'Bloody Sunday'.

The Government of Ireland Act

Already in 1920 the British government had passed the Government of Ireland Act, implementing the 1914 Home Rule Bill but creating two separate Irish parliaments in Dublin and Belfast. There was provision for a Council of Ireland on which northern and southern representatives could sit, but it had limited powers and could never be acceptable to republicans.

Crucially, however, the Act did not regard partition of Ireland into six and twenty-six counties as permanent, and referred to a possible All-Ireland parliament provided both sides agreed to give up their powers to it. Lloyd George may have been genuine in wishing for such a solution, but by now he was desperate to off-load responsibility for what he called 'that beautiful, sad bitch of a country'. However, it stood no chance of realisation while the likes of Carson and Sir James Craig were in power. Just as Pearse had indulged in republican utopianism, they were unbudging and fanatical in demanding, in the first instance, that all nine Ulster counties be handed over even though only four had a Protestant Unionist majority.

The Anglo-Irish Treaty

The 18-month absence of de Valera on a trip to the USA in 1919–20 (which raised $5 million for the Republican cause) kept him out of the turbulent events at home, and made him seem a suitable negotiating partner for the British when he returned to Ireland in December 1920. There was a hiccup when the British authorities mistakenly arrested him in June 1921, but in the event negotiations to end the fighting proved fruitless. De Valera spoke to Craig, representing the Unionists, and Lord Derby, representing the British government, but no substantial progress could be made.

The crucial factor in making the Dáil aware of the need to negotiate was Collins' urgent warning to de Valera that the IRA was on the verge of military defeat. For their part, the British were unaware of the IRA's weakness and were under pressure from public opinion abroad and at home to end the fighting. Due acknowledgement needs to be given here to the role of the British press, notably *The Times*, in bringing the Lloyd George government to the negotiating table. Nevertheless, the negotiating process was long and acrimonious. The Irish side was dominated by de Valera, Collins and Griffith, particularly the first two.

The 'Big Fellow' and the 'Tall Fellow' (de Valera) were as different as chalk and cheese; 'Dev' got bogged down with legal formulae and tautology, while Collins as a military man tended to react more decisively and hot-bloodedly.

Initially de Valera led the Irish delegation and got into a wrangle about whether an independent Ireland was to be a republic or a self-governing dominion like Canada or Australia. When Lloyd George asked what the Irish word for 'republic' was, de Valera had to concede that there wasn't one and that the nearest word to it was 'saorstat' or 'free state'. This was a victory for Lloyd George, who was determined both that the Irish link with the British Crown be preserved, and that the new state should not be described as a republic. The two would have been incompatible anyway.

Needing to report back to the Dáil in Dublin, de Valera decided that as President of the new Irish government he should stay above the negotiating battle, as the symbolic representative of the Irish people. Instead Collins was reluctantly persuaded to go, although he insisted on describing himself as the delegate of the IRB, and staying in separate accommodation from the rest of the Irish delegation.

Then as the negotiations dragged on into December 1921, Lloyd George, himself under pressure from his Conservative coalition partners, began to lose patience with what he regarded as Irish obduracy. In the end he decided to stage a typically melodramatic Lloyd George stunt. He produced two envelopes, saying that one or other would go that night by fast destroyer from Holyhead to Northern Ireland, telling Sir James Craig of the Irish delegation's decision. If they agreed to let six Ulster counties opt out of an independent Ireland and remain part of Britain, all would be well. But if they refused then it would be war again between Britain and the Irish republicans.

This, of course, was a none too subtle form of blackmail and left the Irish delegation to agonise about what to do (these events were very well portrayed in the 1992 Anglo-Irish TV production, *The Treaty*). At one level they were uncertain about whether they had the right to sign an agreement without referring the decision back to the Dáil first; at another several members of the delegation were appalled by the prospect of the partition of their country. Collins and Griffith were the first to realise that there was no real alternative, and to persuade tormented colleagues that this was so. All realised that signing would be divisive, none more so than Michael Collins who remarked, 'I have signed my death warrant.'

The Treaty allowed a month for the suspension of its provisions to the six Ulster counties of Londonderry, Antrim, Down, Armagh, Tyrone and Fermanagh. At the end of that month the counties would then have the right to opt out of the newly created 'Irish Free State'. They did just that. Robert Kee has made an interesting technical point about this, saying that when the Irish negotiators had been invited over to London, they had effectively been representing the whole of Ireland because no mention was made of Ulster. It was Collins and his colleagues who, in the last analysis, were left to decide how the 'national aspirations' should best be served. Confronted with the possibility of a renewed war which Collins did not believe they could win, they opted for the right of the Ulster counties to be excluded. *But* (and this is Kee's point) the delegation had in effect been negotiating for the whole of Ireland, not just the twenty-six counties that were to form the Free State.

It was also clear from the Treaty that even the British government did not expect partition to be permanent. Provision was made for a Council of Ireland which would have both northern and southern representatives on it, and a Boundary Commission to adjust the border between north and south 'in accordance with the wishes of the inhabitants'. Nationalists certainly thought that a plebiscite in Tyrone and Fermanagh, with their Catholic majorities, would bring those counties into the Free State. This would leave the Unionists with just four north-eastern counties, and such a unit was thought by British and Irish alike to be economically unviable.

The issue of the Crown, a sticking point for Lloyd George and his colleagues, was neatly sidestepped by an oath which placed the reference to the monarchy as far away as possible from the reference to the Irish Free State, in this way:

> I do solemnly swear true faith and allegiance to the Constitution of the Irish Free State as by law established . . . and that I will be faithful to H.M. George

V, his heirs and successors by law, in virtue of the common citizenship of Ireland with Great Britain and her adherence to and membership of the group of nations forming the British Commonwealth of nations.

Collins' argument was that part of a loaf was better than no loaf at all, 'You'd take the oath to get rid of it,' as he said. But the oath to the British Crown, let alone partition, was repellent to hardline republicans who regarded Collins and Griffith as traitors. In this division lay the genesis of the Irish Civil War.

As it was the Treaty was narrowly passed in the Dáil by 64 votes to 57, after a bitter debate which reduced de Valera to tears. He declined the presidency of the Dáil, refusing to recognise the validity of the Treaty, and the IRA decided to fight rather than accept it or the legitimacy of the new Free State government.

The Irish Civil War

Having fought the British to achieve independence, Irish men and women now found themselves fighting each other about the validity of the peace settlement. In many ways the Civil War of 1922–3 was even more tragic and wasteful than the War of Independence itself.

The Free State leader Michael Collins, lying in state, after the painting by Sir John Lavery

The war began in Dublin, where anti-Treaty IRA men led by Rory O'Connor seized the Four Courts building and after days of shelling by Collins' Free State artillery (ironically borrowed from the British) were forced to surrender. The anti-Treaty side were stronger in the south-west where they held Cork, but Collins sent Free State forces around by sea to seize the new state's second city. As their cause seemed more and more hopeless, the anti-Treaty IRA fought with desperate courage and atrocities were perpetrated on both sides. Draconian measures were taken by the Free State government which had seventy-seven IRA men shot by firing squads, particularly after Michael Collins himself had died in the conflict.

Michael Collins died as he had lived, with gay abandon driving an open-topped Rolls-Royce with an armoured car escort in a place called Bealnamblath in County Cork. Collins had said, 'Sure, they won't shoot me in my own county,' but shoot him the anti-Treaty IRA did, in that ambush in August 1922. Exactly what happened that evening remains controversial to this day, but the most likely explanation is that Collins was hit and killed by a richocheting bullet. More sensational versions have him shot in the head by his own side. So Collins' prophecy about his own death was only too accurate. He was just thirty-two years old.

Griffith had already died, worn out at fifty by overwork, but most poignant of all was the death of Erskine Childers, the gun-runner of 1914, who had denounced the Treaty and his old comrades. Childers was a propagandist rather than a fighter, but that did not save him. Possession of a small pearl-handled revolver, given to him by Collins, was the excuse manufactured for shooting him.

By May 1923 the Free Staters were victorious, and de Valera ordered the anti-Treaty IRA, 'the soldiers of the rearguard' as he called them, to surrender. In this manner, with 13,000 republicans in jail, was independent Ireland bloodily conceived.

Why did the Free Staters win, when by some estimates they were outnumbered four to one when the Civil War started (although this number was soon made up by vigorous recruitment)? There were practical reasons, like the fact that they had all the artillery, but the most significant factor, as the doyen of Irish historians F.S.L. Lyons pointed out, was that the hoped-for republic was invisible rather than indivisible, and the sincere and moving idealism sought to evoke it roused little echo in a war-weary country, bent upon as speedy a return to normality as possible.

THE LEGACY OF WAR

The pronouncements made by Pearse in 1916 have bitten deeply into the Irish republican psyche. War and violence had driven the British out, and war was used to try and overthrow the 1921 settlement. This ignored the fact that the June 1922 general election gave the Free Staters a majority of the Dáil, in effect the popular endorsement of the Treaty by the people.

Even after the end of the Civil War elements in the old IRA continued to regard the Free State government, and therefore partition, as illegitimate. It followed from that that the republican die-hards rejected the legitimacy of the Unionist government in Belfast; violence was to be used to overthrow it as well. Here lies the root of the current tragedy in Northern Ireland.

Culture

The shadow left by the violence of 1916–21 makes it easy to forget that it coincided with a period of immense cultural achievement in Ireland.

William Butler Yeats

William Butler Yeats (1865–1939), best remembered by many for that phrase in 1916 about 'a terrible beauty', was primarily a poet but his output was prodigious. Inspired by Maud Gonne he tried to stimulate the creation of a distinctive Irish literature with *The Celtic Twilight* (1893) and his plays *The Countess Kathleen* and *Cathleen ni Houlihan*. Yeats helped to found the famous Abbey Theatre in Dublin in 1904 with the playwright Lady Gregory (1852–1932), but later moved away from his association with a nationalist literature. He was awarded the Nobel Prize for Literature in 1923.

James Joyce (1882–1941) was forced like several Irish writers to flee the country before his talent could flower in Paris. He was critical of Yeats and the nationalist school of literature, and of the morbid Catholicism of his youth. His *Portrait of the Artist as a Young Man* (1916) is perhaps the best account ever written of the tensions of a Catholic upbringing, with its memorable 'fire and brimstone' sermon. *Ulysses*, published in 1922, gives an extraordinary account of one day in the life of a Jewish Dubliner. His earlier collection of short stories, *Dubliners* (1914), gave a sharp indication of Joyce's potential.

George Bernard Shaw (1856–1950) was another who took his talents abroad. After a spell as an unsuccessful novelist after moving to London in 1876, he became one of the foremost literary critics there before his own career as a playwright took off with plays like *Man and Superman* (1912), *Heartbreak House* (1919) and *St Joan* (1923). He interested himself in the national question and mounted a campaign to save Roger Casement from execution in 1916. Of the events of Easter 1916 Shaw wrote, 'the shot Irishmen will now take their place beside Emmet and the Manchester Martyrs in Ireland'. He loved the limelight and as an ageing playwright often featured in British contemporary newsreels giving impish (and frequently irreverent) views on all and sundry. He was awarded the Nobel Prize for Literature in 1925.

Ireland is not noted for her contribution to the visual arts but in Jack B. Yeats (1870–1957), the brother of the celebrated poet, she had a painter of distinction. Like his brother, Jack Yeats had literary leanings but learnt to sketch in his youth while on visits to Mayo and Sligo. He really established himself by having five paintings exhibited at the famous Armory exhibition in New York in 1913. Thereafter painting became his life, with a pronounced interest in what one critic has called the 'inconsequential'. Yeats painted poachers, turf-cutters, poets and lovers with equal facility, as he did landscapes like 'On Through Silent Lands'. He had little time for his brother's mysticism or his 'Hermetic Students of the Golden Dawn.'

J.M. Synge (1871–1909) was a friend of Jack Yeats and went sketching with him on the west coast, but his talents were theatrical. After a period in Paris, he was persuaded by W.B. Yeats to settle and work in Ireland. His study of *The Aran Islands* was illustrated by Jack Yeats and gave him the plots and settings for his plays *In the Shadow of the Glen, Riders to the Sea*, and his greatest comedy, *The Playboy of the Western World* (1907). His verse-drama *Deirdre of the Sorrows* was unfinished when he died of cancer at thirty-seven.

Finally, although he properly belongs to an earlier chapter, there was Oscar Fingall O'Flahertie Wills Wilde (1854–1900) who was brought up in Dublin before, like Shaw, moving to London. Reputedly the most brilliant conversationalist and wit of his day, his genius was best expressed in the theatre, in such comedies as *Lady Windermere's Fan* (1892) and *The Importance of Being Earnest* (1895).

CHAPTER FIFTEEN

A Protestant State for a Protestant People,
1920–1973

The Constitutional Framework

The Government of Ireland Act of 1920 was a victory for Unionism in the sense that it gave them a separate parliament in Belfast (something they had not sought); but the original Bill, based on that of 1914, left open the question of what Ulster was to consist of. The British government offered the Unionists the historic nine-county Ulster, but this was turned down by Sir James Craig and his colleagues in favour of a six-county state because it would be more 'homogeneous'. That is, it would have a substantial Protestant majority, whereas a nine-county state would have a Catholic minority of 43 per cent. Nevertheless the Belfast parliament was circumscribed in its powers, and subordinate to the Westminster parliament, which controlled defence, foreign policy, external trade and, crucially, most aspects of finance. This meant that the new Northern Ireland parliament could not pay its way without subsidies from Westminster. Nor could it follow a really distinctive and effective economic and regional policy: Northern Irish slums were the worst in the United Kingdom in the inter-war period.

Worryingly, however, from the Unionist perspective, the 1920 Act also included the reference to a Council of Ireland, which showed that Westminster did not regard partition as permanent. One of the major developments in the period between 1920 and 1925 was how partition *did* indeed become permanent. The Council of Ireland did have authority over minor matters like all-Ireland rail-ways and fisheries, and the northern and southern parliaments each had twenty representatives.

THE CATHOLIC REACTION

The Catholic reaction to the establishment of the Northern Ireland state was consistently hostile. One response, that of the IRA (before and after the Anglo-Irish Treaty), was to use physical force against the new state. This did not prove very successful and gave Sir James Craig (1871–1940), the first prime minister of Northern Ireland, who had replaced Carson as head of the Unionist Party in 1921, the excuse to introduce three classes of paramilitary police to support the new Royal Ulster Constabulary (RUC), of whom the 'B Special' constabulary were especially loathed by the Catholic minority.

Another response, from the old Nationalist Party, was to point out, as Joe Devlin did, the lack of safeguards in the 1920 Act for the minority community, but neither the British nor the Unionists took any notice. Yet a third was to boycott the Northern Irish institutions, so that the RUC never had more than 16 per cent Catholic membership, and Catholic teachers continued to be paid by Dublin rather than Belfast for ten months after the signing of the 1921 Treaty. Catholic schools also opted for voluntary status in the six counties, rather than accept what was seen as a Unionist or British subsidy.

This strategy was conditioned by the expectation that partition would not last long, for as a nationalist leader later observed, 'We thought it was a very temporary thing and that the house of cards would crumble.' Great hopes were centred on the Boundary Commission set up by the 1920 Act, which was confidently expected to reduce Unionist Ulster to an economically unviable rump of four counties.

THE SPECIAL POWERS ACT

The obstructive tactics of northern Catholics played right into the hands of the Unionists, who felt like a beleaguered garrison anyway and saw such behaviour as proof that Catholics were bound to be disloyal to the Northern Ireland state. The Unionist government's response was to enact the Civil Authorities (Special Powers) Act of 1922, often simply known as the Special Powers Act, which gave draconian powers to the authorities. Possession of firearms became a capital offence and republican suspects could be flogged.

SECTARIAN STRIFE

It was inevitable that the tensions of the Anglo-Irish War and partition would spill over into Ulster itself. Between 1920 and 1922 450 people were killed in sectarian rioting in the Six Counties, most of them Catholics, so that many of the minority community fled over the border into the Free State. There were bad episodes in Belfast, where the B Specials were let loose in Catholic areas in a manner calculated to embitter the population there. Neither were matters helped by Craig's appointment of a particularly unsympathetic Unionist as Home Affairs Minister.

In one sense Unionist behaviour, though provocative, was understandable, because hardline republicans were intent on overthrowing the 1920 settlement without waiting for any adjudication the Boundary Commission might make. As the Free State, until 1923 at least, seemed to be encouraging IRA activity in the north, severe measures were deemed necessary and a fatal polarisation of political attitudes took place. True, the nationalist position after 1920 encouraged the belief that all Catholics were against partition, just as all Protestants were for it, but this primitive divide made it harder for a constitutional nationalism to evolve which wanted to change the status of the Six Counties by consent and negotiation.

Such a Catholic grouping would, in any case, have flown in the face of Craig's pronouncement that there was only room in the Northern Ireland parliament for two parties, consisting of 'men who are for the Union, on the one hand, or those who are against it and want to go into the Dublin Parliament on the other'. Such attitudes produced a situation where the Unionist Party did not produce a single Catholic MP in fifty years, and the Nationalist politicians walked out of the Northern Ireland parliament in 1932 in protest at what they claimed was institutional sectarianism. It has to be conceded that there was weighty evidence for such a claim. As early as 1922 Craig had abolished proportional representation in Northern Ireland local government (introduced by the Government of Ireland Act), and gerrymandering of electoral boundaries became common. A classic example was in Londonderry, where a Catholic majority elected a minority of councillors after dextrous meddling with ward boundaries. Unionists responded to accusations of malpractice by pointing to the persistent lobbying of the Catholic minority for a 32-county Ireland.

The result of this political divide was a permanent duplication of the 1921 Northern Ireland election result when forty Unionists were elected to six Sinn Féiners and six Nationalists. It became common for members of parliament in many constituencies to be returned unopposed, and this permanent Unionist dominance seemed to be symbolised by the opening of the new Stormont parliament building by the then Prince of Wales in 1932. Outside it was a statue of Carson in a characteristically obdurate pose.

The Boundary Commission

In the years between 1921 and 1924 attempts to determine the Border question foundered because of the Irish Civil War and the recalcitrance of Sir James Craig. Ultimately the British government was forced to appoint a Northern Ireland representative to the Boundary Commission because Craig refused to do so, with a neutral South African judge as chairman. The judge in fact opted for tinkering with the border rather than making the wholesale changes nationalists expected. This intention was leaked by the British newspaper *The Morning Post* before the Commission report was ever made (it only finally saw the light of day in 1969). It made it clear that the putative report would only give some small, economically insignificant areas to the Free State, while a large slice of East Donegal would be given to Northern Ireland.

This premature leak so embarrassed the Free State government that in 1925 it rushed into agreement with Britain, accepting the existing border in exchange for the writing off of Ireland's part of the British national debt. There was no doubt that Craig and the Unionists were the clear winners, for the agreement also dismantled the Council of Ireland which had always been unpopular with the Unionists. Craig talked of joint cabinet meetings with the Free State, but in the event the rival heads of state did not meet again until 1965. Whatever nationalist aspirations were in the intervening period, the border appeared to be set in concrete.

The Depression

Unionist anxieties were not quietened by de Valera's election victory in the Free State in 1932, with his known ambition of bringing about a United Ireland. These fears appeared to be realised when de Valera's 1937 Constitution (see p. 208) claimed sovereignty over the whole of Ireland. The statement in Article 2 of the Constitution that 'The national territory consists of the whole island of Ireland, its islands and the territorial seas' seemed proof to most Unionists that they should have no truck with the Dublin government. The 'special position' given to the Catholic Church in that same Constitution appeared to be further proof that 'home rule was Rome rule'.

This constitutional development in the South took place against a backcloth of economic depression in the North. Throughout the 1920s and 1930s unemployment in the Six Counties was around 25 per cent, but this did not bring about Protestant and Catholic working-class unity in the face of privation. The brief exception was in 1932 when protests against inadequate welfare benefits sparked off riots in which Catholics and Protestants were involved, resulting in two deaths. But the coincidence of the riots with de Valera's first government in the Free State, which heightened Protestant suspicions about southern policy, meant that this was the first and only example of joint action which stretched across the sectarian divide.

The economic climate in the North throughout the 1930s remained bleak, and F.S.L. Lyons has highlighted the relative poverty of Ulster compared with other parts of the United Kingdom. A 1937 government report stated that the poorer classes in the province were 'mostly residing in homes more or less unfit for habitation'. Infant and maternal mortality in Ulster was higher than elsewhere, and tuberculosis, then a killer disease, was endemic in the under-25 age group. In 1938 87 per cent of houses in the Ulster countryside still had no running water, and there was a puny investment in public housing throughout the inter-war period.

What was the political significance of such deprivation? It did not, as we have seen, bring about working–class unity, but did in fact result in even more rampant and inflexible Unionist discrimination. For, faced with a possibly embittered unemployed element in the Protestant working class, the Craig government chose to emphasise the importance of sectarianism: in effect to make poor Protestants feel that, even in their poverty, they were superior to poor Catholics, who were lampooned as 'Taigs' or 'left footers' (an old Orange gibe which suggested that Catholics only dug with their left feet).

The classic Unionist political statement was made by Lord Craigavon (as Craig had become in 1927) at Stormont in 1934 when he told MPs that he rejoiced in being Grand Master of the Orange Lodge

> far more than I do being Prime Minister ... I have always said I am an Orangeman first and a politician and a member of this parliament afterwards ... all I boast is that we are a Protestant parliament and a Protestant state.

The message given here to the one-third Catholic minority was clear, Catholicism meant exclusion. It was made even clearer by Sir Basil Brooke (later Lord Brookeborough), who was Northern Ireland prime minister 1943–63, when he boasted that he did not employ any Catholics whatever – an extreme position, but it bore witness to the common Unionist assumption that Catholics were disloyal to the Northern Ireland state.

Even so there were positive aspects about the period as well. Rural electrification, for example, was considerably extended by the Stormont government in the 1930s, and there were signs that a more leisured consumer-oriented society was starting to emerge (even if it was largely the province of the Protestant middle class). Motor vehicle ownership increased four times between the world wars, and cinema and radio became available to those on modest incomes, with a regional BBC station being opened in Belfast in 1924. Always, though, the spectre of sectarian bigotry hung over the province. Its worst manifestation was in 1935 when eleven died in rioting in Belfast and hundreds of families, mostly Catholic, were driven out of their homes.

War

World War in 1939 provided an opportunity for the Unionists to prove their complete loyalty to the British Crown, and Northern Ireland provided an important base for guarding Britain's Atlantic sea-lanes. Her aircraft and shipping industries, together with agriculture, made a valuable contribution to the war effort too.

But even then her precarious status seemed to be underlined by Sir Basil Brooke's remark in a 1941 British newsreel, 'As you know, we are a part of the United Kingdom.' It was, as one historian has remarked, as if other British people needed reminding of the fact! And perhaps they did, because mainland Britain generally paid scant attention to Northern Ireland affairs. Stanley Baldwin's (British prime minister 1935–7) reaction to protests from Catholic community leaders about the bloodshed in 1935 was to say that it was a matter for the Northern Ireland government to deal with. Catholics might have felt that the defence obligation imposed upon Westminster by the 1920 Act should have included protecting them from Orange mobs.

Northern Ireland paid for its loyalty to the Crown by suffering four severe raids from German bombers, the worst of which killed 700 people in Belfast in 1941 and rendered 100,000 homeless. But given the experience of 1917, the British government, as Eamonn Phoenix has observed, 'prudently decided not to extend conscription to the six counties'. Nevertheless, Britain's image of loyal, embattled wartime Northern Ireland strengthened the grip of Unionism because of the sharp contrast with the clear-cut neutral stance adopted by de Valera's Free State. Craig and his colleagues were fond of boasting that they were 'King's men', but their patrician aloofness from ordinary Ulster people was demonstrated by the fatuity of discussions about saving Carson's statue, when Belfast was being devastated by German bombers.

Constitutional Consolidation

After the war there was something of a social revolution in the Six Counties. The radical legislation of the Attlee Labour government in Britain was extended to Northern Ireland, so she too got free health, free secondary schooling, grants for university attendance and welfare benefits akin to those in the UK.

But the political stalement continued, with the Unionist government flatly refusing to concede the principle of one man one vote in Stormont or local elections. Nationalist hopes that Labour might be more sympathetic than the British Conservative Party proved illusory in the political sphere, following the Free State's decision to become a republic outside the Commonwealth in 1949. The Attlee government's response was to declare that

> in no event will Northern Ireland or any part thereof cease to be part of His Majesty's dominions and that of the United Kingdom without the consent of the Parliament of Northern Ireland.

No Unionist leader could have asked for more.

Economic Development

In many respects the progress made by the Northern Ireland economy between 1945 and 1968 was impressive. Agriculture was modernised in such a way that export of livestock and cereals to the rest of the United Kingdom went up in leaps and bounds, and there were also generous government grants to encourage the development of industry in the province. Nevertheless unemployment remained ominously high (never less than 6 per cent of the workforce) throughout the immediate post-war period, and it was always the minority Catholic community which suffered most, thus heightening sectarian tensions. Much of this endemic unemployment was not the fault of the Unionist government and resulted from factors like the small size of the domestic Northern Ireland market, but isolated provocative policy decisions made it seem, in Catholic eyes, as if they were part of some conscious strategy. Examples included the building of the new town of Craigavon, the very name having all sorts of sectarian overtones, in a locality well away from the depressed Catholic areas west of the River Bann. Another was the decision to put Northern Ireland's second university in the small Protestant town of Coleraine rather than in the largely Catholic Londonderry.

In other sectors the achievements of the Unionist government, with lavish UK assistance (running to £45 million a year by the 1960s), were neutralised by the time it took to make progress. A notable example was housing, so that although 100,000 houses had been built by 1968 and their allocation was fairer and less discriminatory, by then it was too late.

The Border War

The fact that social and economic progress had been made was strikingly demonstrated when the IRA began a new campaign in the North in 1956, with the utopian object of ending Partition. This dragged on for six years, during which nineteen IRA men and members of the RUC and B Specials were killed and a million pounds' worth of damage was done to the fabric of the Northern Ireland state. When it was called off in 1962, however, the IRA were forced to admit that the campaign had been a failure largely because the Catholic minority had not supported them. For this reason the old 'flying column' tactic, so successful in the War of Independence, achieved little.

There might, perhaps, have been a chance for communal reconciliation here, after the Catholics had remained overwhelmingly loyal to the Crown, and one Unionist politician suggested to the prime minister, Lord Brookeborough, that they merited some reward. He met with a totally negative response. Meantime the rest of the UK lived on in blissful ignorance of the real nature of Northern Ireland's problems. This was hilariously underlined when Brookeborough gave a TV interview to the well-known BBC commentator Richard Dimbleby, who asked him with alphabetical emphasis, 'Just what is this I-R-A?' Too wily a bird to miss this opportunity, Brookeborough then repeated, despite the evidence from the 'Border War', the old Unionist canard about the inevitable disloyalty of all Catholics.

The Troubles

There has been considerable debate amongst modern Irish historians about whether the current phase of republican insurgency in the North, which began in 1969, was inevitable. At a first glance there is much to suggest that it was, given the continuing discrimination against Catholics in education, housing and local government. Taking one example only, in County Fermanagh as late as March 1969 there were just thirty-two Catholics employed in local government against 338 Protestants. But there were particular features about the situation in Ulster in 1968–9 which brought the crisis to a head. One concerned the Unionist establishment which had, since Terence O'Neill (prime minister 1963–9) became Unionist leader, been making some small gestures of reconciliation to the Catholic community. These included visits by O'Neill to Catholic schools, previously unheard of in Unionist circles, and in January 1965 a meeting between him and the then Irish prime minister, Seán Lemass.

None of these things really challenged the dominant Protestant and Unionist position. Yet O'Neill's limited conciliatory gestures unleashed a virulent Protestant extremist backlash led by Ian Kyle Paisley (b. 1926), a Presbyterian minister who had already broken away from his own church, and now haunted O'Neill at his public meetings with taunts about his 'moving towards Rome'. This was a wild exaggeration about a man like O'Neill, who condescendingly explained his modest reform strategy as a way of getting Catholics to 'live more like Protestants' and stop having the stereotypic eighteen children!

Terence O'Neill

Unfortunately this particularly obdurate form of Unionism (Paisley went on to found the Democratic Unionist Party in 1972) coincided with the continuing existence of an equally obdurate utopian form of republicanism. Here, too, there was a moderate alternative, which had been started in 1968 by Catholic students as the People's Democracy movement, inspired by the black Civil Rights movement in the USA to ask for similar concessions by Stormont. According to Unionist legend People's Democracy was a front for the IRA from the start, but there is little evidence to sustain this accusation. What is undoubtedly true is that the Unionist establishment was thoroughly alarmed by this manifestation of Catholic street power and overreacted by letting the B Specials loose on the demonstrations. There was a particularly notorious episode early in 1969, when the police stood by while a Paisleyite mob stoned a civil rights demonstration at Burntollet Bridge about seven miles outside Londonderry.

The situation then escalated when B Specials were allowed to terrorise Catholic areas of Belfast, provoking such civil disorder that

Ian Paisley

British troops had to be sent to Northern Ireland in August 1969. Here it seemed was a situation tailor-made for the IRA, but that organisation had become so enfeebled that its adherents were mocked in Belfast, 'IRA – I Ran Away'.

The Provisional IRA

This weakness was partly a result of a change in outlook in the IRA after the Border War when a new, more intellectual Chief of Staff, Cathal Goulding, tried to move the organisation away from the use of violence towards political militancy of a left-wing variety. Goulding's ideas were not well received by traditionists in the IRA, who accused him of going Marxist and broke away from the organisation in 1970. The secessionists called themselves the 'Provisional IRA' after the 1916 Provisional Government in Dublin, and declared their intention of mounting a determined armed campaign against the Crown forces in the North. The rump of the IRA became known as the official IRA, which abandoned violence in 1972 (other than feuding with the 'Provos') and was sidelined by the more vigorous Provisional IRA (PIRA).

Even then it took some time for the 'Provos' to win significant support in the Catholic ghettos. That they did so was, at least in part, due to mistaken tactics by the British army which had initially been warmly greeted by Catholics who regarded it as their protector against the B Specials. So began the unfortunate convergence between deprived urban Catholicism in Northern Ireland and the Provisional IRA (although it also built up areas of influence in South Armagh), and from it a spiral of brutal Provisional bombings and shootings, which sparked off retaliatory violence from loyalist paramilitary groups. A deadly cycle of violence and counter-violence was established for the next two decades.

CHAPTER SIXTEEN

From Free State to Republic, 1922–1949

The Irish Free State that emerged uneasily from the civil conflict of 1922–3 was built on a seam of bitterness which bedevilled the first years of the new state's life. This bitterness derived in part from the losses suffered by both sides during the Civil War, but also from the fact that de Valera and his followers refused to accept the new political dispensation. This left the new government with no really effective political opposition, not a healthy situation for an infant parliamentary democracy. In fact the republicans won forty-four seats in the 1923 elections to the Dáil, but they refused to take them up.

Kevin O'Higgins

The leader of the Free State government was W.T. Cosgrave (1880–1965) whose official title was President of the Executive Council, which he remained for almost a decade. But its dominant personality for the first few years was Kevin O'Higgins (1892–1927), a disciple of Michael Collins who acknowledged that in every situation which confronted him, 'I always try to do what I think the Big Fellow would have done.'

O'Higgins, who was Minister for Home Affairs and Vice-President of the Executive Council, was able, decisive and, when necessary, ruthless. During the Civil War he had sanctioned the execution of the IRA man Rory O'Connor, even though O'Connor had been best man at his own wedding. Nicknamed by some the 'Irish Mussolini' because of his capacity for work and tough decision-making, O'Higgins did in fact have a strong belief in parliamentary democracy, together with a relentless hostility to paramilitary opponents of it. It was O'Higgins, therefore, who took responsibility for coercive measures against those elements of the anti-Treaty IRA which continued to resist the new government party, which now took for its name Cumann na nGaedheal (Society of Irishmen). Two Public Safety Acts in 1923–4 gave the Free State government draconian powers like flogging and internment to deal with dissident IRA men, and even de Valera himself was imprisoned. This proved to be counter-productive for on release 'Dev' went on attacking the Cosgrave government as before.

The government's authority also suffered a reverse over the Boundary Commission fiasco, when the leak (see p. 194) led to the resignation in 1925 of the Irish representative on the Commission, prior to what republicans regarded as a sell-out on the Border.

THE ASSASSINATION OF O'HIGGINS

This success for Cumann na nGaedheal was counterbalanced by a shattering blow. In July 1927, as Kevin O'Higgins made the short journey from his Dublin home to Sunday Mass in a nearby church, he was waylaid by three assassins (never subsequently caught) who wounded him and, as he tried to flee, ran him down and poured shots into his prostrate corpse. At a stroke, therefore, the Cosgrave administration had lost its strongman, at an age barely older than his

William Cosgrave, guardian of the Irish Free State 1922–32

mentor Collins, and historians can only speculate about the shape events might have taken had O'Higgins lived on. F.S.L. Lyons at least had no doubts about O'Higgins' quality, believing him to be 'of such calibre that he would have played a leading role whatever post he had been assigned'.

The Return of Constitutionalism

In an effort to force de Valera and his newly-formed Fianna Fáil (Soldiers of Destiny) party into parliament, the Cosgrave government passed legislation which forced every candidate for election to take an oath that if elected he or she would take their seat in the Dáil. This faced de Valera with the problem that if elected he would have to take the oath of allegiance to King George V. Ingeniously, however, he pushed the Bible to one side and merely signed his name in the book as all Dáil members were required to do. Honour was then deemed to be satisfied, and de Valera and his followers entered the Dáil. F.S.L. Lyons has aptly described de Valera (remembering his arguments with Lloyd George about a 'free state' or 'a republic') as the 'constitutional Houdini of his generation', but another historian has asked, not unreasonably, why when this constitutional expedient was adopted in 1926 it could not have been adopted in 1922. At all events, the opposition boycott of parliament was now ended, and the Free State entered an era of regular parliamentary rule.

THE CHURCH

From the outset there were the closest of ties between the Catholic Church and the Cumann na nGaedheal government. The Church had made its political position clear by condemning the anti-Treaty IRA in 1922, and it remained hostile to de Valera and Fianna Fáil until the 1930s. By comparison with the Northern Irish State, however, the Cosgrave government was not sectarian, and gave the Protestant minority in the Free State (less than a tenth of the population) a significant role in affairs. There was no specific reference to Catholicism in the constitution, and the second chamber, the Senate (*Seanad Éireann*), was deliberately designed to cater for minority interests.

It was in the area of public morality that Catholic influence was most strongly felt during this period, with severe censorship of films and a ban on publications about contraception. These bans remained in place until the 1960s and 1970s.

EDUCATION

A small newly independent state like Ireland was almost bound to attempt to assert its separate cultural identity, after centuries of cultural domination by England. Whether such an attempt was ever likely to succeed is another matter. Certainly the steps taken by the government were halting ones, which reflected its conviction that Anglo-Irish reconciliation was preferable to Anglo-Irish confrontation. So Cosgrave and his colleagues contented themselves with trying to make Irish the medium of instruction in the nursery schools (this was a failure) and insisting that it be compulsory in the secondary school curriculum.

Fianna Fáil in Power

In 1932 the inevitable transition in Irish politics took place and Fianna Fáil came to power. It was in coalition with the Irish Labour Party, but Fianna Fáil did not have an effective working majority and new elections had to be held a year later. During the campaign the IRA had a high profile in canvassing for Fianna Fáil, using tactics of intimidation and impersonation; some were said to have voted as many as fifty times. In these circumstances it is perhaps not surprising that Fianna Fáil, again in coalition with Labour, won a substantial majority and was to remain in office for a further sixteen years. However, it is probable that the coalition would have won anyway, with or without the assistance of the IRA.

In 1933 a peaceful transition of power seemed unlikely. There was particular concern about the attitude of the Free State army, which was known to be hostile to the IRA, and some members of Cumann na nGaedheal itself regarded Fianna Fáil as little more than a front for the IRA men who had murdered O'Higgins. (There is at least one story about an anxious Fianna Fáil deputy being found in a telephone box assembling a machine-gun, so great was the tension surrounding Fianna Fáil's assumption of power!)

In the event, such anxiety proved to be unfounded because Cosgrave and his lieutenants accepted their electoral defeat with good grace, and the army which they had created remained loyal to the constitution. Cumann na nGaedheal itself was soon to disappear, to be re-formed under the new name of Fine Gael (United Ireland). Together with Fianna Fáil it was to dominate Irish politics down to the present day, following the fissure created in 1921 between those who would and would not accept the Treaty. This was far more meaningful than labels about 'right' and 'left' because on many issues Fianna Fáil and Fine Gael proved to be almost indistinguishable, leaving Labour as the only genuinely left-wing party in the Free State.

De Valera and the IRA

If the IRA expected preferment under de Valera's premiership they were in for a rude awakening, despite the fact that at the beginning of his administration their adjutant-general held a post in the Ministry of Defence. The problem was that the IRA began to flout its paramilitary presence by openly drilling and parading in Irish towns, irrespective of the government's wishes. Even though de Valera had done his best to mollify them by granting government pensions to those IRA men who had fought against the Free Staters in the Civil War, and by offering commissions in the Free State army, when he demanded that IRA drilling should cease, the organisation impertinently demanded that he make the Free State into a republic within five years. This proved too much even for a man with de Valera's republican pedigree (another factor was a series of bloody killings of civilians by IRA men).

Great bitterness then divided the IRA and the Fianna Fáil establishment, even if its rank and file felt some sympathy for the increasingly desperate exploits of the paramilitary organisation. Its flavour is well captured in this song from the 1950s:

> This Ireland of mine has for long been half free
> Six Counties lie under John Bull's monarchy
> And sure de Valera's greatly to blame
> For shirking his part in the Patriot game....

Matters came to a head in 1939 when a daring IRA raid on a government arsenal in Phoenix Park resulted in the loss of a vast amount of arms. De Valera was forced to enact an Offences Against The State Act allowing internment of IRA suspects, and a Treason Act. In the years that followed four IRA men were executed.

Faced with such opposition inside the Free State, the IRA mounted a somewhat desperate bombing campaign on the British mainland in 1939–40 in which a number of civilians were killed.

THE BLUE SHIRTS

Another threat to the Fianna Fáil government in the years after 1933 was posed by the fascist-style 'Blue Shirts' movement led by the former police commissioner, Eoin O'Duffy, whom de Valera had sacked. The Blue Shirts were clearly influenced by Mussolini and his idea of the corporate state, and their avowed aim was 'to promote and maintain social order'. O'Duffy always denied having dictatorial ambitions, and he would have made an unlikely Führer or Duce, but de Valera was sufficiently alarmed by their posturing to set up in 1933 the so-called 'Broy Harriers', named after their first leader, a special police auxiliary force consisting of ex-IRA men.

Ultimately the Blue Shirt threat amounted to little, their most significant achievement being the sending of a division to help the rebel General Franco in his war against the Spanish Republic.

The 1937 Constitution

In office as out, de Valera showed a rare talent for tinkering with constitutional devices. When he came to power a primary objective was the loosening of ties with the British Commonwealth, and this was accomplished between 1933 and 1937 by a slow process of attrition. First of all, the right of appeal to the British Privy Council in London was abolished, then the oath of allegiance to the Crown, and finally, the Governor Generalship (this official represented the Crown in Ireland).

The process was completed by the 1937 Constitution, although de Valera did not leave the Commonwealth and the British did not expel Éire, as the Free State was renamed (the word is Gaelic for Ireland).

They were, though, angered by the phrasing of the new constitution which laid claim in Articles 2 and 3 to all thirty-two counties, while limiting the area of jurisdiction to twenty-six counties 'pending the re-integration of the national territory'.

Such a constitutional revision was calculated to infuriate the Unionists and prompted a broadside from Lord Craigavon who reminded all and sundry that 'we are a Protestant Parliament and a Protestant State'. There was talk in the North of referring to 'Ulster' as a separate state although this did not occur, but Unionist fury was also a result of the special references made to the Catholic Church in the 1937 constitution. Its preamble began 'In the name of the Most Holy Trinity' and, although the Catholic Church was not established in the manner of the Church of England, reference was made to its 'special position . . . as the guardian of the Faith professed by the great majority of the citizens'. In this adroit way de Valera won over the Catholic hierarchy, hitherto suspicious of Fianna Fáil because of its links with the IRA.

On the debit side de Valera's constitution made the likelihood of Unionist acquiescence to the concept of a united Ireland even more remote, and given the avowed intention of the Taoiseach (as Irish prime ministers were to be called) of creating a united Ireland, it is hard to see how the constitution was going to assist in this process. Articles 2 and 3 were to be the object of constant Unionist criticism and com-plaint over the years. They were not impressed by the fact that the new position of President of Éire was occupied by the Protestant Douglas Hyde.

EDUCATION

De Valera and his government were more hostile to the process of 'Anglicisation' in Ireland than Cumann na nGaedheal had been, and therefore more determined to impose the Irish language on a not always enthusiastic population. Irish was declared the 'first official language' in the 1937 constitution, and the historian David Fitzpatrick has commented on Fianna Fáil's 'spirited efforts to infuse the history curriculum with Gaelic and patriotic precepts'. Another method of encouraging the use of Irish was to subsidise the sending of teacher trainees into the Gaeltacht, the remaining Gaelic-speaking areas on the western coast of Ireland. (The author's own mother was educated entirely in Irish by this process in Tourmakeady, County Mayo.)

Did the policy succeed? Statistics suggest not, as the number of Gaelic speakers in the Gaeltacht itself halved between 1922 and 1939. And historians see the policy as fundamentally misguided: the vernacular language was not encouraged, and the earlier Gaelic revival itself was put in jeopardy. It is a historical irony that it was in the Six Counties that Gaelic thrived in the teeth of Protestant and Unionist opposition.

THE ECONOMY

The Cosgrave administration had followed a cautious, budget-balancing economic policy, characterised by a reluctance to allow the state to intervene. But de Valera's nationalistic policy in the 1930s rather undermined this policy which, until the worldwide slump of 1931, had given the Free State a lower rate of unemployment than the Six Counties.

De Valera's refusal to continue payments to the British exchequer by farmers who had been given British subsidies under the pre-war land purchase acts then provoked London into a costly economic war. It has to be seen in the context of the additional provocation, in British eyes, provided by the constitutional reforms. Ireland in the inter-war period was almost totally dependent on the British market for her agricultural products. De Valera's policy of confrontation resulted in a collapse of livestock exports to Britain, which was not counterbalanced by the efforts of the government to extend the area of land under cultivation in the twenty-six counties. All in all, what Fitzpatrick calls 'de Valera's paper victories' were bought at a high economic cost. In 1938 Éire's national income was only 3 per cent higher than it had been in 1931 when the slump started.

THE RETURN OF THE TREATY PORTS

Only in April 1938, when Neville Chamberlain (British prime minister 1937–40) and de Valera negotiated the return of the so-called 'Treaty Ports' to Ireland (those like Cobh, the former Queenstown, which had remained British naval bases under the 1921 Treaty), did relations improve. It is noteworthy that Chamberlain, who was savaged by historians and contemporaries alike for his concessions over Czechoslovakia in that same year, has received little credit for this gesture of good will to a small, neighbouring sovereign state. As for de Valera, the issue of the Treaty Ports was to return to haunt him later.

SOCIAL POLICY

Fianna Fáil's social policies did little to help economic recovery in the 1930s. A striking example was its attitude towards the use of female labour in the workforce. This was laid down in Articles 40, 41 and 45 of the 1937 Constitution and was entirely negative. As Roy Foster remarks tersely: 'The image of rural utopianism was incompatible with an industrialised female workforce, or, it might be added, with any industrialised workforce at all.' Woman's role was to stay at home, and a 1935 measure put the ceiling on the number of women who could be employed in the, admittedly small, Irish industries.

On the credit side, Fianna Fáil was more sympathetic on the question of pension rights and unemployment insurance than Cumann na nGaedheal had been. But curious propagandists lilke Aodh de Blacam (1890–1951) put over visions of an unrealistic rural idyll in which Éire could ignore the realities of modern economic life. Much of this thinking was linked to a fierce nationalism, profoundly Catholic in spirit, which tended to see the country as a likely victim of perverse outside influences. Thus in 1935 de Valera warned his fellow countrymen that 'Ireland remains a Catholic nation, and as such sets the eternal destiny of man high above the "isms" and idols of the day'.

Ireland in the Second World War

Reference has already been made to the involvement of Northern Ireland in the Second World War, and there was an assumption on the other side of the Irish Sea that Éire would join in the conflict too. Why, given the experience of recent Irish history, it is hard to fathom. De Valera's position on the outbreak of hostilities in September 1939 was quite clear-cut. While Northern Ireland remained under British occupation, Éire could not belong to any coalition of which Britain was a member. This position was maintained even after the USA entered the war in 1941 and put considerable pressure on the Dublin government to enter the conflict.

Winston Churchill, who succeeded Chamberlain as prime minister in 1940, reacted to Irish neutrality with a mixture of incomprehension and cold fury, particularly as the loss of the Treaty Ports had put Britain at a disadvantage in her battle with the German U-boats in the Atlantic. British policy was a mixture of 'carrot and stick'. In 1940 there were references to a benevolent British attitude towards Irish unity (bizarrely ignoring the known Unionist position), but when this did not work there were threats of invasion. Nothing, however, would budge de Valera from his position, or bring Britain the return of the Treaty Ports.

In retrospect, it is clear that Irish neutrality was heavily biased in favour of the Allies. When Allied airmen crash-landed in Éire they were driven to the Border and handed over (they included a US Air Force general who crashed in 1944 with the D-Day invasion plans on him!). If their aircraft were still serviceable they were refuelled and sent on their way, often with cockpits full of eggs, butter and milk. British Observer Corps members were allowed to station themselves around the Irish coast, and no attempt was made to interfere with the recruitment of thousands of Southern Irishmen into Crown forces.

Nor was the emergency facing the embattled North ignored. In 1941, when Belfast was bombed, de Valera sent fire engines from the Free State to help (Dublin itself was accidentally bombed by the Germans in 1941 with considerable loss of life). In this context Churchillian rhetoric about 'joining issue with Mr de Valera' seems at the very least inappropriate, particularly when the treatment of German fliers is recalled. Unlike the Allied airmen they were interned in Curragh Camp for the duration.

THE GERMAN DIMENSION

The Nazi regime inevitably saw the encouragement of republican dissidents in Éire as a means of causing trouble for the British. For his part, de Valera was anxious to avoid compromising Irish neutrality in any way and continued his severe repression of the IRA. Feeble

German efforts were made to infiltrate their own agents into Éire, with comical results. On one occasion three agents, one of them an Indian, were found wandering hopelessly in the Irish countryside after being parachuted in. On another an agent escaped from Dublin's Mountjoy Jail disguised as a woman and hawked himself around various republican households before eventual recapture! The Germans also sent the former IRA Chief of Staff, Sean Russell, organiser of the 1939–40 bombing campaign in Britain, to Ireland by submarine in 1941, but he died of a perforated ulcer off the coast of Galway and a colleague was forced to return to Germany where he died later. Overall the IRA did not impress their Nazi allies, whose chief agent in Ireland told one of them, 'You know how to die for Ireland, but to fight for it, you have not the slightest idea.'

Despite this 'Walter Mitty' world of espionage, the neutrality issue was still able to bring Anglo-Irish relations to their nadir in 1945. First of all de Valera, in an excessively legalistic diplomatic gesture, signed the book of condolence at the German embassy when Hitler killed himself. Then Churchill singled de Valera out for abuse in his VE speech:

> Had it not been for the loyalty and friendship of Northern Ireland we should have come to – we should have been forced to come to close quarters with Mr de Valera or perish from the earth ... And we left Mr de Valera's government to frolic with the German and later with the Japanese representatives to their hearts' content.

De Valera's response was more measured, allowing as it did for the 'first full flush of victory' but going on to ask the British premier:

> Could he not find in his heart the generosity to acknowledge that there is a small nation that stood alone not for one year or two, but for several hundred years against aggression, that endured spoliations, was clubbed many times into insensibility, but that each time on returning consciousness took up the fight anew; a small nation that could never be got to accept defeat and has never surrendered her soul.

In many ways this war of words between two very different men epitomised the misunderstandings between the two neighbouring islands over the centuries. Churchill could not comprehend the degree of Irish bitterness after the long struggle for independence, while de Valera could not see how offensive his gesture might seem to those involved in the struggle with Nazism.

The Final Split

Éamon de Valera was voted out of office in 1948 when he was defeated at the polls by an inter-party coalition consisting of Fine Gael, the Labour Party, a new radical republican party called Clann na Poblachta (Republican Family), and a farmers' party.

Surprisingly, it was this Fine Gael-led coalition, under the new Taoiseach John Costello (1891–1976), which finally broke the constitutional tie with Britain in 1949, by declaring Ireland to be a Republic outside the Commonwealth. Surprising because Fine Gael was, after all, the direct descendant of Cumann na nGaedheal, the original pro-Treaty party which seemed to be more in favour of the British link. There were certainly stories at the time that Costello had been incensed, firstly by a toast proposed by British Prime Minister Attlee in Downing Street to 'the King' (leaving out all reference to the Irish President), and then by another incident in Canada when the Canadian prime minister had made exactly the same 'blunder'. Costello always denied that he had been influenced by these slights, or by an equally bizarre incident on the Canadian trip when the Governor General, the Ulsterman Viscount Alexander of Tunis, put a replica of 'Roaring Meg' on the table at which he and the Taoiseach were sitting. As 'Roaring Meg' was the cannon used to defend Londonderry in 1689 and, as F.S. Lyons points out, 'an almost sacred symbol' to Ulster Unionists, Mr Costello could be forgiven for being upset!

In reality these colourful incidents were not the deciding factor; rather was it the unsatisfactorily ambiguous constitutional relationship between Éire and Britain under the de Valera External Relations Act. The new republic was to be known as the Republic of Ireland, but its birth brought a swift response from the British government as we saw in the last chapter.

CHAPTER SEVENTEEN

Towards Europe,
1949–1973

The Fine Gael-led coalition was soon to find itself involved in a welter of anti-partition propaganda, which was encouraged by de Valera but was also the work of Sean MacBride (1904–88). The leader of Clann na Poblachta and son of Maud Gonne, the idolised lover on whom W.B. Yeats had doted so many years before, MacBride was Minister for External Affairs in the Costello government. He was a quixotic figure who had been Chief of Staff of the IRA before the war, and went on to become Chairman of Amnesty International and win both the Nobel and Lenin Peace Prizes.

The Health Crisis

Curiously, however, the constitutional issue was to be overshadowed by a major health row which was eventually to bring down the Costello coalition in 1951. The major figure here was Dr Noel Browne (b. 1915), another maverick political figure who was then a member of Clann na Poblachta and had been given the Health portfolio in the coalition. He had picked up a health reform bill which Fianna Fáil had been considering since 1947 and had shelved when there was known to be opposition from the Catholic Church.

Dr Browne was made of sterner stuff and soon ran into trouble on two fronts. One was the Irish medical profession, which resented his demand that pre-natal provision for mothers should be free and not means-tested; the second was the Church, which was unhappy about the reference to sex education and also believed that such state interference was a violation of family rights. Of the two, the opposition from the Catholic

215

Church was far more significant and caused considerable unease among Clann na Poblachta's less radical partners. In the end, too, it was to cause tension between Browne and his party leader, MacBride, who ordered him to resign. But after doing so Browne then published his correspondence with the Catholic hierarchy, and this caused considerable concern in political, media and intellectual circles. The *Irish Times* went so far as to claim that the Catholic Church was now running Ireland (a view, of course, long held by Northern Unionists). This was obviously an overstatement but, as F.S.L. Lyons has pointed out, the Browne affair did underline 'the extreme difficulty in a Catholic country of drawing the line between morals and politics'. Noel Browne went on to join Fianna Fáil (uneasily), found his own party briefly, and eventually find a home in the Irish Labour Party. His battle with the Church became a cause célèbre in post-war Irish politics, but in the short run the tensions it created forced Costello to go to the country in 1951 and the coalition was defeated.

The Political Game in the Fifties

The Irish system of proportional representation with its transferable votes was very fair, but also made it hard for any one party to obtain an outright majority. This was the case in 1951 when de Valera became leader of a minority Fianna Fáil government which, plagued by balance of payment difficulties and inflation, was then defeated by a second Costello-led inter-party coalition in 1954. The difference this time was that Clann na Poblachta had dwindled to a tiny rump of two seats. Yet it again proved to be an unfortunate period in power because it coincided with the outbreak of the 1956–62 Border War. Costello was forced to consider coercive measures against the IRA, but when he asked the Dáil for stronger powers, his old ally Sean MacBride moved a vote of no confidence against Fine Gael and the coalition and brought the government down.

Nevertheless, the second coalition government of the 1950s was not without interest, especially in the sphere of foreign policy. The neutrality of wartime had become the neutrality of a member of the non-aligned bloc, and Ireland had some understanding for the newly emergent Afro-

Asian countries. Her foreign policy was based on the so-called 'three principles': strict adherence to the UN Charter, non-membership of rival alliances like NATO and the Warsaw Pact, and support for the battle of 'Christian Civilisation' against communism. The last two principles were not strictly compatible and pressure was put on Ireland to join NATO, but she would not. Instead, the Republic played a respectable and sometimes influential role at the United Nations in New York. Individuals like Dr Conor Cruise O'Brien (b. 1917) made a distinguished contribution to international peacekeeping.

The Economy

The major battleground in Ireland during the 1950s was the economy. At the beginning of the decade it was stagnant, over-reliant on agriculture and poorly organised. This was all changed by a relatively obscure Secretary to the Finance Ministry called T.K. Whitaker (b. 1916). It was Whitaker who produced a crucial report in 1958 which formed the basis for a five-year economic plan which had a considerable impact on the Irish economy by the 1960s. The characteristics of the Whitaker-inspired plan were a vast increase in domestic investment, with the private sector working in tandem with the state, and a big effort to attract foreign capital. The success of this strategy can be deduced from the fact that between 1959 and 1968 industrial output rose by 82 per cent in the Republic; exports in 1966 were 88 per cent up on the 1953 figure.

Considerable efforts at improvement were also made in the vital agricultural sector although, as the economic historian L.M. Cullen has noted, 'recovery was ... tied more closely to the growth of industrial output'. In fact the results were disappointing, despite a campaign against bovine tuberculosis and efforts to market products more efficiently and develop agricultural education.

Ireland's trade policy also became less protectionist, but she still suffered from her dependence on the UK market, and the uncertainty about Britain's attitude to the evolving European Economic Community which had been created in 1957. Immediate consequences of the more expansive economic policy were, however, discernible. The 1966 census showed that the population had actually increased by over 60,000 and remarkably emigration, a constant feature since the Famine, began to fall. Equally striking demographic changes were a rise in the birth-rate, so that Ireland began to have one of the youngest populations in Europe, and the falling out of fashion of the ancient Irish custom of late marriage.

Certainly the Fianna Fáil government of the late 1950s and early 1960s seemed to be far more dynamic than its predecessors in economic policy, although some measures to encourage exports and help remote underdeveloped areas had been introduced by the inter-party coalition.

A New Wave

Economic dynamism was not unconnected with the rise of a new and more energetic generation of political leaders in Fianna Fáil, and also in Fine Gael and the Labour Party. Éamon de Valera resigned from the premiership in 1959 and was elected President of the Republic. This remarkable man then held that position, even after he went blind, until two years before his death in 1975. He had served as Taoiseach for no less than twenty-one years. Oblique sometimes in his meanings, legalistic and stubborn when it suited him, 'Dev' could nevertheless make a serious claim to be the founder of modern Ireland.

He was succeeded as Taoiseach by Sean Lemass (1899–1969), by then nearly sixty, who had been 'out' in 1916 but was much more than just a traditional republican activist. Lemass had considerable talents as an economic manager, and under his aegis Jack Lynch (b. 1917), who was to succeed him, Patrick Hillery (b. 1923), a future President, and Charles Haughey (b. 1925), his son-in-law and another future Taoiseach, all began their ministerial careers. Fine Gael could point to considerable figures like the future Taoiseachs Liam Cosgrave (b. 1920), the son of W.T. Cosgrave, and Garret Fitzgerald (b. 1926); while Labour had Conor Cruise O'Brien, Brendan Corish and David Thornley. These younger men marked the divide between those who had been formed by the experience of independence and civil war, and a more managerial genre of politician with the skills to run a modern economy. Certainly the more progressive thrust of Fianna Fáil policy under Sean Lemass did much to account for that party's victories in the general elections of 1961 and 1965, before his retirement as party leader in favour of Jack Lynch, whose political appeal was certainly strengthened by his having been a well-known Gaelic footballer for Cork.

The Northern Troubles

The appearance of the Provisional IRA in 1970 (see p. 202) was perhaps the decisive event in the current phase of 'The Troubles', the term variously used to describe particularly stressful periods of modern Irish history. Throughout the early 1970s there was escalating violence as the Provos stepped up their campaign of urban violence while the British response seemed to some commentators to be unduly heavy-handed. A notable low-spot was on 30 January 1972 when, on so-called 'Bloody Sunday', thirteen civilians were killed by members of the Parachute Regiment in Derry in circumstances which have remained highly controversial to this day. Paradoxically, however, at the same time the then Northern Ireland Secretary, William Whitelaw, did have talks with leaders of the PIRA during a period of ceasefire, although they led nowhere. The Provos wanted an end to British rule in the Six Counties and their evacuation by Crown forces; this was never on the agenda as far as the British government was concerned. It suspended the Northern Ireland parliament, however, in March 1972 and introduced Direct Rule from Westminster.

THE PROVOS IN BRITAIN

Extension of bombing campaigns to the British mainland was an old IRA tactic; indeed it could be traced back to the Fenians. The thinking was that one bomb in London was worth a dozen in Belfast because of the publicity that accrued from it for the republican cause. In 1973 the current wave of mainland bombings started with bombs at New Scotland Yard, the Old Bailey and the Ministry of Agriculture building in Whitehall, planted by a group led by the Price sisters (it was no accident that their father was an old IRA man). The campaign then became far more deadly. Horrific bombings in Birmingham and Guildford in 1974 resulted in much loss of life, and in an atmosphere of anti-Irish hysteria (it is now clear) the wrong people were arrested for these crimes. This allowed the PIRA to make propaganda points against the British government, while condoning the slaughter perpetuated by the real bombers.

In response, the British government rushed through the Prevention of Terrorism Act, one of whose provisions allowed it to exclude Northern Ireland citizens suspected of PIRA sympathies from the mainland. Over the years since its implementation hundreds of innocent Irish citizens have been held under the Act, which makes the point that the real victims of PIRA violence are nearly always Irish people, whether in Northern Ireland itself or in the rest of the UK.

This especially virulent PIRA bombing campaign reached its zenith in 1975 when there were incidents almost every week before the PIRA unit concerned, known as 'the Balcombe Street' gang, was captured.

The Sunningdale Experiment

Northern Irish people tend to feel that undue attention is given to PIRA outrages in Britain, whereas they suffer terrorist violence on a day-by-day, month-by-month, year-by-year basis. This is a valid point, for in 1972 400 people were killed in the province alone, figures which forced the British government to review its policy.

The result was a courageous initiative by the Secretary of State for Northern Ireland William Whitelaw known as the Sunningdale 'power-sharing executive' (named after the place in Berkshire, England, where it was set up). For a while in 1973–4, the power-sharing executive did seem to offer a real political solution to Northern Ireland's problems. This was because the last Unionist prime minister, Brian Faulkner, actually a rather hardline member of former Unionist administrations, was persuaded to co-operate with the Catholic Social Democratic Labour Party and share power with the minority community. Sadly, many of Faulkner's fellow Unionists would not agree, and organised a workers' strike in 1974 which paralysed the province. By then a Labour government under Harold Wilson had come to power in Britain, and it buckled under the pressure and abandoned the Sunningdale experiment. There are some grounds for thinking that the Wilson government lost its nerve unduly quickly.

The European Dimension

The Irish government had long favoured membership of the EEC but was tied to Britain by economic dependence, and between 1957 and 1973 Britain's attitude to the EEC was wildly erratic. But by 1972 Conservative Prime Minister Edward Heath had decided to take Britain in, and negotiated a Treaty of Accession. On 1 January 1973 Britain, Ireland and Denmark all became full members of the EEC.

There were those in the Republic, notably the future Taoiseach Garret Fitzgerald in his book *Towards a New Ireland*, who saw EEC membership as a great step forward in healing Ireland's political division. It has to be said, though, that in the long term such hopes have proved to be an illusion, even if, as Fitzgerald has pointed out in his recent memoirs, the government of the Republic has on occasion got better deals for Northern Ireland out of Brussels than the British government has been prepared to lobby for.

The Republic certainly gained from the application of the EEC Common Agricultural Policy, which heavily subsidised Irish farmers, although the immediate prosperity brought about by Community membership began to taper off in the 1980s. Nevertheless, EEC membership did bring about a general widening of Irish horizons and, it must be said, a lessening of interest in the issue of the Border even if this continued to be a political totem for Fianna Fáil. Just how much this was the case was underlined in 1970 when two government ministers, one of them Charles Haughey, Lemass's son-in-law, were charged with gun-running for PIRA (both were acquitted).

Culture

The rich stream of Ireland's literary heritage continued to flow onwards in the mid-twentieth century. A notable figure who bestrode the Independence era and later decades was Sean O'Casey (1884–1964). Born in Dublin and self-educated, O'Casey was a trade union activist and a member of the Irish Citizens Army, later writing a history of that organisation. But his real talent was as a playwright, and encouraged by Lady Gregory he had his powerful trilogy *The Shadow of a Gunman*

(1923), *Juno and the Paycock* (1924) and *The Plough and the Stars* (1926) staged at the Abbey Theatre in Dublin in the 1920s. The last-named play, which presented a realistic and demythologised portrait of the Easter Rising, caused a riot in the theatre, and after the rejection of another of his plays, *The Silver Tassie* (1928), by the Abbey O'Casey went into permanent exile in England. Only one of his later plays was staged in Ireland. He produced six volumes of autobiography between 1939 and 1954.

Another influential playwright who followed the traditional Irish route into exile was Samuel Beckett (1906–89). In his case, like that of Joyce, Paris was to be his second home after he had found the rather obscurantist nationalism of 1930s Ireland unpalatable. He reputedly told his parents in 1939 that he preferred France at war to Ireland at peace. He began his career as a novelist, but following the failure of *Murphy* in 1938, he switched not just his field from literature to drama, but also his medium of expression from English to French. Strongly critical of those Irish writers who parodied Yeatsian or Gaelic obsessions, Beckett's plays like *Waiting for Godot* (1952) had a stark, if nihilistic, simplicity. It has been suggested by one commentator that the tramps in this most famous of his plays represented the 'now rootless Anglo-Irish middle class', which since independence had been lost in a no-man's-land between the two cultures. Beckett was perhaps eccentric for a modern Irish playwright in his love for that most English of games, cricket!

A theme of Irish literature and drama in the 1950s and 1960s was a yearning for a sort of idyllic Gaelic simplicity, combined with an awareness of the contemporary bleakness of Irish rural life. The first strand was represented by Brendan Behan (1923–64), the Dublin-born playwright who spent some of his early years in prison for IRA activity. Behan initially wrote poems in Irish, had little success, and only obtained public recognition through his plays *The Quare Fellow* (1956) and *The Hostage* (1959). In the first play the theme of innocence is represented by the Blasket islander (the Blaskets are remote islands off the west coast) who queries the right of the state to impose capital punishment. In this search for an innocent Gaelic Ireland, Behan the playwright was the antithesis of Behan the public personality, who was a hard-drinking 'broth of a boy' who frequently appeared on British

Brendan Behan

TV chat shows in the early 1960s. It was the boozy, extrovert Behan who peered out from the pages of his racy autobiography, *Borstal Boy*. Behan died prematurely in his forties, without fulfilling the great potential many contemporaries saw in him.

As a city man Behan perhaps knew less of the realities of rural life than Patrick Kavanagh (1905–67), who made a savage attack on its bleakness and sloth in *The Great Hunger* (1942), a long poem about the boredom and misery of single male life on a County Monaghan farm. But if this theme was palatable to the Irish authorities, other more sexual ones, expressed in the novels of someone like Edna O'Brien (b. 1932), an example being *The Girl with Green Eyes*, were not. Her books remained banned in Ireland in the sixties and seventies, so underlining the tension in Irish life between the creative artist and what some regarded as an almost theocratic state. Yet even in this sometimes discouraging environment, the cultural achievement of a small island like Ireland remains impressive.

CHAPTER EIGHTEEN

Contemporary Ireland

Politics

The politics of contemporary Ireland was dominated by two men: Charles Haughey, the leader of Fianna Fáil until 1992, and Garret Fitzgerald, the leader of Fine Gael until 1987. Contemporaries at University College Dublin, the two had little in common otherwise. Haughey was the thrusting entrepreneur and wheeler-dealer, an owner of racehorses and offshore islands, with an almost miraculous capacity for political survival. Fitzgerald was a former Aer Lingus executive, economics lecturer and son of the External Affairs Minister in the Cosgrave government, with a keen interest in European affairs (he could reputedly speak French even faster than Frenchmen). His qualities of integrity and intellectual vigour acquired for him the nickname of 'Garret the Good', even if his enlightened attitudes on social policy and the North differed from those of some of his fellow countrymen and women. As the son of a Catholic Cumann na nGaedheal politician and a Protestant Unionist mother, Fitzgerald had an understanding of Unionist anxieties rare in Irish politicians.

Fianna Fáil had tended to be the natural party of government in the Republic since 1921, but doubts about Charles Haughey after the gun-running trial of 1970 and a series of other scandals meant that throughout the 1980s he failed to deliver the decisive overall majority his party expected. This happened in 1981, 1982 (twice), 1987 and 1989, forcing Haughey to endure challenges to his leadership on several occasions. But each time he survived, often by using a frankly undemocratic device which forced Fianna Fáil deputies to vote in

Garret Fitzgerald

open session rather than by secret ballot. Few dared to defy Haughey, a renowned machine politician, in front of other members of the parliamentary party. Ultimately a bugging scandal in 1992 brought Haughey down as Fianna Fáil leader and Taoiseach, although it was but the culmination of a series of corruption scandals, the most notorious of which involved Michael Smurfit, the chairman of Telecom *Éireann*.

By contrast, Fitzgerald was the widely-admired leader of Fine Gael who, following a period as Foreign Minister in the 1970s under Liam Cosgrave, was Taoiseach from June 1981 to March 1982, and then from December 1982 to 1987.

Social Policy

The 1980s were decisive years in crucial areas of social policy which were to haunt Irish governments into the 1990s. One was the issue of divorce, which had particular importance because Protestant Unionists regarded its prohibition in the Republic as evidence of the grip of the Catholic Church south of the Border. Garret Fitzgerald was particularly sensitive to Unionist opinion, but also thought he sensed a significant change in attitude over the question in the Republic itself. As Taoiseach Fitzgerald organised a referendum on the issue in 1986 which was bitterly divisive and produced a 63 per cent majority against change. Fitzgerald subsequently admitted that he had underestimated the anti-forces led by the Church.

The Church's position on divorce was clear-cut: marriage was indissoluble unless there were convincing grounds for an annulment. This was not really the issue, for constitutional change would really have benefited Protestants and others who could not legally obtain a divorce in the Republic, whereas such a change would not interfere with the Catholic Church's right to prohibit divorce for its flock. In his memoirs Garret Fitzgerald makes it clear that he thought he had obtained the agreement of the Catholic hierarchy to the principle that the Church would not interfere with the State's right to legislate in this area. Instead, he found the divorce amendment to the constitution being denounced from the pulpit, as well as Fianna Fáil abandoning its official neutrality on the issue. The former Taoiseach admits to finding 'the whole debate extremely depressing'.

Abortion was an equally thorny issue for Irish governments of both political persuasions. In the early 1980s the Pro-Life Amendment Campaign had become exercised about the possibility that, following a judgement by the US Supreme Court, the Irish Supreme Court might intervene to declare anti-abortion legislation unconstitutional. Such an event was most unlikely, but the Irish government, then under Charles Haughey, felt obliged to defer to such anxiety even though the Catholic hierarchy itself was dubious about the need for a constitutional amendment. A convoluted constitutional amendment was therefore produced which declared that:

> Nothing in the Constitution shall be invoked to invalidate or to deprive of force or effect a provision of the law on the grounds that it prohibits abortion.

A referendum was then held on the issue in 1983, and the amendment was passed by a two-to-one majority although only 54 per cent of the electorate turned out. It should be said that there was consensus between the main political leaders that abortion could be condoned only if the mother's life was in danger because of an ectopic pregnancy or a cancer of the womb.

This was not the end of abortion as a constitutional issue, however, for in 1992 a cause célèbre was created when the then Irish Attorney General took out an injunction to prevent a girl who had been raped from going to Britain for an abortion. This, despite the fact that it was widely known that Irish women had been having abortions under the British NHS for years. The Attorney's behaviour provoked an uproar in Ireland, and the new Taoiseach, Albert Reynolds (b. 1932), barely in office as successor to Haughey, referred the case to the Supreme Court. It then ruled that, because the girl's life would be put in danger if an abortion were not carried out (she had threatened suicide if she were forced to have the baby), the injunction was set aside.

A wider constitutional issue also arose in connection with the case in relation to Ireland's position in the European Community. For the original injunction, preventing the girl from going to Britain for an abortion, appeared to be a clear breach of the Treaty of Rome's provisions about free movement between member states. At that stage (before the Supreme Court ruling) the Republic's judiciary seemed to be ruling that it could legislate about the behaviour of Irish citizens inside *another* EC country. Clearly this was an unsatisfactory legal situation, which was not really clarified by the Supreme Court ruling which was based, not on a potential infringement of EC law, but on the grounds that the mother's health might be endangered.

A similar legal minefield existed in the Republic about the sale of contraceptives and the giving of advice about birth control. Ultimately legislation did permit the sale of contraceptives, against Church opposition, but then only to married couples. Once again there was bitter dispute between Irish feminists and traditional-minded Catholics over this issue.

The feminists did, however, win a considerable victory, together with trade union and Labour Party allies, when they secured the election of Mary Robinson to the Irish Presidency in 1990. Mrs Robinson had previously been a distinguished academic lawyer, and a Labour Party member of the Senate, to whom no one had really given much of a

Mary Robinson

chance against the Fianna Fáil nominee, Deputy Prime Minister Brian Lenihan. But Lenihan was fatally damaged by an indiscreet taped interview given to a postgraduate researcher, and this helped Mrs Robinson on to victory. Thereafter she placed particular emphasis on the often forgotten contribution made by women to Irish society, and despite the fact that the Presidency gave her no real political power, kept a high enough profile to ruffle Taoiseach Haughey's feathers from time to time!

The Continued Northern Emergency

At the beginning of the 1980s there was a notable turnaround in PIRA tactics with the revival of the old republican tactic of the hunger strike by PIRA internees in the notorious H Block at Longkesh in Belfast. Ostensibly the hunger strikes were about the right of PIRA prisoners to be treated as prisoners of war, but soon the campaign took on a momentum of its own and the deaths of several young hunger strikers had a powerful emotional appeal. The most celebrated victim was Bobby Sands, who was actually elected a Westminster MP while in his death throes.

If the hunger strikes were intended to move the British government they were a conspicuous failure, because Prime Minister Margaret Thatcher flatly refused to make any concessions or take any responsibility for the deaths. None of this meant in any case that PIRA had abandoned violence, with spectacular episodes in 1979 when eighteen British soldiers died at Warrenpoint, and Earl Mountbatten of Burma was assassinated inside the Republic while on holiday. In 1981 the campaign was switched again to the mainland of Britain, and in 1984 PIRA came perilously close to killing Margaret Thatcher herself by bombing the hotel in Brighton where she was staying during the Conservative Party Conference.

The Anglo-Irish Agreement

Whether her narrow escape from death influenced Mrs Thatcher's decision to look again at the Irish Question must remain a matter for speculation, but in 1985 she came to an important agreement with Taoiseach Fitzgerald. Known as the 'Anglo-Irish Agreement', it provided for joint Anglo-Irish consultations on matters like security, and the siting of a permanent number of Anglo-Irish civil servants in a secretariat outside Belfast. It was this last provision which outraged Unionists, who talked of interference by a foreign power in Ulster affairs. It is difficult for outsiders to understand the depth of Unionist feeling on this matter when the agreement did not materially affect the authority of the UK government in the North.

The Unionist campaign against the Agreement, which actually brought them into physical confrontation with the Royal Ulster Constabulary, proved in fact to be something of a damp squib. Nevertheless, it has to be conceded that some in the Republic, like Mary Robinson, felt obliged to oppose the Agreement because of the failure of the UK government to consult the Unionists adequately beforehand.

It tends to be forgotten that the Anglo-Irish Agreement contained an important codicil about the injection of US and EC cash into the North if conditions stabilised. But it is also true that the Agreement did not bring any noticeable lessening of PIRA or Loyalist paramilitary violence in the North. By 1992 Garret Fitzgerald, its instigator, was wondering whether the Agreement had not been a mistake, and hopes rested on a series of initiatives by the then Northern Ireland Secretary of State, Peter Brooke. These centred on the hope that dialogue between the Unionists and the SDLP would bring about a political solution in Ulster.

THE FOREIGN DIMENSION

Back in the early 1970s PIRA had relied on sympathisers in the USA for guns and money, but its behaviour alienated politicians like Ted Kennedy who had originally sympathised with republican aspirations. Instead PIRA looked to the Middle East for aid, and in 1972 secured considerable help from the maverick Libyan ruler, Colonel Gaddafi, who saw its operations as part of a war against British imperialism. This link was maintained in 1986 when, after the American bombing of Tripoli with British connivance, an enraged Gaddafi authorised huge arms shipments to PIRA. At least one of these shipments is known to have got through to Ireland, before the *Eksund* was intercepted off the French coast and its PIRA operatives arrested. The Provos obtained a large haul of modern weapons and deadly Semtex explosive in the original consignment.

PIRA is also known to have links with the Basque terrorists ETA, but it is by no means as free and easy with its foreign contacts as is sometimes suggested. The Italian Red Brigade, for example, and before it the German Baader-Meinhof group of urban terrorists, were regarded by the Provos, as Mallie and Bishop have pointed out in a recent study, as 'indulgent middle-class nihilists'.

REPUBLICAN FEUDS

The history of the Republican movement after 1972 was a bloody one not only because of operations in the North, but also because of internecine feuds inside the movement itself. These centred on the appearance in the mid-1970s of INLA (Irish National Liberation Army) and its political wing, the IRSP (Irish Republican Socialist Party), led by Bernadette McAliskey, the former Westminster MP Bernadette Devlin, who had attained some notoriety for slapping the then Home Secretary's face in the House of Commons. Both were really 'hive-offs' from the Official, now Marxist, IRA and its political wing, Sinn Féin.

There was a trail of bloody murder and assassinations of rival leaders for which both INLA and the Officials were responsible before a truce was called in 1977. Afterwards the Officials sponsored the Workers' Party in the North, which preached non-sectarian working-class solidarity.

All this Republican violence, it should be noted, was paralleled both inside and outside the Loyalist UDA (Ulster Defence Association) and its illegal paramilitary wing, the Ulster Volunteer Force.

Culture

Contemporary Ireland has a lively cultural life, and one which is perhaps more catholic than in the past. There has been notable success in the sphere of popular and folk music where names like Van Morrison, Bob Geldof, the Chieftains, Clannad and Sinead O'Connor have international renown. Why Ireland should not have produced a major classical composer like Sibelius or Mahler, as other small European nations have done, is something of a mystery, although latterly instrumentalists like James Galway have made considerable reputations for themselves.

Literary excellence has been a continued feature, with the North of Ireland well to the fore through the work of the poet Seamus Heaney (b. 1939) and the playwright Brian Friel (b. 1929). Friel's *Translations* (1981) is a fascinating reconstruction of the 'hedge school' era of the 1830s and, while raising the ongoing issue of the use and relevance of Gaelic, has also been seen by some as an allegory for modern Ireland's attempts to come to terms with its past without betraying it. The Field Day Company of Derry has been prominent in drawing attention to Friel's work, but paradoxically the more overtly political *The Freedom of the City* (1973) was less successful.

The theme of the Troubles was more successfully addressed by Heaney, notably in his fourth collection of poems, *North* (1975), with past and present Ulster starkly interwoven. He went on to win the Nobel Prize for Literature.

In another important sense, too, Ireland has come to terms with its cultural heritage. Censorship is now much less intrusive, and in the 1960s tax exemptions were granted on artists' incomes in a praiseworthy effort to attract artists and writers to the Republic.

A cultural élite known as the Aosdána was set up, which provided for government sponsorship of 150 creative people, and the new atmosphere was underlined in 1987 when Charles Haughey made Brian Friel a member of the Irish Senate.

Changing Ireland

The Irish Republic has changed a good deal from four or five decades ago, when the writer first visited it as a child. Then it was a land of thatched cottages, turf cutting, ponies and traps and horses and carts. In many ways it seemed remarkably insulated from the outside world. But by the 80s and 90s Ireland had become a society where cars, TVs and refrigerators were the norm, and one in which the Republic had joined the European Economic Community and provided Eurocrats of distinction. More importantly the 'terrible beauty' of which W.B. Yeats had written, and which had left the scar of partition in 1921, had receded considerably in significance. Politics were no longer dominated by the Border issue and a younger generation had grown up with other aspirations than Irish unity. Many would have argued that this was a healthy and long overdue development.

Perhaps too as the need for a 'blood sacrifice' disappeared, Irish culture could be valued for its own sake and not just as an adjunct to sectarian politics. It was no accident that long after de Valera's government-inspired language drive in the 1930s, there was a growth in the number of Gaelic speakers: a 1981 census showed that one in three claimed to be able to speak Irish, compared to one in four in 1961. There were now numerous Gaelic language prizes in the Republic and the music festival Stogadh – attended by 10,000 bi-lingual young people each year. Above all, Ireland was now a young country with the highest proportion of under 25s in Europe, even if in the 80s and 90s high unemployment had begun to draw off some of this vital lifeblood through emigration (the trend was starting to reverse by 2000).

What of the North by the opening decade of the twenty-first century? It would have been foolish to imagine that peace was easily attainable after 3,000 civilians, Crown forces and IRA men and women had died since 1971. Indeed, the very growth in the use

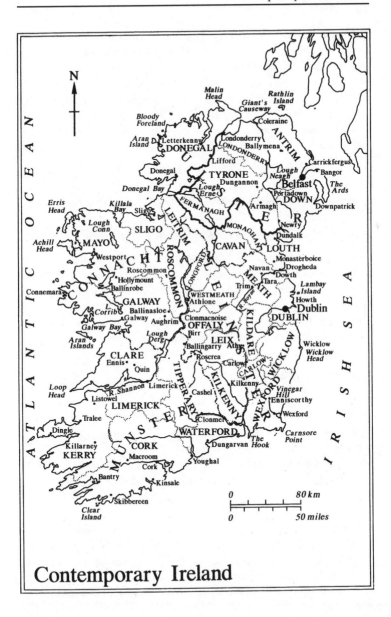

Contemporary Ireland

of Gaelic (at the time, forty per cent of under 25s in the Catholic community claimed to be speakers) in the Six Counties could be seen as a sign of cultural nationalism in opposition to Anglo–Saxon Protestant culture. Dozens of night classes in Belfast attested to the popularity of the original vernacular language of the island. And yet the paradox of Irish history remained. For it was the 1507 liturgy of John Knox, the stern sixteenth Protestant divine, which was the first book to be printed in Irish and its then owner Ian Adamson reminded fellow islanders that:

> Those who equate the Gaelic tongue with Catholicism and Nationalism forget the important role of Protestant unionists in its preservation - when Catholics were voluntarily abandoning it in favour of English, the language of the upwardly mobile.

Some would have queried the use of the word 'voluntarily', but the point was well made – Nationalist historians might have reported that the discriminatory penal laws and the Protestant ascendancy gave eighteenth century Catholics little option, but the force of the argument remained. Only when the terms Catholic and Gaelic, Protestant and English were no longer synonymous, would Ireland be at peace with itself.

An Illusion of Peace?

The most important event in Ireland in recent decades was the decision by the Provisional IRA to call a ceasefire in August 1994 (the loyalist paramilitaries followed suit shortly afterwards). This followed the Downing Street Declaration of 1993 when the British Prime Minister John Major and the Irish Taoiseach Albert Reynolds made it clear that Provisional Sinn Féin could be included in all-party talks if it renounced violence.

There were real hopes that this peace might prove to be a longlasting one, especially after President Clinton's highly successful visit to Northern Ireland in November 1995, which was well received by Catholics and Protestants alike. In an unprecedented move, a UK minister Michael Ancrum had also met Martin McGuiness of Provisional Sinn Féin, and Northern Ireland Secretary Patrick Mayhew had put forward a proposal to set up an international commission on the decommissioning of paramilitary arms. Ultimately this was to be led by US Senator George Mitchell, and the American role was highlighted when, for the first time, Ulster Unionist leaders visited the White House.

Such hopes were rudely shattered on 9 February 1996 when a huge IRA bomb devastated Canary Wharf in London's Docklands. The Provos declared themselves dissatisfied with the peace process, and Sinn Féin had already refused to accept the principle of surrender of arms prior to all-party talks. Another huge explosion devastated Manchester's Arndale Centre in June of the same year, and further Provo attacks were made on British army bases in Germany and Northern Ireland. By the autumn of 1996 there were real dangers that a loyalist paramilitary backlash would follow, putting the Province back to the seemingly hopeless situation of the 1970s. Only an agreement between the moderate Catholic SDLP and the official Unionist Party on the agenda for all-party talks offered any real hope for the future.

A new dimension was provided however with the victory of the British Labour Party in the general election of May 1997. The new Secretary of State Mo Mowlam provided a more hands-on sense of urgency, and was even able to persuade hardened loyalist paramilitaries of the need for change. At the same time in the background the SDLP leader John Hume had strengthened negotiating links with Sinn Féin.

THE GOOD FRIDAY AGREEMENT

The upshot of all this was that on Good Friday 1998 Prime Minister Tony Blair and Taoiseach Bertie Aherne were able to announce a new Anglo-Irish agreement. This provided for a new Northern Ireland Assembly and an executive on which all the Northern Ireland parties would be represented. David Trimble as leader of the majority Ulster Unionist party would become chief minister with Seamus Mallon of the SDLP as his deputy. However, the continuation of the Assembly and the devolved government in Belfast would also depend on IRA willingness to 'decommission' arms and the reform of the overwhelmingly Protestant Royal Ulster Constabulary (a key nationalist demand).

Both these elements in the agreement proved to be ongoing problems. Republicans and nationalists were disgusted when the Patten report on the police service was not fully implemented (a key demand was that the word 'royal' be deleted from the title). On the other side, Unionists did not believe IRA assurances that weapons would be neutralised, when there was no evidence that a single Provo weapon had been destroyed. They also pointed to the activities of republican splinter groups such as the Real and Continuity IRA responsible for an appalling outrage in Omagh, and bombings of Hammersmith Bridge and Ealing in London. Republicans could counter (with some reason) that indiscriminate attacks on Catholics by loyalist paramilitaries had continued after the Agreement.

By the summer of 2001 the situation had reached something of a stalemate with Trimble resigning because of lack of progress on weapons decommissioning. Further assurances by the IRA about decommissioning were not accepted on the Unionist side. Some even demanded a Unionist presence at the sealing of arms caches or their neutralisation, something the Provisionals would never accept. All parties (save the Paisleyite extreme) agreed about the desirability of retaining the devolved assembly. But the issues of decommissioning and policing remained unresolved, creating a dangerous vacuum. When in August 2001 the Unionists refused to accept an IRA offer to put its arms caches out of operation, the offer was abruptly withdrawn by the IRA Army Council, although it maintained its cease-fire. The only positive development was that the SDLP accepted the British government's police reforms when Sinn Féin had rejected them outright. Then suddenly in October the IRA announced that it would put some of its arms out of use. The process was verified by the head of the decommissioning body, General de Castellan, and the Ulster Unionists seem prepared to re-enter the Assembly.

This major breakthrough was undoubtedly accelerated by the terrible outrages in New York and Washington on 11 September, which made terrorism a global issue in a new and more horrific way. The US administration would now have little patience with Provo recalcitrance on the issue of decommissioning.

Northern Ireland now had an assembly in which power was to be shared between Unionists and Sinn Féin. By the time of the 2003 election the Democratic Unionist Party (DUP) headed by Ian Paisley had replaced the Ulster Unionist Party (UUP) as the majority Protestant party, while Sinn Féin got majority Catholic support.

Slowly but surely there was movement towards peace. On 28 July 2005 the Provisional IRA ordered an end to its thirty year campaign of bombing, in favour of a political settlement. There were still mutual suspicions, and only in October 2006 did the two sides agree to share political power, something that had been tried and failed in 1973.

In an extraordinary historical twist Ian Paisley (1926-2014) became First Minister of Northern Ireland, while his old foe Martin McGuinness of Sinn Féin (1950-2017) became his deputy. This would have been an unimaginable scenario in the 1970s and 1980s, and observers of the Northern Ireland scene were amazed when Paisley and McGuinness were so friendly that they were nicknamed 'the Chuckle Brothers.' When the two men were inaugurated in May 2007 the 2005 track *You Raised Me Up* by the pop group Westlife was played in the Chamber. The wheel had turned full circle.

Matters changed somewhat in 2008 when Paisley stepped down and was replaced by Peter Robinson, who adopted a far more abrasive attitude to McGuinness and Sinn Féin. Earlier in his career Robinson had taken part in an attack on a Garda station in the Republic. Nonetheless progress was shown in 2012 when Queen Elizabeth II visited both parts of Ireland, the first British monarch to visit the South since King George V.

Robinson was severely embarrassed in a bizarre scandal in 2010, when his wife Iris was involved in an affair with a teenage boy, for whom she had obtained a £50,000 loan. Robinson had to stand down briefly in favour of Arlene Foster as DUP leader. He was cleared of any inappropriate conduct over the loan. In 2015 after suffering a heart attack, Robinson stood down again and was permanently replaced as First Minister by Arlene Foster.

Her tenure of the post was also controversial. In particular over a scandal about heating boilers, whose sale benefitted DUP members and led to a Sinn Féin refusal to stay in the power sharing executive.

The situation was compounded by the DUP refusal to grant the Irish language the same rights as English.

Foster was in post during the acute UK crisis between 2016 and 2020 over leaving the European Union commonly known as Brexit. Her party favoured Brexit, but a majority in Northern Ireland voted against it in the 2016 referendum on the issue. Another strange situation arose when the Conservative Party – led by prime minister Teresa May – failed to achieve a working majority in 2017. She had to resort to an unsavoury alliance with the DUP in the House of Commons which involved what pundits called 'a bung' (what amounted to a billion pound bribe). This kept May in office, in alliance with Foster, although she only sat in Belfast and did not have a Westminster seat.

The Republic

Politics in the Irish Republic proceeded to the backcloth of such dramatic events in the North. The government of Albert Reynolds fell in 1994 after a scandal involving a paedophile priest and a high court judge, but it was replaced in the traditional Irish way by another coalition. This so-called 'rainbow coalition' was led by Fine Gael leader John Bruton and included the Democratic Left and the Labour Party (whose leader Dick Spring was to play a major role in the Northern Ireland peace process). The inclusion of the Democratic Left was especially important as it had evolved from the old official Sinn Féin and Workers' Party. Its leader Proinsias de Rossa (an old IRA man who had spent time in prison) was included in Bruton's Cabinet.

Bruton's major preoccupation was, not unnaturally, with the North and he made use of the Forum For Peace and Reconciliation set up by Reynolds in 1994, to meet Provisional Sinn Féin leaders like Gerry Adams. But a worrying rise in crime, especially drug-related crime, in the Republic was highlighted in June 1996 by the brutal shooting (at traffic-lights in Dublin) of the courageous investigative journalist Veronica Guerin. This gave all the appearance of a contract killing at the behest of drug barons, and caused great shock throughout Ireland, forcing the Bruton government to consider emergency measures to combat such a threat to everyday existence.

Nevertheless, Ireland played a significant role in Europe: its investment in information technology was praised by august journals like the British *Economist* magazine, and it proved to have a golden touch in popular culture with repeated wins in the European Song Contest, and the runaway success of the Irish dance phenomenon 'Riverdance'.

The End of the Armed Struggle

While the economy of the Republic boomed (causing it to be called the 'Celtic Tiger'), vital changes were taking place in the North. There were setbacks, as when the DUP polled more votes than the UUP in the 2003 Assembly elections, and the Provos were accused of stealing £26 million from the Northern Bank in Belfast in 2004. But in July 2005 the Provos ordered the end to their armed campaign, and the dumping of all arms. The Unionist response was sceptical, but in September PIRA followed up by announcing the decommissioning of all its armaments (a key Unionist demand). Paisley's DUP complained that no photographs were supplied, but the head of the decommissioning body General de Chastelain confirmed the veracity of the process. But the government of Northern Ireland remained a problem. The elected Assembly was suspended between October 2002 and April 2007 because of political feuding. Devolution was finally restored in 2007 with Ian Paisley as Chief Minister, as his Democratic Unionist Party was the largest assembly party.

Up to 2003 the Irish economy was a runaway success, but from 2007–8 it ran into a very dark period. Speculation in the property market, akin to that in the U.K., put Irish banks in a difficult position and the property market collapsed. From being the European country with the second largest GDP between 2001 and 2003, by 2008-9 Ireland had enormous debts and had to agree to punitive loans from the E.U. and the International Monetary Fund (IMF). It was humiliating for Ireland to await the sanction of other E.U. parliaments before it could obtain needed funds. During this grim period it was not unusual to drive right across Ireland from Dublin to Galway, and see whole estates of abandoned new houses.

The political fallout from this disaster was devastating for Fianna Fáil. Voters had not been impressed by the rather casual attitude of Taoiseach Bertie Ahern to the financial disaster. It was his successor Brian Cowen who was left to sort out this mess before the 2011 general election in the Republic. Unsurprisingly, he could not. Fianna Fáil was massacred at the polls, its vote share going down to just seventeen per cent. The leader of Fine Gael, Ireland's other main party, became Taoiseach.

Recovery and Brexit

After years of hard slog, during which the Irish people showed admirable self-discipline, the economy began to recover. The new Taoiseach Enda Kenny faced servicing a huge loan of 85 billion euros at six per cent interest. By 2016 the economy was starting to recover. At this point Ireland was hit by what was effectively a double whammy. Ireland had always been closely linked to the economy of its larger neighbour the United Kingdom, but in 2016 the U.K. electorate (albeit by the narrow margin of 52 to 48 per cent) voted to leave the E.U. Even though Northern Ireland had rejected Brexit by a margin of 62 to 48 per cent, the Republic was faced with the perilous prospect of what Brexit might do to the All-Ireland economy. Since 1973 both parts of Ireland had been inside the E.U., now the Republic had a new land border in prospect with the U.K., with Northern Ireland staying in the European Union Single Market.

The sheer political instability in the U.K. was alarming for Irish people. Endless knife edge votes in the House of Commons could not produce a decisive vote on what sort of Brexit the British wanted. And the appointment of the rabidly pro-Brexit Boris Johnson in 2019 as prime minister did not allay Irish fears. Kenny's successor Leo Varadkar (appointed in June 2017), received a poisoned chalice with the Brexit imbroglio. He was fortunate only in receiving absolutely solid support from the other twenty-six E.U. states, despite inept efforts by Johnson to divide them on the issue of the Northern Ireland border. His own political position was shaky, and in 2020 Fine Gael could only come third in a new election (Sinn Féin showed new strength by coming second). Varadkar stood down as Taoiseach, and was replaced by Fianna Fáil's Micháel Martin in a three party coalition (Varadkar became his deputy). The Irish government was unable to stop Johnson defecting from the E.U. in 2020, and the status of the Northern Ireland border was not settled until late 2020. Northern Ireland, whose people had voted against Brexit, remained in the E.U. Single Market and had a border with the Union. In an extraordinary turnabout, Johnson's government – supported by the D.U.P. – then claimed that the Northern Ireland Protocol based on the 1998 Good Friday Agreement was unsatisfactory, even though Johnson had signed an international treaty accepting the Protocol just months before. This behaviour did not please the incoming Democratic President in the United States Joe Biden, a man with strong Irish roots. His stance in favour of the Protocol was strongly supported by both political parties in Congress. This fact seemed to have escaped the British government which was apparently unaware of the strength of the Irish lobby in the U.S. Irish people were not surprised when, in 2019, the Northern Ireland Secretary showed amazing ignorance when she remarked on her surprise at the sectarian nature of Northern Ireland politics.

Ireland Now

The Ireland of the 2020s is markedly different from the one of the 70s and 80s, let alone of the forty-year-old De Valera dispensation. The much reduced influence of the Catholic Church is a striking feature of modern Ireland. Mass attendance is down drastically and many young Irish people are no longer churchgoers. The era when the entire population of Irish towns went to church on Sundays has passed, is gone forever. Instead, the Church's reputation has been undermined by horror stories about dead babies taken away from their mothers, and unmarried girls exploited in laundries run by nuns. Pope Francis II felt obliged to apologise for this behaviour, as well as sexual misbehaviour by prelates, when he visited Ireland in August 2018.

On the other side of the coin is the cultural virility of the new Ireland. Irish films have done well, from *Michael Collins* (1996) to *Intermission* (2009) and *Angela's Ashes* (1999). Ireland continues to produce many, many distinguished actors like Gabriel Byrne, Colm Meany (star of *The*

Damned United), Saoirse Ronan – an Irish American actress (*Brooklyn* and *Mary Queen of Scots*), Colin Farrell (with Brendan Gleeson the star of *In Bruges*) and James Nesbitt.

The twenty first century has also been a golden area for Irish rugby, a sport showing a uniquely Irish unity when other sports have not (even during the worst of the Troubles the North-South rugby team played on). The team that played in the 2000s won three Triple Crowns (2004-6) and the long overdue Second Grand Slam, when Ireland beat all of the other five nations came in 2009. The visit by England to Croke Park Dublin in 2007 was especially symbolic. In use at the time because the former Landsdowne Road stadium was being rebuilt, it was the historic centre for Gaelic football and hurling, and for many years players of the Gaelic games would have been banned if found playing 'English' games like rugby. Appropriately, Ireland won 43 – 13. Ireland had arguably the greatest rugby player in the world: Brian O'Driscoll, although retirement meant that O'Driscoll missed out on the first win over the famous New Zealand All Blacks in 2017. His protégé Jonathan Sexton masterminded the third Grand Slam win at Twickenham in 2018, but importantly the captain was Rory Best, a Northern Protestant.

New cultural influences have played upon Ireland after the E.U. expansion in 2004. You are as likely to find a Polish restaurant in Tralee in the far west as in the major cities. Ireland is now very much a European country in a way that its larger neighbour England increasingly is not.

Rulers and Monarchs

Famous Irish Kings

Domnall Uí Néill   *956–80*
Brian Boru   *975–1014*
Mael Sechnaill II (Uí Néill)   *980–1022*
Muirchetach O'Brien   *1086–1119*
Rory O'Connor   *1166–86*

English Monarchs

Plantagenet
Henry II   *1154–89*
Richard I   *1189–99*
John   *1199–1216*
Henry III   *1216–72*
Edward I   *1272–1307*
Edward II   *1307–27*
Edward III   *1327–77*
Richard II   *1377–99*
Henry IV   *1399–1413*
Henry V   *1413–22*
Henry VI   *1422–61*
Edward IV   *1461–83*
Edward V   *1483*
Richard III   *1483–85*
Tudor
Henry VII   *1485–1509*
Henry VIII   *1509–47*
Edward VI   *1547–53*
Mary   *1553–58*
Elizabeth I   *1558–1603*

Stuart
James I   *1603–25*
Charles I   *1625–49*
(Commonwealth   *1649–60*)
Charles II   *1660–85*
James II   *1685–88*
William III and Mary II   *1689–1702*
Anne   *1702–14*
Hanover
George I   *1714–27*
George II   *1727–60*
George III   *1760–1820*
George IV   *1820–30*
William IV   *1830–37*
Saxe-Coburg-Gotha
Victoria   *1837–1901*
Edward VII   *1901–10*
Windsor
George V   *1910–36*
Edward VIII   *1936*
George VI   *1936–52*
Elizabeth II   *1952–*

Prime Ministers of the Free State and Republic

Presidents of the Executive Council

W.T. COSGRAVE *1922-32*
E'AMON DEVALERA *1932-37*

Taoiseachs

ÉAMON DEVALERA   *1937-48*
JOHN COSTELLO   *1948-51*
ÉAMON DEVALERA   *1951-54*
JOHN COSTELLO   *1954-57*
ÉAMON DEVALERA   *1957-59*
SEAN LEMASS   *1959-66*
JACK LYNCH   *1966-73*
LIAM COSGRAVE   *1973-77*
JACK LYNCH   *1977-79*
CHARLES HAUGHEY   *1979-81*
GARRET FITZGERALD   *1981-82*
CHARLES HAUGHEY   *1982* (March–December)
GARRET FITZGERALD   *1982-87*
CHARLES HAUGHEY   *1987-92*
ALBERT REYNOLDS   *1992-94*
JOHN BRUTON   *1994-97*
BERTIE AHERNE   *1997–2008*
BRIAN COWAN   *2008–2011*
ENDA KENNY   *2011–17*
LEO VARADKAR   *2017–20*
MICHÁEL MARTIN   *2020–*

Presidents of the Free State

DOUGLAS HYDE *1938-45*
SEAN T. O'KELLY *1945-48*

Presidents of the Republic

SEAN T. O'KELLY *1948-59*
ÉAMON DE VALERA *1959-73*
CEARBHALL O DALAIGH *1973-76*
PATRICK HILLERY *1976-90*
MARY ROBINSON *1990-97*
MARY McALEESE *1997-*

Prime Ministers of Northern Ireland

SIR JAMES CRAIG (later Viscount Craigavon) 1921–40
J.M. ANDREWS 1940-43
SIR BASIL BROOKE (later Viscount Brookeborough) 1943-63
TERENCE O'NEILL 1963-69
JAMES CHICHESTER-CLARK 1969-71
BRIAN FAULKNER 1971-72

Secretaries of State for Northern Ireland

WILLIAM WHITELAW 1972-73
FRANCIS PYM 1973-74
MERLYN REES 1974-76
ROY MASON 1976-79
HUMPHREY ATKINS 1979-81
JAMES PRIOR 1981-84
DOUGLAS HURD 1984-85
TOM KING 1985-89
PETER BROOKE 1989-92
SIR PATRICK MAYHEW 1992-97
MO MOWLAM 1997-99

PETER MANDELSON 1999-2001
JOHN REID 2001-2
PAUL MURPHY 2002-5
PETER HAIN 2005-7
SHAUN WOODWARD 2007-2010
OWEN PATERSON 2010-12
TERESA VILLIERS 2012-16
JAMES BROKENSHIRE 2016-18
KAREN BRADLEY 2018-19
JULIAN SMITH 2019-20
BRANDON LEWIS 2020-

Chief Minister of the Northern Ireland Assembly

DAVID TRIMBLE 1998-2002
OFFICE VACANT 2003-7
IAN PAISLEY 2007-8
PETER ROBINSON 2008-16
ARLENE FOSTER 2016-21
JEFFREY DONALDSON 2021-

Chronology of Major Events

AD

77-84	Agricola, Roman governor of Britain, considers invasion of Ireland but desists
c. 130-80	Ptolemy's account of Ireland
367	Major attack on British Isles by Picts, Irish and Saxons
431	Palladius sent as bishop to the Irish by Pope Celestine
c. 432	St Patrick's return to Ireland
563	Foundation of Iona by St Columba
597	Death of Columba
697	Synod of Birr
c. 700	Eastern Eóganacht become dominant in Munster
704	Death of Adomnán, ninth abbot of Iona
721-42	Cathal mac Finguine, king of Munster
c. 725	Uí Briúin dynasty dominant in Connacht
734	Cenél Conaill excluded from Uí Néill overkingship
743	Clann Cholmáin takes over Uí Néill overkingship
793	Vikings raid Lindisfarne
795	Viking raids on Iona, Rathlin, Inishmurray and Inishbofin
c. 800	The Uí Néill dominate north Leinster
807	New monastic foundation at Kells
836	Raids by Vikings into Central Ireland
837	Viking fleets on the Liffey and the Boyne
840-1	Viking fleet winters on Lough Neagh
841-2	Viking fleet winters in Dublin
842	First report of a Viking-Irish alliance
845	Forennán, abbot of Armagh, captured by Vikings
846-62	Reign of Mael Sechnaill I of the Uí Néill
914	Viking fleet in Waterford
919	Death of Niál Glúndub of the Uí Néill in Battle of Dublin
956-80	Domnall Uí Néill overking of the Uí Néill
975-1014	Brian Boru reigns in Munster and claims high kingship of Tara

980–1022	Mael Sechnaill II overking of the Uí Néill
999	Boru defeats Leinstermen and Vikings at Glenn Ma'ma
1014	Battle of Clontarf; death of Boru
1086–1119	Muirchetach O'Brien king of Munster (1088–1119) and claimant to the high kingship of Tara
1101	Synod of Cashel; Cashel becomes metropolitan seat
1106–56	Turlough O'Connor king of Connacht and claimant to the high kingship
1111	Synod of Raith Bressail divides Ireland into territorial dioceses under Armagh and Dublin
1134	Cormac's chapel consecrated at Cashel
1142	Consecration of Mellifont, first Cistercian house in Ireland
1152	Synod of Mellifont
1166	Death of Murtough MacLoughlin, claimant to the high kingship; Dermot MacMurrough, king of Leinster, seeks aid from Henry II of England
1169	Norman invasion restores MacMurrough as king of Leinster
1170	Strongbow marries Aoife, daughter of MacMurrough
1171	Death of Dermot MacMurrough; Strongbow king of Leinster; Henry II visits Ireland
1172	Second Synod of Cashel; Henry returns to England
1175	Treaty of Windsor; Rory O'Connor, high king of Ireland, becomes Henry's vassal
1176	Death of Strongbow
1177	Prince John made lord of Ireland
1185	Prince John's first visit to Ireland
1210	King John visits Ireland
1235	Conquest of Connacht completed by Richard de Burgh
1260	Battle of Downpatrick; defeat and death of Brian O'Neill
1261	Battle of Callan; defeat and death of John FitzThomas
1263	Earldom of Ulster given to Walter de Burgh, lord of Connacht
1315	Edward Bruce invades Ireland
1316	Battle of Athenry; Connacht rebels defeated
1318	Battle of Dysert O'Dea; Richard de Clare defeated and killed by O'Brien
1333	William de Burgh, earl of Ulster, murdered; Crown control of Ulster and the Irish chieftains lost
1366	Statutes of Kilkenny
1394–5	Richard II's first expedition to Ireland
1398	Death of Roger Mortimer in battle against Leinster Irish
1399	Richard II's second visit to Ireland, followed by deposition in England
1414–47	Struggle between Talbot and Butlers for control of Crown

	administration in Ireland
1449–50	Richard of York sent to Ireland as Lord Lieutenant
1459–60	York's second visit
1467–8	Tiptoft, earl of Worcester, appointed Lord Deputy
1487	Earl of Kildare has pretender Lambert Simnel crowned Edward VI in Dublin cathedral
1494	Poyning's Law
1496	Kildare reappointed Lord Deputy
1513	Death of Gerald, eighth earl of Kildare
1534	Ninth earl of Kildare dies in Tower of London
1534–6	Revolt in Ireland results in arrest and execution of tenth earl of Kildare and uncles in London
1541–3	Meeting of English parliament which declares Henry VIII 'king of Ireland'
1557–8	Establishment of plantation in Laois/Offaly
1561–4	Warfare between Lord Deputy Sussex and Shane O'Neill
1567	Defeat and death of Shane O'Neill
1570	Queen Elizabeth excommunicated by the Pope
1579	Fitzgerald-Desmond revolt in Munster
1580	Revolt against Crown in Leinster
1582–3	Suppression of Munster-Leinster revolt
1595	Hugh O'Neill assumes title of 'the O'Neill' and revolts against English Crown
1598	O'Neill defeats government forces at the Yellow Ford
1599	Earl of Essex sent to suppress O'Neill's revolt
1600	Essex superseded by Mountjoy
1601	Spanish troops arrive in Kinsale and are supported by O'Neill forces; government victory ends revolt
1607	Flight of the earls of Tyrone and Tyrconnell
1609–10	Government implements plans for the plantation of Ulster
1616	Death of Hugh O'Neill in Rome
1633–41	Thomas, Viscount Wentworth (later earl of Strafford) serves as Crown governor in Ireland
1641	Catholic uprising in Ireland
1646	Owen Roe O'Neill defeats Scots at Benburb
1647	Dublin falls to English parliamentary forces
1649	Cromwell sacks Drogheda and Wexford
1650–2	Completion of Cromwellian conquest of Ireland
1654–5	Cromwellian plantation
1660	King Charles II states that he will preserve Cromwellian settlement
1662	Ormond appointed governor in Ireland
1681	Execution of Oliver Plunkett, archbishop of Armagh

1687	Appointment of Richard Talbot, earl of Tyrconnell, as Lord Deputy in Ireland; policy of making Catholic appointments
1688	Flight of James II from England
1689	Arrival of James in Ireland; siege of Derry
1690	William III lands in Ireland; Battle of the Boyne
1691	Williamite victory at Aughrim; Treaty of Limerick
1695	Penal legislation restricts Catholic rights in education, armsbearing and horse-owning
1699	Acts restricting Irish woollen exports
1704	Laws restricting Catholic rights in respect of landowning and public office
1713	Jonathan Swift becomes dean of St Patrick's cathedral in Dublin
1719	Toleration Act for Protestant Dissenters
1720	Act gives Westminster parliament the right to legislate for Ireland
1724	William Wood granted patent to mint copper Irish half pence
1726	Publication of Swift's *Gulliver's Travels*
1780	Colonial trade open to Irish goods
1782	Henry Grattan and Irish Volunteers call for legislative independence
1791	Foundation of the Society of United Irishmen
1795	Foundation of Orange Order
1796	Hoche's French army fails to land at Bantry Bay
1798	Irish revolt in Wexford crushed at Vinegar Hill; Humbert defeats British at Castlebar but is then defeated at Ballinamuck; arrest and death of Wolfe Tone
1800	Act of Union between Britain and Ireland
1803	Emmet's revolt
1823	Catholic Association founded
1828	Daniel O'Connell elected MP for Clare
1829	Catholic Emancipation Act allows Catholics to sit in Parliament
1831	Introduction of elementary schools in Ireland
1840	Foundation of O'Connell's Repeal Association
1843	Repeal meeting at Clontarf cancelled by government
1845	Beginning of the Potato Famine
1846	Peel repeals British Corn Laws
1848	Failure of 'Young Ireland' revolt at Ballingarry
1858	Irish Republican Brotherhood founded
1859	'Fenian Brotherhood' established in USA
1867	Failure of Fenian uprising in Ireland
1869	Gladstone disestablishes Church of Ireland
1870	Gladstone's first Land Act

1873	Home Rule League founded
1877	Charles Stewart Parnell elected president of Home Rule Confederation
1879	Irish National Land League founded
1880	Parnell elected chairman of Irish party at Westminster
1881	Parnell imprisoned in Kilmainham
1882	Murder of Lord Frederick Cavendish by 'the Invincibles' in Phoenix Park, Dublin
1884	Gaelic Association founded
1886	Catholic hierarchy endorses Home Rule campaign
1889	Captain O'Shea names Parnell as co-respondent in divorce case
1890	Parnell repudiated by Irish MPs
1891	Death of Parnell
1893	Gaelic League founded; Yeats' *The Celtic Twilight* published
1895	Oscar Wilde's *The Importance of Being Earnest* appears
1900	John Redmond elected chairman of Irish Parliamentary Party
1903	Yeats publishes *Cathleen ni Houlihan*
1907	First staging of J.M. Synge's *The Playboy of the Western World*
1908	Foundation of Sinn Féin
1912	Liberal government introduces third Home Rule Hill
1913	Formation of Ulster Volunteer Force, Irish Citizens' Army and Irish Volunteers; transport strike in Dublin
1914	Outbreak of First World War and shelving of Home Rule Bill
1916	Easter Rising in Dublin; Battle of the Somme
1918	Arrest of republican leaders following alleged 'German plot'; formation of Dáil Éireann, following Sinn Féin election victory
1920	Government of Ireland Act; 'Bloody Sunday' in Dublin
1921	Anglo-Irish Treaty; Unionist victory in Northern Ireland election
1922	Outbreak of Irish Civil War; death of Michael Collins; foundation of Irish Free State; publication of James Joyce's *Ulysses*
1923	Anti-Treaty IRA defeated; foundation of Cumann na nGaedheal
1925	Collapse of Anglo-Irish Boundary Commission
1926	DeValera founds Fianna Fáil; riots at opening of Sean O'Casey's *The Plough and the Stars*
1927	Assassination of Kevin O'Higgins; Fianna Fáil deputies enter the Dáil
1932	De Valera replaces Cosgrave as President of the Executive Council; riots by unemployed in Belfast

1933	Fine Gael founded
1937	Constitution of Éire replaces that of Irish Free State
1938	Treaty ports agreement between de Valera and Chamberlain
1939	IRA bombing campaign in Britain, and raid on Phoenix Park government magazine; Irish declaration of neutrality; death of W.B. Yeats
1941	German air-raids on Belfast and Dublin; death of James Joyce
1945	Churchill attacks de Valera in VE Day speech
1946	Northern Ireland insurance system aligned with Britain's
1947	Northern Ireland gets universal secondary school system
1948	Costello government declares Éire a republic; National Health Service introduced in Northern Ireland
1949	British declaration securing status of Northern Ireland
1951	Noel Browne resigns after hierarchy opposes Mother and Child scheme
1952	Beckett's *Waiting for Godot*
1954	Brendan Behan's *The Quare Fellow*
1955	Republic of Ireland joins the United Nations
1956–62	IRA 'Border Campaign' in the North
1958	Start of Republic's first Five Year Plan
1961	Republic fails to join EEC; military courts introduced to deal with IRA
1965	Meetings between Lemass and Northern Ireland premier O'Neill
1967	Northern Ireland Civil Rights Association founded
1968	Clash in Derry between CRA and RUC
1969	British troops sent to Northern Ireland
1970	'Provisional' IRA defects from traditional IRA; gun-running trial in Republic
1971	British government introduces internment without trial in Northern Ireland
1972	Stormont Parliament prorogued and direct Westminster rule imposed after episodes like 'Bloody Sunday' in Derry
1973	Sunningdale agreement sets up power-sharing executive in Northern Ireland; Republic becomes EEC member
1974	Workers' strike in Ulster destroys Sunningdale agreement; IRA bombings in Britain lead to passage of Prevention of Terrorism Act
1975	Seamus Heaney's *North* appears
1976	Assassination of British ambassador in Dublin
1979	Assassination of Earl Mountbatten in Co. Sligo; eighteen British soldiers killed at Warrenpoint, Co. Down
1980	Foundation of Aósdana in Republic; first performance of Brian Friel's *Translations*

1981	Death of Bobby Sands and other republican hunger-strikers in 'H Block', Longkesh
1983	Referendum approves ban on abortion in Republic
1984	IRA narrowly fails to assassinate British Prime Minister Thatcher in Brighton
1985	Garret Fitzgerald and Margaret Thatcher sign Anglo-Irish Agreement
1986	Referendum approves keeping ban on divorce in Republic
1987	Provisional IRA assassinate eleven civilians at Enniskillen Armstice Day service
1990	Mary Robinson becomes first woman President of Ireland
1992	Charles Haughey forced to resign as Taoiseach after series of scandals; abortion case forces further referendum in the Republic; Republic votes in favour of Maastricht Treaty; Secretary of State Patrick Mayhew bans UDA
1993	Downing Street Declaration
1994	John Bruton replaces Albert Reynolds as Taoiseach; PIRA ceasefire followed by loyalist ceasefire
1995	Talks between Sinn Féin and UK Government; International commission (Mitchell Commission) set up; visit by President Clinton to Northern Ireland and Republic; Referendum removes ban on divorce in Republic
1996	PIRA ceasefire ends with Canary Wharf bombing; elections to N. Ireland Constitutional Forum; Manchester bombing; murder of Irish journalist Veronica Guerin
1997	Labour electoral victory in Britain
1998	Good Friday Agreement
1999	Persistent difficulties about IRA decommissioning
2001	Government defeated in Republic European referendum; David Trimble resignation as Northern Ireland chief minister; IRA agrees to put some of its wea pons beyond use
2003	The Republic adopts the euro
2005	IRA agrees to ceasefire
2006	Power sharing agreed between D.U.P. and Sinn Fein
2007	Paisley becomes Northern Ireland Chief Minister; England rugby team play at Croke Park, Dublin
2008	Economic Crash hits Ireland. Peter Robinson Northern Ireland Chief Minister
2009	Ireland win Second Grand Slam
2011	Fianna Fáil routed in Republic general election
2012	Queen Elizabeth II becomes first British monarch to visit the South since George V
2013	Republic leaves EU bailout programme

2014	President O' Higgins becomes first Irish President to visit the UK; Enquiry into Mother and baby homes scandal announced in the Republic
2015	Arlene Foster succeeds Peter Robinson as Chief Minister
2016	UK votes for Brexit, but Northern Ireland does not
2017	Leo Varadkar becomes Taoiseach of the Republic
2018	Referendum removes ban on abortion in Republic; Ireland wins third Grand Slam
2020	Northern Ireland Protocol included in UK–EU agreement; Micháel Martin becomes Taoiseach

Further Reading

BERESFORD ELLIS, P. *A History of the Irish Working Class* (London, 1985)

BRADY, O'DOWD and WALKER (eds) *Ulster: An Illustrated History* (London, 1991)

BROWNE, N. *Against the Tide* (Dublin, 1986)

COOGAN, T.P. *The Troubles* (London, 1996)

CULLEN, L.M. *An Economic History of Ireland since 1660* (London, 1976)

DILLON, M. *25 years of Terror. The IRA's War against the British* (London, 1994)

FITZGERALD, G. *All in a Life. An Autobiography* (London and Dublin, 1991)

FOSTER, R. *Modern Ireland 1600–1972* (London, 1988)

FOSTER, R. (ed.) *The Oxford Illustrated History of Ireland* (Oxford and New York, 1989)

GALLAGHER, T. *Paddy's Lament* (Dublin, 1990)

HARKNESS, D.W., *Northern Ireland since 1920* (Dublin, 1983)

JENNER, M. *Ireland through the Ages* (London, 1991)

KEE, R. *Ireland. A History* (London, 1980)

KEE, R. *The Green Flag* (London, 1990) (3 vols: The Most Distressful County, The Bold Fenian Men, Ourselves Alone)

KEOGH, D. *Twentieth Century Ireland. Nation and State* (Dublin, 1994)

LYONS, F.S.L. *Charles Stewart Parnell* (London, 1977)

LYONS, F.S.L. *Ireland since the Famine* (London, 1990)

PAKENHAM, T. *The Year of Liberty* (London, 1969)

DE PAOR, L. *Divided Ulster* (London, 1970)

RICHTER, M. *Mediaeval Ireland. The Enduring Tradition* (London, 1988)

STEWART, A.T.Q. *The Narrow Ground. Aspects of Ulster* (London, 1977)

WOODHAM SMITH, C. *The Great Hunger* (London, 1954)

Cassette Collection

BRADY, C. (ed.) *The History of Ireland* (6 cassettes), Hidden Ireland Productions, Dollanstown, Kilcock, Co. Meath

Historical Gazetteer

Numbers in bold relate to the main text

THE REPUBLIC

Adare (Limerick) contains some medieval ruins plus the Gothic revival Adare Manor, begun in 1832. Access to Desmond Castle and the 15th-century Friary is unfortunately blocked by a golf course (although permission to visit is obtainable from the clubhouse), but there is an Augustinian priory site near the village bridge. The Trinitarian Abbey dates from 1230.

Aran Islands (Galway) The three islands, Inishmore, Inishmaan and Inisheer, lie some 30 miles out into Galway Bay. In 1912 a writer noted how their inhabitants believed them to be the nearest land to the mythical island of Hy Brasail, the paradise of the pagan Irish. They are Gaelic-speaking and in the 1890s, during the Gaelic revival, attracted a good deal of literary interest (especially from J.M. Synge). There are early ring forts, and church remains dating from the 8th century. The most memorable prehistoric site is Inishmore's ring fort, Dun Aengus. Inishmore was also the subject of Robert Flaherty's famous documentary *Man of Aran* (1934). A special feature of island life is the use of currachs, light woodframed boats about 20 feet long, formerly made of cowhide but now constructed with tarred canvas. **43**

Ardmore (Waterford) is genuinely medieval with its cathedral and round tower on the site of St Declan's original 6th-century monastic foundation. The cathedral dates from the 12th century and a particular point of interest is the ogham inscriptions. The graveyard contains St Declan's Oratory where he is supposed to be buried. **10**

Arklow (Wicklow) had an interesting history as a centre for fishing, shipbuilding and the export of copper ore, pyrites, and even gold which was mined further up the valley. Its Maritime Museum has a motley collection of local finds which claim a history for the town going back to Ptolemy's famous 2nd-century map. Arklow was a major arms-smuggling centre during the revolts of 1798. **122**

Athlone (Westmeath) An 11th-century castle has withstood numerous sieges, notably in the Williamite war of 1690–1. There is also a fine 17th-century Jacobean mansion and close by the ruins of a 17th-century

abbey. The museum has some interesting Stone, Bronze and Iron Age
artefacts. And an old gramophone is
available for fans who want to play
the records of the legendary Irish
tenor John McCormack (1884–1945)
who was born in the town. **112**

Aughnanure Castle (Galway) was
an O'Flaherty stronghold dating from
the 16th century, which has been
restored after previous depradations.

Aughrim (Westmeath) was the
site of the important battle in 1691; a
small museum has artefacts linked
with it. **112**

Ballintubber Abbey (Mayo) was
built by Cathal O'Connor, king of
Connacht, for Augustinian monks in
1216.

Ballymahon (Longford) There are
numerous associations in this region
with Oliver Goldsmith who was born
at Pallas near Abbeyshrule. **129**

Banna Strand (Kerry) Here Sir
Roger Casement was arrested in 1917
after landing from a German U-boat;
he had taken shelter in a ring fort
known locally as 'McKenna's Fort'.
169

Bannow (Waterford) was reputedly the site for the first Anglo-
Norman landing in 1169 (it was then
an island). Another version has it that
this tiny force under Robert Fitz-
Stephen landed on Baginbunn Head
on the Hook Head peninsula, the
name of which according to legend
came from the two Norman ships,
'Bagg' and 'Bunn'. **48, 50**

Bantry Bay (Cork) was the site of
the famous failed French invasion of
1796. In the town itself Bantry House
is an elegant example of the life-style

of the Anglo-Irish aristocracy with
many treasures, while the Bantry
Museum is a source of information
about local history. Appropriately
perhaps a statue of St Brendan the
Navigator looks out to sea. **121–2**

Birr (Offaly) is notable for its
castle, the home of the earls of Rosse.
The Victorian grounds are worth a
visit. Only the shell remains of the
famous Rosse telescope built by the
3rd earl in 1845 and until 1920 the
largest telescope in the world, with a
diameter of 72 inches. There is an
explanatory exhibition.

Blarney (Cork) is for ever associated with its stone and the (alleged)
loquaciousness of the Irish. The stone
is 4 foot by 1, on a limestone block 83
feet up. Visitors with a head for
heights are held by the shins over the
battlements so they can kiss the stone
and benefit from its magical powers in
giving what the Irish call 'the gift of
the gab'! According to the story, the
legend derives from one McCarthy, a
lord of Blarney, who dazzled Elizabeth I with his charm and kept his
rebellious head. The castle was actually built in 1446 by Dermot
McCarthy, king of Munster.

Blasket Islands (Kerry) are worth
a visit for an insight into an older rural
Irish way of life. They have inspired a
remarkable amount of Gaelic literature (e.g. *Twenty Years A-Growing* by
Maurice O'Sullivan).

Boyle (Roscommon) has a Cistercian monastery dating from 1220
which was founded by monks from
Mellifont. **45**

Bruree (Limerick) is the child-
hood home of Éamon de Valera. The

cottage where he was brought up now has a small memorial consisting of family possessions, and the village museum also contains a lot of de Valera memorabilia. **174, 218**

Bunratty Castle (Clare) is on what was formerly an island in the River Shannon. It is the largest of the Irish tower houses and has an international reputation for the way it recreates medieval Irish banquets for tourists. Despite this, it does have convincing historical antecedents as the home of the MacNamaras, who built the existing castle on what was originally a Norman site. There is also a reconstruction of a 19th-century village in the castle grounds.

Cahir (Tipperary) has a castle which dates from the 13th century, although most of the surviving stonework is of a later vintage. The Butlers, earls of Ormond, made it one of the strongest fortifications in the whole of Ireland. The keep is distinctly medieval, with a portcullis, and a prison which can only be reached through a trap-door. **81, 104**

Carlow (Carlow) has an interesting history and was for centuries an Anglo-Norman stronghold; hundreds of rebels were massacred there in 1798. But few historic buildings now remain other than the remnants of the Norman castle, and a courthouse with a portico modelled on the Parthenon in Athens. The museum, which is in the Town Hall, has items on local history. **59, 122**

Carrick-on-Shannon (Leitrim) has the Costello Chapel but this only dates back to 1877, and for those interested in real history Co. Leitrim is, alas, a disappointment. A Georgian house in the town contains one of only two existing 150-year-old Irish harps.

Cashel (Tipperary) The impressive Rock of Cashel, a limestone outcrop allegedly formed when the Devil dropped a rock after the shock of seeing St Patrick below, provides the site for a formidable collection of medieval buildings which are generally in very good condition. Most memorable is Cormac's Chapel, dating from the 12th century, the most beautiful of Ireland's Romanesque churches; Cormac himself is said to be buried here. The chapel shows evidence of continental influence with its twin square towers, an unusual feature in Irish churches of the period. The Vicar's Hall nearby contains the original Cross of St Patrick which used to stand outside, and the cathedral is a 13th-century foundation without aisles, in the contemporary Irish fashion. Last of all is the Round Tower, actually the oldest building on the Rock, which may date from as far back as the 10th century. **44, 46**

Castlebar (Mayo) has little in the way of historic interest despite being the site of the French defeat in 1798 after Humbert's invasion. **127**

Cavan (Cavan) is most notable as the burial place of the most famous Irish soldier of the wars of the Confederacy, Owen Roe O'Neill. Otherwise only a round tower marks the site of the former abbey, which was the focal point early in the town's history. **3**

Clonmacnoise (Offaly) Ireland's most famous Celtic monastery, is in a fairly remote part of western Offaly near Shannonbridge. Founded by St Keran in the 6th century, it could originally only be reached by boat. Despite being sacked by the English in 1552, much of great historic interest remains. There are 8 churches, a cathedral, two round towers, high crosses and a 13th-century ring fort. Clonmacnoise was also much more than just a monastic settlement, being a royal city and the burial place of the kings of Connacht and Tara (Rory O'Connor was buried here in 1198). The cathedral dates from 904, the South Cross from the 9th century, and O'Rourke's tower, a round tower built just after the cathedral, is also 10th-century. **11, 28, 60**

Clonmel (Tipperary) is the most impressive town in Tipperary although its historic buildings only date from the 18th and 19th centuries. These include the 19th-century Catholic St Mary's Church, the Old St Mary's Church of Ireland Church, and the Palatinate Court House from the 18th century.

Coblooney (Sligo) has the Teeling Monument which commemorates one of the most colourful episodes in the revolt of 1798. Teeling was an Irish-born officer with Humbert's French army who single-handedly charged a British gun in the nearby skirmish at Carricknagat. But being Irish, unlike Humbert and his French officers, Teeling was hanged as a traitor. **127**

Cork (Cork) is the Republic's second city; it takes its name from one of the islands in the River Lee (Cor-

caigh, meaning 'marshy place') on which St Finbarr founded a monastery in 600. Raiding Vikings took such a liking to the place that they settled there in 917, and the city was then taken by the Normans in 1172. Parts of the city's medieval structure can be discovered in the lanes in the city centre, but the most striking public buildings are from the 18th and 19th centuries. Among them is the 19th-century Butter Exchange and the 18th-century Church of St Anne's Shandon. The work of the famous British architect Pugin is on view in the Church of St Peter and Paul on Friar Matthew Quay, and there are several other interesting Gothic-style churches. The Cork Public Museum is perhaps a bit of a disappointment for visitors since it concentrates on the history of the Republican movement. **52, 59**

Croagh Patrick (Mayo) is where St Patrick is supposed to have spent Lent fasting in 441, and the mountain is a place of pilgrimage today for Catholics who climb it in bare feet. **11**

Dingle Peninsula (Kerry) The Gallarus Oratory is a fascinating early Christian remnant which dates from between the 9th and 12th centuries, and a slightly older church can be seen near by at Kilmalkedar. **16**

Donegal (Donegal) has little of historic interest to see other than what remains of its castle, which dates from the early 17th century. It was built by Sir Basil Brooke whose family provided one of the prime ministers of Northern Ireland. On the left bank of the River Eske the ruins of Donegal Friary can be seen. **196**

Drogheda (Louth) On the River Boyne, the town began with the Vikings, who arrived in 911 and founded separate settlements on each bank. The ford linking them gave the town its name Droichead Atha, the Bridge of the Ford. By the 14th century the walled town was one of the most important in the country. Most of it is now 18th-century although sections of medieval wall remain. The Millmount with its Martello tower gives an excellent view of the town, and the Millmount Museum is one of the finest urban museums in Ireland. There are fascinating historic examples of the work of brogue-makers, carpenters and weavers. St Lawrence Gate is perfectly preserved, with two round towers and a portcullis entry and retaining wall. It is the most important surviving part of the old town.

On the top of the hill opposite Millmount is the 14th-century Magdalene tower, the surviving remnant of a large Dominican friary founded in 1224 by the archbishop of Armagh (and in which Richard II received the submission of the Ulster chiefs in 1394). In the centre of the town is the Catholic Church of St Peter on West Street which contains a gruesome relic, the head of Oliver Plunkett, archbishop of Armagh, who was executed in London. The head is on view in a tabernacle-shaped box in the left-hand aisle, so making the church a place of modern pilgrimage. The church itself dates only from 1791; Drogheda was, of course, the site of the Cromwellian massacre in 1649. **106–7**

Dublin

College Green stresses the consistency of Dublin topography since Viking days when they had their Haugen and Thenginote (burial ground and central meeting place) there. Formerly known as Hoggen Green, it was the administrative centre of Ireland until the Act of Union, **30, 32**

The Bank of Ireland, facing Trinity College, is central to the Anglo-Irish ascendancy. Begun in 1729 as the putative Irish parliament building: the Grattan parliament met there in 1782. It was sold to the Bank of Ireland after 1800 for £400,000. Care is taken to keep it in period today, with ushers in 18th-century costume showing visitors around. **120**

Trinity College, founded in 1591 by Elizabeth I, had a major role in developing Anglo-Irish tradition. Statues outside of Burke and Goldsmith, two of its most famous graduates. Strongly associated with Protestant tradition and until 1966 Catholics had to get dispensation to study there. Best known recently as the site for *Educating Rita*, the successful English film. Stern grey college buildings are arranged around quadrangles in Oxbridge manner. Chapel and Theatre were both designed by Sir William Chambers, a Scots architect who never actually visited Ireland; beyond the Chapel is the Dining Hall, designed by the German Richard Cassels in 1743. The bell tower in the middle of the square was erected in 1853 and may have marked the site of a priory which predated the university. A 'startling element' of colour was introduced by the red brick of Rubrics, student accommodation dating from 1712 and one of Trinity's oldest surviving buildings.

Trinity College Library contains the famous 8th-century Book of Kells and other priceless early Irish manuscripts. Some doubt whether Kells was copied in Ireland at all; 680 pages long, rebound in 1950s into 4 volumes, it has illuminated pages with magnificent designs facing pages of text. The Book of Durrow is equally interesting, the first of the great Irish illustrated manuscripts, dating from between 650 and 680. TCL also contains two early Irish harps, one of which is known as Brian Boru's harp although it almost certainly dates from a much later period. **29, 103**

Kildare Street nearby has several interesting buildings. Notably *Leinster House*, an elegant Georgian building designed by Cassels in 1745 as a town house for the Duke of Leinster, which now houses the Dáil Éireann and the Seanad Éireann when in session. To its left and right are the entrances to the *National Library* and the *National Museum*. The former has a good collection of first editions of works by Irish writers like Swift, Goldsmith, Yeats, Shaw and Joyce, while the Museum has priceless treasures like the Ardagh Chalice and the Tara Brooch, both dating from the 8th century. Around the corner in Merrion Row in the

National Museum Annexe are the Viking artefacts found during the digs in Wood Quay and other Dublin sites.

St Stephen's Green has pleasant gardens with an ornamental pond, and No. 86 on the south side was the former site of the Catholic University College Dublin (now moved into the suburbs). Founded in 1853, it had Padraig Pearse, de Valera and James Joyce among its graduates.

Merrion Square, the heart of Georgian Dublin, was the home of distinguished Irishmen like O'Connell, Wilde and Yeats. Now a selling place for Dublin's artists, on its south side is St Stephen's Church dating from 1825 with its Greek-style columns.

In Merrion Street and also next to Leinster House is the *National Gallery of Ireland*, with over 2,000 paintings on show. Though small by the standards of other European galleries, the collection does include some Rembrandts and French impressionists, together with Irish artists like Edwin Hayes. One of the paintings on display is the massive 'Marriage of Strongbow and Eva' by the 19th-century Irish artist Daniel Maclease. The National Gallery collection does not cover the modern period, and for this you will need to visit the Municipal Art Gallery in Parnell Square.

Dublin Castle is to be found to the west of the Bank of Ireland and Dublin City Hall on Dame Street. Inside there is a mishmash of architectural styles with a gothic fantasy-style church contrasting with the red brick of the castle itself. The term 'castle' is somewhat misleading because, although the original castle dates from 1207, only the Round Tower survives from that period (out of four original Anglo-Norman stone towers); otherwise it is 18th-century. It was, of course, the symbol of the British presence in Ireland for centuries, and in 1990 adopted a new role when, for a while, it was the home of the European parliament. **61, 169**

Moving down towards the River Liffey, visitors can find the *Wood Quay* excavation site where large amounts of Viking and Norman remains have been found. **42–3**

Close by is *St Patrick's Cathedral* (the national centre for the Church of Ireland) which is full of mementoes of Jonathan Swift. These include table and chairs used when writing, and a death mask. Memorials to him and Esther Johnson, whom he immortalised as 'Stella' in his writings, can be seen near the porch. The nearby 'Swift's Hospital' was one of the first psychiatric hospitals in the world. There is also a monument to the Boyle family, whose most famous son was the scientist Robert Boyle. **61, 113**

Christchurch Cathedral is at the other end of Patrick Street and is another Church of Ireland building. It was the site of Dublin's first wooden cathedral, founded by the Viking Sitric Silkenbeard (the first Christian Norse king of Dublin) in 1038. This was demolished by Strongbow who built a stone cathedral in 1172 and is himself buried there. **37, 49–53**

On the north side of the Liffey is *O'Connell Street*, reputedly one of the widest (and most expensive) in Europe. Little of real historic interest has been preserved, but one historic site is the General Post Office at the corner of O'Connell Street and Henry Street. Here it was that Padraig Pearse raised the republican flag on Easter Monday 1916, although the original building was completely destroyed in the fighting and had to be restored before being reopened in 1929. A statue of Parnell at the top of O'Connell Street has had a better fate than the one of Nelson which used to stand opposite the Post Office and was blown up by the IRA in 1966. **169–72**

Phoenix Park is on the west side of Dublin. Its name is a corruption of the Gaelic *fionn uisce* (clear water) and the park began as part of church lands, confiscated after the Reformation and made into a royal deer park. It contains the Viceroy's Lodge, which was build in 1817 as a tribute to the Duke of Wellington who was born in Dublin; it is now the official residence of the President of Ireland. The Park also contains Dublin's zoo and the old duelling grounds or so-called 'Fifteen Acres' (now used for Gaelic football and other sports). There is a flea market there every Sunday as well. **158, 161, 208**

Another notable landmark is the

Custom House on Custom House Quay, which is to the west of O'Connell Street on the banks of the Liffey. It is a long elegant building with a portico and dome which was burnt down during confused fighting between the IRA and the British in 1921 before restoration. Completed originally in 1791 by the famous Georgian architect James Gandon, it was apparently built because a large stone in the river-bed further up the Liffey prevented ships from reaching the old customs house. **180–1**

Durrow (Laois) Castle Durrow (1716), the first Palladian house built in the area, is now a convent.

Dysert O'Dea (Clare) is the site of the important battle between the de Burghs and O'Briens in 1318 which prevented Anglo-Norman encroachment into Co. Clare. It is also on the site of St Tola's 8th-century monastic foundation, and the remains of a medieval church and round tower can be seen. The O'Dea castle is now a museum and archaeology centre. **66**

Ennis (Clare) The Friary in the town centre was founded in 1242 by the O'Brien kings of Thomond. The Creagh tomb incorporates the 15th-century MacMahon tomb. Ennis played an important role in the history of modern Irish nationalism and a statue of Daniel O'Connell, plus a square named after 'the Liberator', commemorate the famous Clare by-election of 1828. De Valera was TD (member of parliament) for Ennis 1917–59, and his links with the town

are marked in the de Valera Library Museum. **65–6, 174**

Faughart (Louth) north of Dundalk, was reputedly the birthplace of St Brigid. You can see her holy well in the local churchyard together with the grave of Edward Bruce, who was killed after the Battle of Faughart in 1318. Legend has it that he was beheaded on a nearby stone. **66**

Ferns (Wexford) is of historic interest, with the remains of a 6th-century abbey in St Eden's churchyard, and (more strikingly) what is left of a 13th-century castle. **13**

Galway (Galway) was granted a royal charter by Richard III in 1484 as a reward for its loyalty to the Crown in the face of attacks by the fearsome O'Flaherties. This loyalty forced it to suffer a lengthy Cromwellian siege in 1652. Amongst buildings of interest are the Collegiate Church of St Nicholas, the largest medieval church in Ireland, dating from 1320, and the Cathedral of Our Lady Assumed into Heaven and St Nicholas. Built only 30 years ago, the cathedral has an architectural style which evokes mixed reactions! Otherwise there is the building housing University College, Galway, dating from 1849, and Lynch's Castle, reputedly the finest medieval house in Ireland (the Lynches were the most important family in Galway for three centuries). **137–8**

Glencolumbcille (Donegal) the Glen of Columbcille or Columba. This verdant glen has the ruins of St Columbcille's Church with the 'resting stone' where the saint is supposed to have rested and prayed after his labours. **14–15**

Glendalough (Wicklow) meaning the valley of two rivers, is notable for its monastery. Founded by St Kevin in the 6th century, it became famous throughout Europe as a centre for Celtic learning (despite being sacked twice by the Vikings). There is also a 9th-century cathedral and a 12th-century 'Priest's House', so called because Catholic priests were buried there during the years of penal legislation. Most famous of all is St Kevin's Church, which may date from the 6th century although it has been rebuilt with an 11th-century round-tower belfry. **37**

Inishowen Peninsula (Donegal) is notable for the early fort, Grianan of Aileach, an early, though much restored, drystone circular fort, and several early Christian crosses (Cloncha, Mura, Carrowmore and Cooley).

Kells (Meath) is another historic site, with an 11th-century oratory, a round tower and a square bell tower. Its most famous artefact, the Book of Kells, is of course in Trinity College Library. The monastery was founded by St Columba in the 6th century, and the round tower dates from before 1076, the year when Murchadh Mac Flainn, a claimant to the high kingship, was murdered inside it. **29**

Kildare (Kildare) Best known now for its racing (it is the home of the Curragh racecourse) but still with points of historic interest. The town is dominated by a huge 13th-century Church of Ireland cathedral, named after St Brigid who founded a religious community in the town in 490. It was reconstructed in a medieval style in 1875. Its 12th-century round tower is notable for its unusual doorway and odd 19th-century battlements. **83–5**

Kilkenny (Kilkenny) is arguably Ireland's finest medieval city. It is dominated by the castle, on the site of a fort built by Strongbow, and parts of the original medieval castle remain. The Confederate Parliament ruled Ireland from here 1642–8, but the 19th-century restoration gives the castle a Victorian look today. The picture gallery inside is lavishly decorated, and the Butler Gallery houses an exhibition of modern art. St Canice's Cathedral, dating from the 13th century, is of outstanding interest, with a fine selection of monuments from the 16th century, notably the likenesses of the Butler family (the earls of Ormond). There are several other medieval churches, including the Black Abbey (dating from 1225), St John's Priory and St Francis' Abbey. **71–3, 81**

Killarney (Kerry) is overcommercialised and has little of historic interest apart from St Mary's Cathedral, which has been described as 'Pugin's masterpiece in Ireland'. There is no evidence of a settlement here before the 17th century. **4**

Killybegs (Donegal) is best known for its fishing but does have the MacSweeney Tombstone which is decorated with Celtic carvings. Three galleasses from the doomed Spanish Armada were beached outside the town in 1588.

Killykeen Forest Park (Cavan) has a 13th-century circular tower called Clough Oughter.

Kinsale (Cork) was where the Spanish and O'Neill combined force was defeated by the English in 1601. The town then became an important British naval base 1700–1900, and its 16th-century tower house was used to hold French prisoners during the Napoleonic Wars. The chief claim to fame of the town's museum is that it was where the inquest was held in 1915 into the sinking of the *Lusitania*; otherwise there are items of local interest like royal charters and maps. Just outside the town is the Charles-fort which served as a fort 1677–1922. **92**

Limerick (Limerick) has a paucity of historic relics despite its status as Ireland's third city. The Treaty of 1691 which ended the Williamite wars is commemorated by a plinth on which it was reportedly signed on Thomond Bridge. In the past it was used as a stepping stone for mounting horses. There is also St Mary's Cathedral, which dates from the 12th century, although only a small portion of the surviving building is original. By contrast, King John's Castle has kept much of its original early 13th-century stonework. **52, 81, 112**

Lismore (Waterford) has been described as 'a gem of ecclesiastical history'. A monastic foundation dated from the 7th century, although the former medieval cathedral site is now occupied by St Carthage's Church of Ireland Cathedral (he was the saint who founded the monastic settlement), dating from 1633. The castle is a 19th-century copy of a Tudor castle, which does not do justice to the long connection between it and the Anglo-Irish baronage. A medieval fort stood on the original site, which is now surrounded by leafy parkland.

Lough Mask (Mayo) Loughmask House, on its shores, gave the word 'boycott' to the English language when it was the home of Captain Boycott whose ill-treatment of his tenants caused Parnell to advise them to leave 'him severely alone' (i.e. boycott him).

Maynooth (Kildare) is the site of the 19th-century Catholic seminary St Patrick's, but also has the ruins of Maynooth Castle, one of the two strongholds of the Fitzgeralds. Carlton House, built by Richard Castle and lying at the other end of the main street, has been described as 'a Georgian gem'. Castletown House, designed by the Italian Galilei in 1722 for the then speaker of the Irish parliament, is also worth a visit; the long gallery is especially impressive.

Mellifont (Louth) was the first Cistercian foundation in Ireland and the inspiration of St Malachy. Although suppressed, like other Irish monasteries, by Henry VIII in 1539, the surviving stonework gives some idea of the abbey's magnificence during the four centuries when it was one of Ireland's great monastic foundations, and the meeting-place for the Synod of Mellifont. Thereafter it fell into a sad decline, which included use as a pigsty in the 19th century. A ground plan makes it easy for visitors to identify the monastery's original shape from the ruins. **45, 46**

Mohill (Leitrim) is of particular importance to American visitors because one of its sons, Turlough O'Carolan, wrote 'The Star Spangled Banner'.

Monaghan (Monaghan) is a product of the Jacobean plantation and there is a 17th-century Scots settlers cross in Old Cross Square. Church Square has a Regency Gothic church and some other 19th-century buildings, while Market Street has the Market House built at the end of the 18th century. The Monaghan County Museum has a wealth of archaeological finds, notably the early 15th-century Cross of Clogher. The county has plenty of Bronze Age sites, and there are megalithic sites at Lisnadarragh, Tiravera and Tullyrain. **99–100**

Monasterboice (Louth) to the north of Mellifont, was a much smaller foundation, but among the ruins are two of the finest 10th-century high crosses in Ireland. The site also contains the finest example in the country of a round tower, which is 110 feet high. The ruins of two 13th-century churches which antedate the monastic settlement can also be seen. **45**

Mostrim or Edgeworthstown (Longford) was the home town of Maria Edgeworth, the author of *Castle Rackrent*, and her family vault can be seen in the graveyard of St John's Church which also contains the grave of Oscar Wilde's sister Isola. **130**

Muckross Abbey (Kerry) was a 15th-century foundation paid for by McCarthy Mor on behalf of the

Franciscans. The ruins are said to be among the best preserved in Ireland (the abbey was suppressed during the Henrican Reformation).

Mullingar (Westmeath) has a couple of good museums, the Market Hall and the Ecclesiastical Museum (which has items belonging to St Oliver Plunkett). The cathedral, a neoclassical structure, is not a particularly memorable one. **109**

Newgrange (Meath) Near to the site of the Battle of the Boyne at Oldgrange is the area known as Brugh Na Boinne, which is made up of some 40 prehistoric remnants between Tullyallen and Shane. The three most important are Dowth, Knowth and Newgrange, which consist of passagegraves, stone burial chambers with high round mounds raised above them; they are reputedly several centuries older than the Egyptian pyramids. **4**

Oldgrange (Meath) It may come as a surprise to visitors that the site of the Battle of the Boyne in 1690, with all its northern associations, is so far south. It actually took place at Oldgrange, 5 miles south of Drogheda. A path leads to a viewpoint where William III's troops were stationed. **111–12**

Portarlington (Laois) Although built by the Earl of Galway in 1667, it was settled by French Huguenot refugees. The local church, St Michael's, is still known as 'the French church' and some of its inscriptions are in French.

Portlaoise (Laois) founded by the O'Mores in 1547, was soon involved in the first English plantations and renamed Maryborough (after Mary Tudor) in 1556. Little of note in the town but outside it is the Rock of Dunamase, used by the O'Mores as a fort. It has a 12th-century ruined castle, which was included by the king of Leinster, Dermot MacMurrough, in his daughter Aoife's dowry when she married Strongbow. **51**

Roscommon (Roscommon) has two medieval ruins. The castle dates from 1269, was then burnt down by the Irish and rebuilt in 1280, and the Dominican priory is also 13th-century.

Ross Castle (Kerry) was the last place in Munster to surrender to the forces of Oliver Cromwell in 1652. **107**

Slane (Meath) on the Boyne, is of considerable historic interest, with a Transport Museum and a castle which is the seat of the Conyngham family (a former marchioness was reputedly the mistress of George IV). The Hill of Slane is said to be where St Patrick lit his paschal fire in 433 to announce the arrival of Christianity in Ireland. On the top of the hill is a ruined friary church which dates from 1512. St Erc, who was bishop of Slane and St Patrick's greatest friend, is reputedly buried in the churchyard. **10–12**

Sligo (Sligo) has a Dominican abbey with sizeable ruins, although its effective religious life ended in 1641. The Municipal Art Gallery has some of Jack B. Yeats' paintings, and his brother W.B. Yeats is commemorated in the Yeats Memorial Museum. Nearby Lissadell House is a 19th-century country house best known for its association with the poet. It is the home of the Gore-Booth family, the best known of whom was Constance Gore-Booth Markiewicz. **58**

Strade (Mayo) has a Michael Davitt Museum containing exhibits linked with this seminal figure in the history of Irish nationalism. **149**

Tara (Meath) is the hill on which the high kings of Ireland were crowned, and on its slopes today is a medieval banquet hall. The Rath of the Synods marks the series of mounds on which saints like Patrick and Brendan are supposed to have held church synods. **6**

Thomastown (Kilkenny) contains the ruins, which are not extensive, of its former medieval walls, a castle and a 13th-century church.

Tipperary (Tipperary) only has a museum with relics of the Irish Civil War of the 1920s. Much of this is military, apart from a violin belonging to Joseph Plunkett, the poet who was executed in the Easter 1916 Rising. **109**

Tory Island (Donegal) has some relics from Columba's time, notably the Tau Cross, supposedly of Egyptian origin and one of only two such crosses left in the country. There are also some round-tower remains.

Tralee (Kerry) is a historical disappointment although a plaque on the local sports ground commemorates the heroic feats of the author's grandfather on the football field. There are some remains of a Desmond castle on the outskirts.

Trim (Meath) has the largest Anglo-Norman castle in Ireland, although the existing impressive

13th-century structure is not the original, which was built by Hugh de Lacy in 1172 and destroyed by the Connacht Irish in 1173. **52**

Tullamore (Offaly) has two claims to fame: 'Irish Mist', a whiskey liqueur, and Charlesville Forest, a Georgian Gothic mansion built in 1779 to the designs of Francis Johnston. The estate is distinctly Gothic horror in the Mary Shelley mould, with castellated turrets and wall-clinging ivy. Four miles to the north is Durrow Abbey, founded by St Columba, where the Book of Durrow (now in Trinity College Library) was written and illustrated. **18**

Tullynally Castle (Westmeath) is the seat of the earls of Longford, who have been there for 10 generations. The park was laid out by the 1st earl in 1760. The site of a 2nd-century palace here has left little in the way of archaeological remains.

Vinegar Hill (Wexford) the site of the final defeat of the rebels of 1798, is near Ferns. **125**

Waterford (Waterford) The rather grim-looking port conceals much of interest inside the city. There are two cathedrals, which share the distinction of being built by a native of Waterford, John Roberts. Christchurch, the Protestant cathedral, was built 1770–9 and partly restored in 1818 after being damaged by fire in 1815. The Catholic Cathedral of the Holy Trinity was built 1793–6 during the time of the penal laws.

Remnants of Waterford's Viking past still remain, notably Reginald's Tower (where the marriage of Strongbow and Aoife took place), part

of the city walls, and two stone arches inside what is now a grill bar! The best-preserved towers from the former Norman walls can be seen in Railway Square, Castle Street and Jenkin's Lane. Waterford has a reputation for toughness going back to Viking times when those who failed to pay the settlement tribute had their noses cut off – thus known as 'nose money'. Cromwell also boasted in 1649 that he would capture Waterford 'by hook or by crook', but he failed; alone of Ireland's major towns, it held out against him. It retains a reputation for producing fine cut glass. **32, 107**

Westport (Mayo) has much of historic interest. Built largely in the Georgian style, with an octagonal-shaped Georgian square, it was formerly an important centre for linen and cloth. Places of interest include Westport House, dating from 1730, which contains among other things a painting by Rubens and a violin once owned by Synge. It is the seat of the Brownes, marquesses of Sligo.

Wexford (Wexford) has a long history, but there are disappointingly few reminders of it. The site of Cromwell's bloody massacre in 1649 is hard to find in the Bull Ring, more attention being paid, by means of a monument, to the 1798 uprising. The Westgate, dating from 1300, is the only survivor of the town's five medieval gates. The remnants of Selskar Abbey, where Henry II reputedly spent Lent in penitence for willing the murder of Thomas à Becket, are nearby. **52, 124**

Wicklow (Wicklow) Little of interest here save the remains of Black

Castle, one of the fortifications built by the Fitzgeralds in return for lands granted by Strongbow after the Anglo-Norman invasion of 1169. **51** *Youghal* (Cork) is a little port and seaside resort with an interesting history as a Norman settlement, but its present walls date from the reign of Edward I. On Main Street the Red House dates from 1710, and there are some 17th-century almshouses. The 13th-century Collegiate Church of St Mary's has some interesting contemporary monuments. The most striking landmark is the Georgian clock tower.

NORTHERN IRELAND

Armagh (Armagh) is named after the Celtic queen Macha (ard Macha, the height of Macha) and is the senior metropolitan seat in Ireland for both the Catholic Church and the Church of Ireland. Fine Georgian architecture can be seen in the Mall, which also has the County Museum, containing as well as the usual local artefacts a small art gallery. Of the two major churches, St Patrick's Church of Ireland Cathedral is on the site of the saint's first church; the structure is a composite of 13th- and 19th-century styles. Fragments of an 11th-century Celtic cross can be found near the unusual timber porch as you enter. Nearby are the Chapter House and cathedral library. St Patrick's Catholic Cathedral is, of course (given the penalties against Catholic worship after 1691), of much more recent vintage, but is a large, impressive Gothic-style 19th-century building. It is the seat of the Cardinal arch-

bishop, the historic head of the Catholic Church in Ireland. Armagh Priory was a Franciscan foundation dating from 1263, although only the ruins of the priory church remain today. **11, 16**

Belfast began its history guarding a ford over the Farset, a river which now runs below the High Street. Although a Norman castle was built there in 1177, there was no effective conquest and by the 13th century the area was again dominated by the O'Neills of Clandeboye. Only at the end of the 17th century did the expansion really begin, partly with the help of French Huguenots fleeing from persecution by Louis XIV. Belfast was granted its charter as a city by Queen Victoria in 1888.

Despite the ever-present 'Troubles' (actually restricted to a comparatively small part of the city), Belfast has much to offer. The Crown Entry, for example, was where the 'Society of United Irishmen' was founded, and where the playwright Sheridan had his 'pathetic' school of comedy. The Prince Albert Memorial, dating from the 1860s, stands at the docks end of the High Street. The Protestant cathedral of St Anne's can be found at the junction of Donegal and York Street. Dating only from 1899 it is built in a neo-Romanesque style, and is best known for being the last resting place of the great Unionist and anti-Home Ruler, Edward Carson. The west door of the cathedral is memorable but otherwise the building is a disappointment, indeed it has been described as Carson's mausoleum.

Queen's University, designed by Charles Lanyon, dates from 1849 and is surrounded by an attractive Georgian terrace, and in the nearby Botanic Gardens is the Ulster Museum. Among a multiplicity of other exhibits, the museum does have early Irish jewellery and archaeological specimens. A special section is given over to treasures seized from unfortunate survivors of the Spanish Armada during its catastrophic voyage around the Irish coastline. The City Hall which dates from just before the First World War has a Whispering Gallery and Dome which are modelled on those of St Paul's Cathedral. Its marble entrance hall with a statue of Queen Victoria in it is also striking. A mural dating from the 1950s can be found on the main landing commemorating Belfast's now largely lost industries of weaving, spinning, rope-making and ship-building.

In the southern part of the city is an impressive megalithic remain known as the Giant Ring, which some think superior to the ruins on the Hill of Tara in the Republic. North Belfast has its castle but it only dates from 1870, apparently inspired by the royal residence of Balmoral in Scotland. Stormont Castle is an imposing building four miles outside Belfast which was, until 1972, the seat of Unionist power in Northern Ireland. It has an impressive, if rather remote solitude about it. **153, 194**

Bonamargy Friary (Antrim) on the main road between Ballycastle and Cushendun, was founded by the local MacQuillan family in 1500.

Now in ruins, it contains the tombs of the first two earls of Antrim.

Carrickfergus (Antrim) has an Anglo-Norman castle built in 1180 which has withstood many sieges, the first in 1315 when Edward Bruce took a year to reduce it during his Irish campaign. It was briefly captured by the French in 1760 as well. There is a Cavalry Regimental Museum inside the castle, and the Restoration playwright William Congreve lived there as a child. The Andrew Jackson Centre attempts to make a link, not very convincingly, between the town and this US president (1829–37) – Jackson's parents emigrated from Carrickfergus to the USA in 1765. **76, 111**

Cushendun (Antrim) has the distinction of being designed by Clough Williams-Ellis of Portmeirion fame, but it does not compare with its 1920s Welsh cousin which it predates. Otherwise it is close to the supposed grave of the legendary Ossian, son of the equally legendary Finn Mac Cumaill (Finn McCool). **22**

Derry (Londonderry) has very ancient roots, St Columba founding a monastery there in 546. Its distinctive modern history started with the plantation under James I which was anglicised to Doire. It became Londonderry in 1613 following the grants of land made to London companies in the surrounding country. Then followed the famous siege of 1689 which holds such a prominent place in the Protestant tradition.

Derry's old walls survive and the ancient cannon can also be seen over the Magazine and Shipquay Gates. St Columb's Cathedral dates from 1633; outside is a cannonball which was fired into the city by James II's besieging army in 1689 with surrender terms for the garrison. There are more relics from the siege in the cathedral chapter house. More intrepid souls may venture into the Protestant Fountain area and the Catholic Bogside, where wall murals point up the clash between the rival Unionist and Republican traditions. **15, 110–11**

Downpatrick (Down) is, as its name suggests, best known for its association with the saint. The Heri-

tage Centre concentrates on telling St Patrick's own story with details culled from his *Confessions*. It is possible that he is buried in the town although his exact burial site is uncertain. Otherwise there is the Cathedral, built on the site of de Courcy's original abbey on the 'Hill of Down', which had considerable strategic value and was the site of a Celtic fort; however, it only dates from the end of the 18th century although extensively remodelled in the 20th century. St Patrick's Shrine on the Strangford road and St Patrick's Well on Ardglass road maintain the area's strong links with the saint. **10–12, 54**

The fifteenth-century tomb of Cooey-na-Gall O'Cahan, Dungiven Priory

Dungiven   Priory (Londonderry) dates from 1100 and the church contains what many regard as the finest medieval tomb in Northern Ireland (a member of the O'Cahan family). When the town (there is little of interest there) was given to the Skinners' Company, they built a manor house on the priory site in the 17th century.

Enniskillen (Fermanagh)   now has sizeable   17th-century   remains although it was built on the site of a Maguire castle. The Watergate dates from this period and the Fermanagh County Museum is inside the Watergate building. The famous Portora Royal School, founded in 1608, moved to its present site in 1777, and just outside the town is Castle Coole, in the 18th-century Palladian style; it is the former home of the earls of Belmore.

Grey Abbey (Down) founded in 1193 by John de Courcy's wife for the Cistercians, has considerable segments intact.

Killyleagh (Down)   was the site of the 12th-century Anglo-Norman de Courcy castle, which was rebuilt in the 19th century by the Hamilton family. **53–4**

Lisnaskea (Fermanagh)   Castle Balfour is one of the finest examples of 'planter castles', built to protect English and Scots settlers from the native Irish in the county. The town also has a 19th-century cornmarket. **99–100**

Londonderry *see* ***Derry***

Longhall village (Armagh) is significant because here the Orange Order was founded in 1795. The Orange Museum has a collection of memorabilia associated with the Order. **165–6**

Monea Castle (Fermanagh) built in 1618, is another of a series of 'planter castles' in the county. **99–100**

Mount Stewart House near Newtownards (Down) was the seat of the marquesses of Londonderry, one of whom as Viscount Castlereagh was Chief Secretary of Ireland as well as a famous British Foreign Secretary 1812–22. The link with international diplomacy has been maintained by the presence in the house of chairs used by the Duke of Wellington and the French statesman Talleyrand at the 1815 Congress of Vienna.

Navan   Fort (Armagh)   was the northern rival of the Hill of Tara for centuries, possibly as Emain Macha, the capital of legendary Ireland, and the centre of power for the kings of Ulster. Although nothing more than an earthen mound is visible today, recent excavations have confirmed the antiquity of the site, showing traces of human activity *c.* 2000 BC and a round house from *c.* 400 BC. **5**

Nendrum Monastic Site (Down) is worth a visit although the original round tower, church and school are now in ruins.

Omagh (Tyrone) Its   historic associations with the O'Neill family are long gone, and all it has to offer today are an 18th-century courthouse and   the   Sacred   Heart   Catholic Church.

Rathlin Island (Antrim)   is 6 miles offshore but has an interesting history, which begins with its status as the first location in Ireland to be attacked by the Vikings, in 795. Those who love legends will want to see Bruce's Cave where Robert the Bruce allegedly saw his famous spider before going home to Scotland to defeat the English at Bannockburn in 1314. **29**

Torr Head (Antrim) is only 13 miles from the Scottish coast. It is said that in the 17th century local Presbyterians rowed across for Sunday services as Irish penal laws prevented them from worshipping at home. **101**

Tullaghoge Fort (Tyrone) outside Cookstown, is the place where 'the O'Neill', the head of the clan, was inaugurated. Early Christian earthworks are clearly visible on the site. **23**

Ulster American Folk Park (Tyrone) some 5 miles north of Omagh, uses the heritage technique to tell the story of early Ulster emigrants to the USA. The museum has artefacts linked with the American War of Independence. **119–20**

White Island (Fermanagh) has a curious mixture of early Christian carvings (at least one seems to be based on a pagan fertility symbol) on the walls of the now ruined abbey.

Index